# Global Christianity and the
# Black Atlantic

## STUDIES IN
## WORLD CHRISTIANITY

*The Nagel Institute for the Study of World Christianity*
Calvin College

Joel A. Carpenter
*Series Editor*

### OTHER BOOKS IN THE SERIES

*The Making of Korean Christianity*
Sung-Deuk Oak

*Converts to Civil Society*
Lida V. Nedilsky

*Evangelical Christian Baptists of Georgia*
Malkhaz Songulashvili

*China, Christianity, and the Question of Culture*
YANG Huilin

*The Making of Korean Christianity*
Sung-Deuk Oak

*The Evangelical Movement in Ethiopia*
Tibebe Eshete

# Global Christianity and the Black Atlantic

Tuskegee, Colonialism, and the Shaping
of African Industrial Education

*Andrew E. Barnes*

BAYLOR UNIVERSITY PRESS

*Cover design* by AJB Design, Inc.
*Cover image*: Johnston, Frances Benjamin, 1864–1952 (photographer), interior view of library reading room with male and female students sitting at tables, reading, at the Tuskegee Institute, ca. 1902. Image courtesy of the Library of Congress.

This book has been cataloged by the Library of Congress.

Printed in the United States of America on acid-free paper with a minimum of 30 percent post-consumer waste recycled content.

# Series Foreword

It used to be that those of us from the global North who study world Christianity had to work hard to make the case for its relevance. Why should thoughtful people learn more about Christianity in places far away from Europe and North America? The Christian religion, many have heard by now, has more than 60 percent of its adherents living outside of Europe and North America. It has become a hugely multicultural faith, expressed in more languages than any other religion. Even so, the implications of this major new reality have not sunk in. Studies of world Christianity might seem to be just another obscure specialty niche for which the academy is infamous, rather like an "ethnic foods" corner in an American grocery store.

Yet the entire social marketplace, both in North America and in Europe, is rapidly changing. The world is undergoing the greatest trans-regional migration in its history, as people from Africa, Asia, Latin America, and the Pacific region become the neighbors down the street, across Europe and North America. The majority of these new immigrants are Christians. Within the United States, one now can find virtually every form of Christianity from around the world. Here in Grand Rapids, Michigan, where I live and work, we have Sudanese Anglicans, Adventists from the Dominican Republic, Vietnamese Catholics, Burmese Baptists, Mexican Pentecostals, and Lebanese Orthodox Christians—to name a few of the Christian traditions and movements now present.

Christian leaders and institutions struggle to catch up with these new realities. The selection of a Latin American pope in 2013 was in some respects the culmination of decades of readjustment in the Roman Catholic Church. Here in Grand Rapids, the receptionist for the Catholic bishop answers the telephone first in Spanish. The worldwide Anglican communion is being fractured over controversies concerning sexual morality and biblical authority. Other churches in worldwide fellowships and alliances are treading more carefully as new leaders come forward and challenge northern assumptions, both liberal and conservative.

Until very recently, however, the academic and intellectual world has paid little heed to this seismic shift in Christianity's location, vitality, and expression. Too often, as scholars try to catch up to these changes, says the renowned historian Andrew Walls, they are still operating with "pre-Columbian maps" of these realities.

This series is designed to respond to that problem by making available some of the coordinates needed for a new intellectual cartography. Broad-scope narratives about world Christianity are being published, and they help to revise the more massive misconceptions. Yet much of the most exciting work in this field is going on closer to the action. Dozens of dissertations and journal articles are appearing every year, but their stories are too good and their implications are too important to be reserved for specialists only. So we offer this series to make some of the most interesting and seminal studies more accessible, both to academics and to the thoughtful general reader. World Christianity is fascinating for its own sake, but it also helps to deepen our understanding of how faith and life interact in more familiar settings.

So we are eager for you to read, ponder, and enjoy these Baylor Studies in World Christianity. There are many new things to learn, and many old things to see in a new light.

Joel A. Carpenter
Series Editor

# Contents

# Preface

The idea for this book came about quite inadvertently while I was in the middle of researching another project. I came across the African newspapers available online via the World Newspaper Archives. The websites for the archives were searchable, allowing me to type in names or events and then call up all of the articles in selected newspapers published on the subject for a given time. At first, I just read through the newspapers out of fascination for what they revealed. Later, I had occasion to present a paper on missionary social thought during the early decades of the African colonial period. In the discussion that followed, a question was asked about what African Christians were thinking at this same time in regard to missionaries and the colonization of their continent. I had to admit that I did not know. So I returned to the newspapers for African opinions on issues of social development. My discoveries prompted me to put my other project aside and work on the study presented in this text.

I did not begin seeking to illuminate the importance of Booker T. Washington for African Christians. I will admit to having known very little about Washington and of Tuskegee, the school he founded. But I became intrigued by the glorification in African newspapers of Washington as a Christian trailblazer and of Tuskegee as a new "Geneva," that is, a training school for leaders of a new, consciously African form of Christianity, as John Calvin's work in Geneva set new parameters for the Protestant Reformation. Such images are not to be found in any of the books on Washington's historical legacy or those about the planting of Christianity in Africa. Yet the images were integral to the collective efforts made by African Christians in the decades around the turn of the twentieth century to regain some initiative against European colonization. The efforts were made in the only thing that might be labeled shared public space among the different ethnic groups that made up African Christian society at that time—that is, in Anglophone Christian media, most importantly newspapers. Not surprisingly, colonial authorities endeavored to suppress these efforts, primarily by suppressing the newspapers. Still, modern African Christianity grew out of this ultimately blocked effort to appropriate and apply what was seen as Washington's vision of Christianity to African circumstances.

I learned about industrial education, the approach to education Washington perfected at Tuskegee, primarily from the reports I read that were sent in to their superiors by both missionaries and colonial administrators in the 1930s and 1940s. These reports could be a source of humor, given that few colonial schools pursued industrial education in any systematic way. The term generally characterized any type of manual training taught in any nominal way at a mission or government school. The historical literature has tended to reinforce the assessments found in European colonial writing that Africans reacted to the science and knowledge behind modern Western technology much like deer staring into headlights, with an immobilizing incomprehension. Yet, and this is what comes through in the newspapers, for African Christians industrial education as taught at Tuskegee under Washington had connotations of Promethean fire. Africans talked among themselves about industrial education as a vehicle for the widespread acquisition of the science and knowledge Europeans insisted Africans could not understand but also made sure that Africans did not have opportunity to learn. Once they had access to schools like Tuskegee, Africans believed they would be in possession of the knowledge that would allow them to become technologically and industrially competitive with Europeans. Building industrial societies involves more than building a few schools. Still, African ambition here requires better understanding. The reactions to European conquest that had African societies falling apart have been well studied. The reactions to conquest that have African societies collectively striving to meet challenges merits more attention.

I learned that African Christians went looking for guidance in their efforts to build schools that would provide Africans with the technological knowledge required to push back against European domination. Significantly, they did not turn to Christian missions for assistance in their search. Rather, they looked at missions and missionaries as the great-est opponents to the African acquisition of technological expertise. One picture of the European Christian missionary movement that reached its apogee in the era under discussion highlights the faith and courage of individuals who, without any safety net, ventured to the remotest parts of Africa to preach the Christian word. The fairness of this image should not be doubted. The image, however, does not completely reflect the missionary encounter with Africa. Another picture gained more currency among Africans already practicing Christianity. In this assess-ment, European missionaries invoked racial superiority as justification for turning away any African effort at Christian leadership. The fairness of this image also should not be doubted. Many missionaries followed other Europeans into the exaltation of white supremacy. The missionary enthrallment with scientific racism lasted only a few generations, but it left an imprint. A broad spectrum of African Christians concluded that missionaries had not left their racism behind in Europe and America but were determined to introduce it into Christian life in Africa. African Christians developed a distrust of missionaries, and in particular mis-sionary rationales for the limitations of the educational content of mis-sion schools, a distrust that only grew and hardened as missions began to collude with colonial governments in the erection of school systems offering education "adapted" to African needs.

African Christians identified another, to their mind, superior Chris-tian source for the knowledge that they needed. Already before the emergence of Washington and Tuskegee, African Christians were look-ing to the example of African Americans living in the American South as a model of how to develop as a group in the face of white subjugation. African editors filled pages of their newspapers with stories about Afri-can American achievement. Washington and his success only confirmed what African Christians already believed, that African Americans could teach Africans how to build their own Christian civilization.

Scholars talk about a Black Atlantic existing from the time of the first slave ships docking in the New World in the sixteenth century, yet there has been a paucity of study of that world of origin from the point of view of the ties Christians of African descent identified as binding it together. What attracted me to the story told in this study was the affinity both Protestant Anglophone Africans and Protestant Anglophone Afri-can Americans affirmed as existing between them, an affinity based as much on faith and language as race. This presumed affinity gave concrete meaning to Ethiopianism, a term that scholars have used with contradictory meanings but that, for the people who endeavored to live their lives by its presumed tenets, involved black people saving other black people materially, spiritually, and racially. Casting themselves as coprotagonists in a Christian parable, African and African American Protestants, through speeches, newspaper articles, and books, shared plans and dreams across the Atlantic of bringing the African race into the Christian fold. As I show in my analysis, at the heart of these plans and dreams, at least for the years in question, were schools like Tuskegee, the engine that would empower the Christian regeneration of African peoples and of the African continent.

# Acknowledgments

This book grew out of research made possible through advancements in modern technology. Even a generation ago, the amount of data through which I have sorted would have taken perhaps a decade and tens of thousands of miles of travel to process. But online archives and Internet search engines allowed me to complete the research in a much shorter time and primarily from the computer in my den. So, with all seriousness, I thank the Internet for making this book possible. More specifically, I must thank the Center for Research Libraries (CRL), which made the African newspaper collection available via the World Newspaper Archive, the chief database I used, accessible online. I must also acknowledge my debt to the Hayden Library, Arizona State University, through which I gained entrée to the website of the CRL.

I first learned about the African newspaper collection from conversations with Edward Oetting, the subject librarian for history at Hayden Library. During the course of the project, Oetting continued to serve as my mentor, introducing me both to new data sources and to the new research strategies online investigation demands. I offer my deepest thanks to him. I also thank my colleagues at Arizona State University, Edward Escobar, Gayle Gullett, Retha Warnicke, and Chouki El Hamel, who listened patiently, perhaps stoically, as I thought and then rethought what I was trying to show with the data I had discovered.

I attend the meetings of the Yale-Edinburgh Group on the History of the Missionary Movement and World Christianity, and I depend on the comments I have received from the organizers and regular participants in this group for guidance in my research. To them, I tender this book as evidence that I was listening to the questions they raised about the papers I presented based upon this material. I offered the first conception of this book as an invited lecturer at the Nagel Center for the Study of World Christianity at Calvin College in Grand Rapids, Michigan, in 2011, which was an important step in shaping what I understood to be the audience for this text. I thank Joel Carpenter, director of the Nagel Center, for his support and encouragement. I have presented papers that became part of chapters at the Biennial Conference of the Association for the Study of the Worldwide African Diaspora in Santo Domingo, Dominican Republic, in October 2013; the Annual Conference of the American Society of Church History in Washington, D.C., in 2014; and the conference "The US South in the Black Atlantic: Transnational Histories of the Jim Crow South since 1865" held by the German Historical Institute in Washington, D.C., in 2015. Again, I hope that what I say in the book conveys how much I learned from the comments I received at these events.

I appreciate and express my gratitude for the commitment Baylor University Press and Director Carey Newman made to this project from the start. I extend thanks to the two anonymous readers at Baylor University Press who read the manuscript and in their comments recommended some directions in which the manuscript might grow. To the extent that I could, I have followed their advice. Whatever clarity of exposition the book may claim is traceable to the editorial work of Gladys S. Lewis, who nurtured the manuscript through six months of reshaping and restructuring. I see what I was trying to say much better, thanks to her efforts.

Finally, I acknowledge gratitude to my wife, Scarlett, and my three sons, Luke, Aaron, and Joshua. I do not think they have ever understood what I was doing when I disappeared into my office for long stretches of hours. Yet they have always been eager to see me when I came out again. For this, I am eternally grateful.

# Introduction

In the early decades of the European colonial era, African Christians challenged European domination through use of a strategy of social development via Christianization appropriated from their understanding of African American Christian life. The strategy built upon the establishment of schools like Booker T. Washington's Tuskegee Institute. African Christians pictured Tuskegee as a place that turned indigent African American freed slaves into morally disciplined, economically competitive, community-minded Christians. Establishing versions of Tuskegee, they believed, would bring about the Christian regeneration of Africa. Attempts by African Christians to copy Tuskegee failed, in part, because of lack of money and community cooperation and, in part, because European missionaries and colonial authorities opposed the initiatives.

During the early decades of the colonial era, 1880–1920, colonial regimes lacked the bureaucratic apparatus and experts that came to shape colonial policies in later decades. Relations between European governments and subjected African peoples remained sufficiently open for Africans to advance their own agendas. African peoples, specifically African Christians, claimed this space to promote the establishment of school systems based upon the principles of industrial education followed in the United States for African Americans. African Christians believed these principles had produced a black Christian community capable of withstanding white domination. African Christians wanted to institute the same principles among Africans to trigger a pan-tribal, pan-denominational, ultimately pan-African response to European conquest.

1

African Christians learned about African American life in African-edited newspapers. Beginning in the 1880s, mostly as denominational newsletters and circulars, African newspapers grew rapidly through the 1920s, increasing in circulation and coverage. The newspapers aspired to both represent and shape westernized Christian African consciousness. African authors published articles from what they understood to be a civilized perspective, while the newspapers selected and reprinted stories and articles from European and American sources. African American life and the achievements of African Americans held great interest for the readers of African newspapers. The newspapers dubbed the Americans "Africans in America" and treated them as successful cousins whose survival strategies in the racist American South merited examination for application in Africa.

Of the various strategies adopted by African Americas, none had more appeal than the building of schools like Tuskegee. From 1895, when he gave his speech at the Atlanta Cotton Exposition, to the time of his unexpected death in 1915, Booker T. Washington and his school, Tuskegee, were constantly in the international press. African newspapers reprinted many of these stories and added some of their own. Their readers learned about Washington and his wisdom. They learned about Tuskegee and the effectiveness of its program. As a result, the readers of African newspapers looked upon Washington as a leader to emulate and his school as a model to be copied.

In both West Africa and South Africa, African-edited newspapers played an essential role in movements for the establishment of industrial institutes as alternatives to mission schools for African students. African newspapers identified Christian missions, which were denominational and staffed by missionaries whom Africans increasingly indicted as white supremacists, as the opponents to their efforts to build nondenominational African Christian communities. The newspapers characterized mission schools as having the capacity to educate only ministers and clerks, who could only serve as support staff for mission churches and colonial governments. The proposed institutes were presented as secondary, as distinct from primary schools where students would acquire a technologically sophisticated education that would allow them both to understand and to re-engineer European technology for African needs. Schools like Tuskegee would provide a racially empowering alternative to the racially demeaning training provided at mission schools.

More broadly, in promoting the establishment of industrial institutes, the newspapers tapped into African Christian sympathies for Ethiopianism, the notion that Africa's regeneration would be an outcome of African agency. Ethiopianism called for an African-led Christian evangelization of Africa. It advocated for African initiative in the economic, social, and political development of Africa as well. "Princes shall come out of Egypt and Ethiopia shall stretch forth her hands unto God," Psalm 68:31 (KJV) proclaims. Ethiopianists read this passage as a clarion call for people of African descent to build their own Christian civilization.

In both regions the movements grew through the development of concrete proposals based upon the Tuskegee model. In West Africa, industrial education schools were posed first as alternatives, then as complements, to denominational mission schools. In South Africa, where notions of industrial education were already followed in mission schools, the Tuskegee approach was pursued as a counter to existing practices. In both regions, however, the movements ultimately failed, victims of missionary antipathy and more importantly government opposition. Still, for a brief moment, African Christians looked across the Atlantic to Tuskegee Institute in Alabama for guidance. During the time when Booker T. Washington was Tuskegee's principal, African Christians had high hopes that schools like Tuskegee would help them fight back against racial subjugation.

The first chapter of this study, "The Spectacle Reversed," provides background on the subjects of focus, beginning with an examination of African newspapers and their role in shaping the African response to missionary Christianity and European conquest. The discussion then moves to the image of the African American in the Christian African mind and the American practices Africans hoped to apply to their own struggles. African and African American Christians spoke to each through the language of Ethiopianism, a language mostly developed in the New World and then exported back to Africa by black Christian intellectuals. The teachings of these intellectuals, mostly communicated through newspaper articles, created an African mind-set that saw only affinity and joint purpose across the Atlantic. As these same Christian intellectuals affirmed, African American society had been regenerated through the establishment of industrial education institutes. African Christians figured that the strategy would work equally well for their societies.

The second chapter, "Making People," discusses the notion of ethnogenesis through education developed first at Hampton Institute under General Samuel Armstrong and then refined toward black sensibilities at Tuskegee under Booker T. Washington. Today, both the Hampton and the Tuskegee of the era would be labeled Bible colleges. However, their goal was not the training of ministers and missionaries but, rather, the training of educators and entrepreneurs. Most of the graduates of the two schools spent their lives as elementary school teachers. Yet, at both Hampton and Tuskegee, students received technical training in some vocation to which the students were expected to turn when they were not teaching. All teaching at Hampton and Tuskegee was imbued with a Christian entrepreneurial spirit. The students were taught to believe that God helps those who help themselves. Their education envisioned that the students eventually would make enough money from the marketing of their technical skills that they would no longer need to teach. With financial security, both Armstrong and Washington anticipated that the graduates of their schools would lead from the pews to shape and subsidize community development. The unabashed glorification of the "Gospel of Wealth" that took place at Hampton and Tuskegee does not sit well with the intellectual and academic sensibilities of contemporary times. Still, in the latter part of the nineteenth century, Hampton and Tuskegee were widely celebrated for their ability to instill the "Protestant ethic" into black people.

Chapter 3, "The Advancement of the African," returns to the subject of Ethiopianism and suggests a new conceptual framework within which to think about the term as it applied in Africa. Ethiopianism was one among several types of adversarial Christianity, that term denoting the stances African Christians took in response to missionary racial and cultural presumptions. African Christians recognized the excesses of missionary Christianity. Ethiopianists stood out for their claims, addressed to other African Christians via African newspapers, that they could right the things missionaries got wrong. Education was high on that list. Ethiopianists proposed to use American-style industrial education to correct the deficiencies in mission education.

The fourth chapter, "An Attentive Ear," provides information about the reception of Washington and his school in West Africa. Washington had an impressive presence in West African newspapers. His articles and articles by others about Tuskegee were regularly reprinted, and his aphorisms filled space at the end of columns. Some of the greatest and most influential Christians in West Africa spent time thinking about how Tuskegee and its approach could aid in the development of what Edward W. Blyden, the most influential of these Christians, called "the African personality." Efforts at finding funding for industrial institutes, however, presented an ongoing story of frustrated hopes. Ethiopianists had hoped industrial education schools would provide a path away from mission schools. In the end Ethiopianists turned to missions in search of funding.

Chapter 5, "On the Same Lines as Tuskegee," considers the reception of Washington and Tuskegee in South Africa, where Washington and his school were covered in papers more than they were in West African papers. In South Africa, however, Tuskegee and its import were contested, with African Christians and European Christians offering opposing understandings first of industrial education and second of Washington and his achievements. Ethiopianist initiatives went further toward their goals in South Africa, but their success elicited government intervention. For all of the attention Tuskegee had generated during the height of Washington's international prestige, by 1920 it was rarely a subject of discussion in African newspapers.

The sixth chapter, "Men Who Can Build Bridges," starts with a discussion of Washington's attempt to guide Ethiopianists and missionaries toward common ground. Washington built his strategy around calling what he announced as an "International Conference on the Negro," to take place on the grounds of Tuskegee itself. The conference did take place, in April 1912. And its outcome was some thawing of relations in Africa between Ethiopianists and missionaries. But at the moment of Washington's sudden death in late 1915, there had been little reconciliation. By that time also, however, colonial governments were beginning to take control over all forms of education in Africa. Washington's death provided an occasion for Ethiopianists to reassess industrial education as a response to European domination, typically in a comparative context against the advocacy of W. E. B. Du Bois for more direct political activism. For the most part, African writers continued to appreciate the utility of Washington's approach for social and economic development. The years immediately following Washington's death were characterized by a declining interest in industrial education in African newspapers. Debate on the topic was revived, however, in 1920, when two new sets of ideas, both alleging Booker T. Washington as an ancestor, arrived in Africa from the United States. Marcus Garvey explicitly identified his ideas as derived from those of Washington. His movement promised to finally fulfill the African demand for schools like Tuskegee. Thomas Jesse Jones, who headed the two Phelps Stokes Education Commission tours that traveled through Africa beginning in 1920, likewise insisted that his educational ideas came from Washington. In addition, Jones brought with him J. E. K. Aggrey, whom he presented to African audiences as their own version of Booker T. Neither Garvey nor Jones convinced many African Christians, however, that their claims were true.

African Christian movements to build industrial education schools have been noticed by scholars but mostly dismissed as not important. Yet the movements help make sense of a good deal of the negotiations between colonial governments and Christian missions in early colonial British Africa. The British Colonial Office feared the movements as breeding grounds for Ethiopianism and endeavored to suffocate them, mostly by attempting to shut down the pipeline of exchange and interaction between African and African American Christians. The Colonial Office then built its educational policy in Africa around Jones' promise of schools that would suppress the African's instinct toward Ethiopianism. In a series of decisions they themselves questioned later, Christian missions colluded with British colonial governments in these efforts.

The study following will demonstrate the substance behind European concerns. The industrial education movement served as a leading edge of the African challenge to European conquest of Africa. It linked together Protestant Africans with Protestant African Americans around the idea of racial uplift. It provided race-conscious African Christians with concrete objectives to pursue beyond tribal and denominational boundaries. It prompted African Christians to speculate about the contours of an African Christian civilization. In sum, it got African Christians excited about the future in ways inimical to racial subjugation.

# 1

# The Spectacle Reversed

*Shaping the African Response to Missionary
Christianity and European Conquest*

Africa begins to speak for herself. An old fable tells us that once upon a time there was being exhibited to a lion a graphic picture in which a man was killing a lion. "Ah," said the lion, "that picture was painted by a man; wait till the lion paints and the spectacle will be reversed."[1]

## AFRICAN NEWSPAPERS

In the nineteenth century, Africa experienced the great age of European Christian missions. Across Africa, but especially along the western coast north of the Cameroons and the Atlantic and Indian Ocean coasts of what became the Union of South Africa, thousands of missionaries from Europe and North America traveled to the continent to preach the Christian message. The missionaries and their missions achieved their goal. Tens of thousands of Africans became Christians. The Africans who accepted Christian faith never ceased to thank the missionaries for bringing them the good news of the gospel of Christ. Many African Christians aspired to imitate the missionaries by becoming missionaries themselves. European missionaries dismissed their efforts, suggesting that Africans as a race were not yet sufficiently mature to take the lead in evangelization, even of other Africans.

Implicit in the missionaries' efforts was the introduction of Christian civilization to Africa. But the Christian civilization introduced was European civilization, or at least European civilization stripped of the secular materialism that Christians saw as dominating more and more of European life. The process of introducing Christian civilization was broadly understood among European thinkers in the eighteenth and nineteenth centuries as the process of regeneration. In the twentieth century, secular thinkers broke down the holistic notion of regeneration into various ideas of social, economic, and political development. Christians continued to think, however, in terms of regeneration—that is, the bringing to life of the God-fearing spirit within every individual, group, and community. Accordingly, this spirit was lost or repressed in individuals, groups, and communities that did not know Christ. Once found or reignited by Christian conversion, the spirit of God would change all peoples and things for the good. As preached by Christian evangelists and abolitionists from the eighteenth century forward, Christian regeneration was understood to have the capacity to free Africa from the slave trade and Africans from their propensity to trade in slaves. As classically framed in midnineteenth-century Britain, Christian regeneration would teach Africans, as proclaimed by David Livingstone, "commerce and civilization," meaning that Africans would learn to live Christian lives through some African version of European yeoman capitalism.[2]

Whether this idea of Christian life would have ever worked is hard to say. Europeans never allowed such concepts to take root. The opportunities for capitalistic enrichment opened up by the greater economic interaction between Africa and Europe in the last decades of the nineteenth century were simply too lucrative for Europeans to pass up. Thousands of European traders, adventurers, and settlers sailed to Africa during these decades. Like the missionaries, they endeavored to maintain control of whatever power, authority, and rewards that accrued from the European presence on the African continent.

In the decades surrounding the turn of the twentieth century, the number of Europeans living in Africa progressively increased. Administrators and soldiers representing European imperialist interests joined the missionaries, traders, adventurers, and settlers already there. Who first called the period and developments under discussion "the scramble for Africa" in 1884, and what for, is not certain. But since that time it has become the term historians commonly use to speak of the rushed, haphazard way Europeans partitioned the African landmass. The time is also known as the era of the Berlin Conference, so determined by historians to call attention to the diplomatic conference held in Europe to make sure the competition in Africa did not trigger a war in Europe among Europeans.[3] Both expressions signify a time when to Europeans the thoughts and opinions of Africans did not factor into decision making, when the conquest of the lands and peoples of Africa was conceived as a game to be played by Europe's rulers, with their European subjects rooting on the sidelines. Missionaries had little say in this game, but they looked upon the winners in the competition with favor, reasoning that God in his providence had sent missions, in the form of the conquering colonial armies, a stick with which to beat down African resistance to the gospel message.

African peoples fought European domination in a number of ways. Africans who had become conversant through Christianity with European civilization responded with strategies to take over the evangelization and regeneration of Africa themselves, with an ambition to use the African Christian civilization that emerged from their efforts to blunt the pernicious effects of European subjugation. These strategies were laid out in African-edited newspapers, an underinvestigated source for the understanding of African reactions to conquest.

African newspapers began appearing regularly in the 1880s. Most of them started as circulars put out by church people for church communities. Over time the newspapers grew, both in terms of coverage and in terms of audience, to reflect larger Christian constituencies.[4] Initially, African newspapers aimed to address the interests and concerns of denominational audiences. They were newspapers for Methodists or Anglicans or Congregationalists or other denominations. As the readership for the publications expanded, the editors and writers of African newspapers enlarged their conception of the issues they needed to address. The newspapers evolved to provide African Christians with alternatives to missionary sources for news about the world. Their columns opened up to serve as substitutes for church meetings, where Africans could air their frustrations with missionaries and talk about what Africans perceived as the racism increasingly influencing the actions and policies of missions. Their letters to the editor sections became forums where Africans debated the best ways to respond to European domination.

Three characteristics of African-edited newspapers help explain their import on events in Africa at this juncture. First, they should be recognized as Christian, both in expression and in ambition. In nineteenth-century Africa, to turn to newspapers for knowledge and insight presupposed a literacy and a cultural predisposition that typically were the results of Christian education. The writers and readers of African-edited newspapers were mission educated and, in general, believing Christians. Modern scholars have mined African newspapers for the earliest articulations by Africans of a number of secular and social notions and ideas. While these notions and ideas certainly can be found, they were uttered by people who self-identified as Christians and who both wrote and read the articles in the newspapers in the pursuit of a Christian understanding of the world around them.

Faith shaped what was said and discussed in African-edited newspapers. In the process of their development, African newspapers added something to the denominational viewpoints they originally represented. The argument here presented claims that what they added was Ethiopianism, a body of spiritual and cultural descriptors for African Christians. Of fundamental impact for understanding, faith was always an endpoint to the arguments and debates played out in African newspapers. African Christians were sorting out what it meant to be African and Christian at a time when the intellectual edifice of Western civilization was rejecting the commensurability of those two qualities.[5]

A second characteristic collectively exhibited by African newspapers of this era was an editorial distrust of Christian missions. The critique of missionary arguments and actions may have been the primary way the newspapers outgrew denominationalism. One body of contemporary research on African newspapers reveals how, during the period under investigation, African newspapers sought to protest against the imposition of European rule. While important and useful, this literature suffers from an anachronistic assumption. Many African newspapers came into existence before effective European colonization and only gradually turned to a critique of government as colonial rulers made obvious their determination to exclude Christian Africans from political participation in the colonial state. In the years before the nature of colonial rule became clear, newspapers and their readers were preoccupied with other issues, of greatest interest being those connected with faith and education.

A verb other than "protest" becomes more appropriate to convey the ambitions of African-edited newspapers, at least through the end of the first decade of the twentieth century. Through that time, the newspapers printed stories and articles that sought not so much to protest as to contest European interpretations of ideas and events. Until that decade, African Christians still presumed that they shared a common public culture with Europeans and that European explanations of things were open to challenge and debate. The newspapers sought to supply their readers with information and arguments that could shape debates between Africans and Europeans, thus justifying the idea of contest.

The European interpretations that African Christians were most inclined to contest were offered by missionaries, and the missionary interpretations they were most inclined to confront had to do with race. African newspapers demonstrate the extent to which, from the 1880s onward, African Christians saw racism as creeping into missionary discourse. In Europe and America, spreading notions of scientific racism prompted an intense debate in missionary journals and newspapers about whether Africans were capable of assimilating to Christian civilization. A number of the articles published in Europe and America in the context of this debate saw secondary life in African newspapers, where they served as starting points for refutations of what Africans read as articulations of missionary racism.[6] Many of the chapters in Edward W. Blyden's *Christianity, Islam and the Negro Race* got their start as such refutations. So throughout the chapters of the collection Blyden offered, as an answer to the European query why Christianity had failed to take hold in Africa, a contrast of the willingness of Muslims to acknowledge African intelligence and ability versus the fixation of (European) Christians on the African's incapacities.[7]

By 1910 colonial and settler regimes existed across Africa. From that time onward, European governments moved to suppress as subversive the types of criticisms Africans in their newspapers leveled at missions and increasingly at colonial governments themselves. European missions and white governments changed benign contest into subversive protest. The African critique of Christian missions and, more broadly, all African intellectual challenges to white supremacist thought became threats to the established colonial governments functioning as the state in the various African geographical locales. African-edited newspapers did not stop their previous activities, though what they were doing did take on increasingly more of a political complexion. Radical changes came in the penalties the newspapers suffered for their actions, with colonial and settler governments turning to fines, jail time, physical coercion, and ultimately suppression of the right to publish articles on prohibited subjects.

The third characteristic African-edited newspapers came to display was a growing sophistication in the presentation of their critiques. African newspapers and their editors employed a strategy of authorship by proxy. Stephanie Newell's study of the use of anonymity and pseudonymity in West African newspapers during the colonial era reveals that hiding their authorship behind stories with no byline or with a nom de plume was a strategy African writers used to protest colonial policies without fear of government legal reprisal.[8] However, the practices she describes existed before colonial states had the legal apparatus to contemplate reprisal. Her focus on the contest between African authors and the colonial state misses the previous contest between African-edited newspapers and European missionaries. The earlier contest witnesses the evolution of the strategy of authorship by proxy. African editors became adept at finding and publishing articles from foreign newspapers that made arguments that expressed opinions that the editors and their readers shared but missionaries and government officials did not. These articles typically either had bylines that attributed authorship to a European or American writer or listed the originating newspaper as the source. Whole pages in African newspapers could be dedicated to reprinted articles from Britain or the United States that to a casual reader might appear random but for regular African readers added to the arsenal of arguments that repudiated European intellectual hegemony.

A pertinent illustration of the strategy exists in an article printed in the *Lagos Weekly Record* in 1897. Ostensibly a reprint of an interview given to the *Liverpool Courier* by Richard B. Blaize, one of the richest and most successful African merchants in Lagos, upon his arrival in Britain for a visit, the article was a presentation of Blaize's ideas on most of the subjects contained in this current study. Interjected into the article at an early point, without any clue as to its author, was the curious anecdote about the man and the lion quoted at the start of this chapter. The most famous nineteenth-century British missionary was David Livingstone. One of Livingstone's most thrilling stories had to do with his shooting a lion. The story became the subject of innumerable graphic artistic visualizations, printed in European newspapers, missionary journals, and church pamphlets (see figure 1.1). The anecdote would have been an undecipherable non sequitur to any reader outside the African Christian versus European missionary contest. Its meaning would have been immediately apparent to Christian Africans, however, and discerning missionaries, as well. The man was Livingstone, who was emblematic of the missionary enterprise and beyond that the European in Africa. The lion was Africa, who was not as dead as the man's story suggested. And as the contents of the article went on to demonstrate, "the lion had now begun to paint."

LIVINGSTONE ATTACKED BY THE LION

FIGURE 1.1
David Livingstone attacked by a lion in Africa.
*Lithograph. Wellcome Library, London.*
*Image courtesy of Wellcome Images, under a CC BY 4.0 license.*

## AFRICAN AMERICANS IN AFRICAN NEWSPAPERS

More than with any other African-initiated discourse, the strategy of authorship by proxy was employed in the debate about race. And, more than with any other topic, writers and editors of African newspapers looked across the Atlantic to report both the strategies African Americans used to challenge white racial domination and the success they experienced using the strategies. At the end of the nineteenth century, a perception widely shared among the reading public in Africa, and in Europe and Asia as well, held that, in the decades since the end of the American Civil War, no group of humans had developed or, to use the terminology of the period, had "evolved" as rapidly as had African American freed people.[9] Further, and this made the freed people's achievements all the more remarkable, their evolution had occurred in the American South, widely reputed to be the worst place on earth to be black.

Articles republished in African newspapers projected two mutually reinforcing images of African Americans. One elevated African Americans as the sort of capitalist yeomanry, about which missionaries bound for Africa preached, to show economic prowess as the driving force behind African American evolution. Black Americans had learned how to make money and had captured essential parts of the American economy, especially in the agricultural sector. As John L. Dube summed up, in an article congratulating African Americans on "fifty years of freedom," at the end of the American Civil War, African Americans had been a "down-trodden people possessing nothing." Fifty years later, however, they were a people "of increasing importance" with "a large balance sheet to [their] credit." "It was scarcely possible," Dube concluded, "that any other people under such circumstances would have effected more good in the same number of years."[10]

The other was an image of African Americans as Christians. Pictured as bereft of faith and culture and thus open to all sorts of exploitation in 1865 at the end of the Civil War, by the turn of the twentieth century, freed people were seen as holding their own as a Christian, civilized folk and as displaying, as Christians, a collective willingness to help uplift the rest of their race. During the period under discussion in this study, the majority of African Americans remained mired in poverty and victimized by white racism. Still, Christian readers worldwide shared the conviction that the civilized ethos discernible in the actions of the small African American elite, the group later dubbed by W. E. B. Du Bois as the "talented tenth," ultimately would ameliorate the travails of the much larger African American underclass. The racial uplift of the African in America was not argued to be complete. The secular trend of the social evolution of the African American, however, was argued to be obviously going in positive directions.

African newspapers ascribed African American success to Christianity. The transformation African American freedmen had experienced was a powerful demonstration of Christian regeneration. Yet, as Saint Augustine long ago taught, Christian regeneration works only on those whom God has elected for salvation, and, even then, he constantly tests his elect through ordeal. African Americans, as pictured in the African press, demonstrated their election through their perseverance in the face of Jim Crow white racism. They were, as observed by Blaize in the interview mentioned above, "another example of the Hebrews in Egypt. They have been preserved by suffering—salted by fire."[11] The notion, "salted by fire," provides a key to the Protestant Christian African differentiation between African Americans and other New World African peoples. African Americans, as the newspapers sought to show, were the chosen portion of the African diaspora. That which set them apart was the evidence of their capacity to prosper in a hostile environment. John Tengo Jabavu, editor of *Imvo Zabandstundu*, published in South Africa's Cape Province, quoted Frederick Douglass:

> Some talk of exterminating our race, and others say we will soon die out, but I tell you both are impossible, for as they say in the colored prayer meeting—"Brethern, we has been wid ye, we is still wid ye, and we is gwine to stay wid ye." If slavery could not kill us, liberty won't.[12]

E. Cornelius May, editor of the Sierra Leone *Weekly News*, in the same vein commented:

> It is said of Africans in America as it was said of the Hebrews, "the more they afflicted them, the more they multiplied and grew." The Egyptians were grieved because of the irrepressible vitality of the children of Israel. The same is the case in America. The all-conquering Anglo-Saxons, before whom all other darker races have disappeared, are surprised and indignant at the unyielding tenacity of this black race.[13]

Suffering and hardships, in sum, did not signal racial annihilation; rather, they set the stage for the demonstration of the African American's spiritual election.

Providential design, an argument promoted most prominently by Alexander Crummell and Edward W. Blyden from the 1860s onward to black people on both sides of the Atlantic, claimed that through divine providence the Christian God had sent a portion of the African people into slavery in the New World to learn the inner workings of European civilization. From the beginning, went the notion, God's purpose had been that those Africans in America, whose economic success provided evidence that they had acquired an understanding of the world Europeans had fashioned, would come back to Africa, would leave exile and return home, as Blyden posited, and share their knowledge.

African American advocates of the repatriation of black Americans to Africa, such as the African Methodist Episcopal (A.M.E.) bishop Henry M. Turner, insisted that all African Americans would be welcome in Africa.[14] However, writers and publishers of African newspapers showed greater selectivity in their framing of the invitation. They hoped for a portion of that talented tenth that was displaying so much ingenuity in the face of white Southern hostility. As the *Lagos Weekly Record* reported, Africans had in mind the "limited repatriation of those of [Africa's] sons who have her true interest in heart, and who possess qualifications that her indigenous peoples cannot yet so well command."[15] Blyden, making the case for African American repatriation to an audience in Lagos, emphasized

> the advantages which would flow from the return of experienced agriculturalists and skilled mechanics; the influence they would exert upon the tribes in reconciling their differences, settling their wars as disinterested mediators and arbitrators, and the lessons they would impart in the various elements and appliances of civilized life.[16]

Enormous hope rested in the knowledge African Americans would bring with them when they returned to Africa.

African Christians turned to the example of African Americans to refute arguments they heard Europeans make. When Europeans talked about the African's inability to grasp and assimilate civilization, African newspapers reprinted articles that attacked the argument. One set of reprints called into question the collective level of civilization of Europeans. Stories about lynch mobs in America served for African Christians as a counter to claims about the evolved stature of the white race. In the Sierra Leone *Weekly News* under the headline "Civilized Barbarians" appeared a piece from an unidentified London newspaper about the lynching of two black brothers in Texas.[17] The editor of the *Lagos Weekly Record*, in a meandering editorial entitled "The Civilization of Europe," reported one story about two black men who were lynched and burned by a white mob in Missouri in the United States and another about native churches being burned by white settlers in Natal in South Africa. From these stories the editorial reached the conclusion that

> the Civilization of Europe in its practical aspects exhibits features of a kind calculated to bring the whole system into disrepute and disfavor. Glaring instances occur from time to time of doings that shock humanity by their atrocity, while the indifference displayed by the [European] civilized world to such doings tend but to confirm the conclusion, that they are but the symptoms of the depravity and corruption underlying civilized life.[18]

Editorials in African newspapers rarely questioned the characterization of Africa as needing civilization. The editorials suggested instead that Europe and America were in equal need.

This set of articles contrasted with another, which focused on the cultural achievements of African Americans, with the largest number of these stories having to do with Booker T. Washington and the school that he opened July 4, 1881, Tuskegee Institute. Other achievements were cited. An article in the Sierra Leone *Weekly News* in 1898 noted the foundation of the American Negro Academy under the presidency of Alexander Crummell.[19] An obituary of Paul Laurence Dunbar, "The African Poet," in the *Gold Coast Leader* memorialized him as the most poetic of "Ethiopia's sons."[20] To these can be added numerous articles on Du Bois and his book *The Souls of Black Folks*. E. Cornelius May, editorializing in the Sierra Leone *Weekly News*, declared that black American cultural achievements, again in the fifty years or so since the end of the Civil War, "give a lie to the oft repeated slander that the Negro is incapable of high intelligence."[21]

European Social Darwinists, writing to an audience sympathetic to European imperialism, claimed that, as an inferior species, the African in both America and Africa was fated to disappear. With this argument in the background, the *West African Reporter* (Sierra Leone) published in 1881 an article taken from the African American newspaper the *Philadelphia Recorder*. The article summarized the data collected for the United States census for 1880. The key passage for African readers in the reprinted article was this sentence: "The number of colored persons to each 100,000 whites is 15,153 [in 1880 as] against 14,528 in 1870." As the article triumphantly concluded, "The above exhibit can but prove satisfactory to all save the class who insisted that the negro was bound to die out. To these it must prove exceedingly distasteful, and the more as it is looked into. The negro not only refuses to die out, but insists on holding his own."[22] Census data on the African in America proved the lie to the claims of the social Darwinists in Europe.

John Tengo Jabavu in South Africa took information about African American vitality along a different path. In 1890, in an editorial in *Imvo Zabandstundu*, responding to the argument of an unidentified group of Europeans who suggested that the solution to conflict between European and African peoples was the racial extermination of the latter, Jabavu observed:

> The position of the Negro freed slaves in the social and political economy
> of the United States of America is just now exercising the minds of some
> public writers. Naturally by people in South Africa the questions raised
> by the presence of Africans in America are studied with a peculiar interest
> since they are supposed to run parallel to the problems that are offered
> for solution by the aborigines of this country. . . . The results of the public
> discussion of the subject are very satisfactory, as it gives no encouragement
> to those who would exterminate the Natives in this country because such a
> course may have been pursued in America.[23]

If the African minority in the United States could survive genocidal public policies, what hope did whites have with applying similar policies
against the African majority in South Africa? Jabavu saw the African
American example as proving to white policy makers the need to move
on to other types of solutions to race problems in South Africa.

## ETHIOPIANISM

As Jabavu illustrated, in their newspapers African Christians called African Americans "Africans in America" and typically characterized the
latter simply as African peoples transported across the Atlantic. Editors of African newspapers took for granted that African Americans
were Christian kin whose experiences had heuristic value for Africans.
The way of thinking that facilitated these assumptions can be called
Ethiopianism, a difficult term to explain. During the period under consideration, black people used the term in a positive sense while whites
employed it in a negative sense. For black Christians, Ethiopianism
existed simultaneously as a racial and intellectual precept as well as a
religious and social set of behavioral aspirations. Ethiopianism com-
prised an ideology of how they were supposed to think and act and
provided the language through which African American Christians and
African Christians talked about the bonds that united them. Ethiopianism articulated a set of common goals that black people in America and
Africa assumed they were mutually pursuing. The construct made possible the strategies African Christians followed to contest the monopoly
claimed by Europeans over civilization and gave them confidence that
they had history on their side.

Ethiopianism as a shared idiom among English-speaking peoples
of African heritage relates to a passage from Psalm 68:31: "Princes
shall come out of Egypt and Ethiopia shall stretch forth her hands unto
God." Most narrowly, as a theological concept, Ethiopianism affirmed

the idea that a Christian civilization would emerge on the African continent among African peoples through African agency. More broadly, as a race-conscious Christian mind-set, Ethiopianism organized the discussion among black people from different parts of the Atlantic world around a shared ambition to create a common Christian community that would touch on the shores of Africa, the Anglophone islands in the Caribbean, and North America. These people understood that Protestant Christianity was already planted and spreading in the last two of these locales. Thus, they saw themselves to be collectively engaged in a common effort to nurture a modern Christian civilization on the African continent, a modern Christian civilization in which Africans would be proud to live and to which the Africans' New World relatives would be eager to migrate.

Accepting that all Christians recognize as part of their religious identity the obligation to spread or assist in the spread of the gospel, Ethiopianism helped black Christians conceptualize this obligation in terms of racial uplift. Africa and Africans should be saved, and the children of Africa needed to be the ones who saved them. Africans needed to be introduced to modern, capitalistic civilization, and civilized African peoples should be the ones to serve as their mentors. Ethiopia prophetically would stretch forth her hands unto God, and only black people who already knew of Jesus could serve in the task.

Four men, all ordained Protestant ministers, crisscrossed the Atlantic to create and maintain a discourse based upon these shared ambitions. The bridges these men helped construct served as conduits for the exchange of ideas across the Christian Black Atlantic for the forty years under review. The first two, Alexander Crummell and Edward W. Blyden, born in the New World and considered here the first generation, traveled to West Africa to preach and teach. The second two, Orishetukeh Faduma and John L. Dube, recognized here as the second generation, were born in Africa and studied in the United States before returning to Africa to teach and preach.

Alexander Crummell, the first African American ordained by the Anglican Church, spent a significant portion of his adult life preaching in Britain, West Africa, and the United States on the "Christian regeneration of Africa." Crummell provided a four-part argument to the discourse. First, he questioned the effectiveness of European or, as he called them, "foreign" missionaries. "Christianity never secures through entrance and complete authority in any land, save by the use of men and minds somewhat native to the soil," Crummell postulated.[24] With Livingstone clearly in mind, Crummell lauded the "heroic, almost god-like self-sacrifice" of European missionaries. Yet he believed that they lacked the endurance and perseverance to change Africa. The foreign missionary was an "exotic" in Africa, and because of this "he withers and pines, and alas too often dies, a glorious martyr for Christianity."[25] After their deaths, the families of missionaries return to their homes in Europe, the end result being that European missionaries "rarely have permanent influence in Africa." Thus, for Crummell, the argument against the need for "foreign" missions in Africa was their lack of permanency.[26]

The second part of Crummell's argument claimed that only New World African Christians had the knowledge, social discipline, and physical disposition to initiate Christian regeneration in Africa. They had acquired the knowledge and social discipline through divine providence, which had allowed "millions of the Negro race" to be "stolen from the land of their fathers." Now "permeated and vitalized by civilization and Christian principles," the descendants of these stolen Africans were Christians making a living for themselves in New World societies. Although reared in the New World, these descendants remained "indigenous in blood, constitution and adaptability. Two centuries of absence from the continent of Africa had not destroyed [their] physical adaptation to the land of [their] ancestors."[27] Because of this quality of indigeneity, this "somewhat native[ness]," the New World black evangelist would not, like the foreign missionary, "wither and pine away" in Africa. Rather, with "Bibles and Prayer Books, and Tracts and Sermons and family altars," New World African Christian evangelists would journey across the Atlantic "seeking a new home amid the heathen population of Africa."[28]

The third part of Crummell's argument gave his proposal for the regeneration of Africa prominence. Years of living in Africa as a missionary were perhaps behind his conviction that individual missionaries, working on their own, could only precipitate scant change. He continued, "The greatest of saints can only represent a partial Christianity. His work will have to be followed by others." On the contrary, Crummell argued, with a "company of Christian emigrants," "you send a church." For Crummell, organized groups of African American emigrants returning "from the lands of their past thralldom" were the key to the Christianization of Africa. With such companies of people, he insisted, "you send Christianity to Africa." Planted in Africa, the "rootlets" of the churches of these emigrants would "burst forth on one side and another like little daughters of the plantain in a tropical soil."[29]

The fourth part of Crummell's plan and argument supplied answers to the questions about costs that bedeviled all proposals for Christian regeneration. As a solution to all these sorts of issues, Crummell identified what can be called Ethiopianist capitalism—that is, capitalism harnessed by black people in service to the Christian regeneration of black people. Black Protestants were to cover all the costs but also reap all the profits from spreading Christianity across Africa. In one of his earliest pieces of writing, Crummell appealed to "self love," by which he meant the entrepreneurial spirit of New World black Christians to come to Africa to help "open" the "treasures of the lands of their fathers."[30] Crummell had no interest in individual adventurers. From the beginning, he recommended that aspiring emigrants pool their resources and go to Africa as corporations.[31] From this notion, he arrived at his idea of settler communities as missions. In the process of building capitalist industries, African American Christian entrepreneurs would introduce Africans to European technology and Christianity.[32] Crummell visualized the racial uplift of Africans as the outcome of communities of African American settlers migrating to Africa. Through putting Africans to work in their communities, the settlers would assimilate Africans into the Christian world. Crummell's strategy gave priority to the social experience of living a Christian life and focused on the nurturing of the processes through which Africans could be socialized as Christians.

Crummell's ideas wielded a tremendous impact on the thinking of African American Ethiopianists as to what they would actually do if they migrated to Africa for purposes of resettlement. On the American side of the Atlantic, people assumed that African Americans who returned to Africa would settle down as civilizing Christian entrepreneurs. Bishop Henry M. Turner, who served as chief organizer and promoter of the back-to-Africa movement among African American Christians in the last decades of the nineteenth century, certainly had that idea in mind in his speeches and publications. Through Turner and others, Crummell influenced the way African American missionaries conceptualized the ways they would missionize Africa. Yeomen Christian farmers, artisans, and traders of the sort idealized by Crummell were to be the end products of African American evangelization in Africa.[33]

Crummell's direct influence on thinking in Africa is more difficult to gauge; he returned to the United States to live in 1872, after twenty years of travel and proselytizing. He preached and wrote extensively in the United States, yet few if any of his writings made it into African newspapers. Still, Crummell was known in West Africa. In the context of reporting the establishment of the American Negro Academy, the *Lagos Weekly Record* noted that Crummell was "well known in this country as an able and persistent advocate of race preservation and integrity."[34]

Edward W. Blyden, Crummell's onetime colleague in Liberia, gave greater weight to the question of how Africans were to learn to think like Christians. Blyden, considered first generation with Crummell, was the most tireless promoter of the repatriation of African Americans to Africa. Central to his advocacy was his idea that African Americans were experts on all the things Africans needed to know about European technology and the society that nourished it.

Blyden did not view African Americans as evangelists bringing Christianity to Africa. Christianity was already there. What Africa required, rather, was the careful nurturing of African expressions of Christianity in the direction of further manifestations of what Blyden called variously "the African personality" or "the African nationality." Blyden revealed his thinking on the nature of the African personality in an article in the Sierra Leone *Weekly News* entitled "The Religion for the African People," where he praised a sermon by the African Baptist Mojala Agbebi for being the "first instance" of a "Native African" uttering views "intrinsically African and valuable for the guidance of his people."[35] Africans were already directing Africans in the development of African spiritual instincts.

What Blyden sought from African Americans was guidance in the development of the African's technological instincts, guidance Europeans could not be trusted to provide. Blyden thought different civilizations provided different bodies of knowledge on different topics. The task before Africans lay in the choice of which civilization to follow on which topics. Blyden believed that the Islamic world had developed political and social forms far better suited to African needs than the comparative institutions of Christian Europe and America. So, he endeavored to persuade Christian Africans to learn from their Muslim neighbors in terms of political and social organization. In the areas of science, technology, commerce, and industry, Blyden recognized Europeans as being much further ahead than any other group. As a result, he counseled Africans to acquire that knowledge from Europeans. Blyden thought of all civilization as derived from religion, as stemming from the human effort to decipher the insights of sacred texts. European science and technology developed from Christianity, from the efforts of those who shared what Blyden variously called the "Anglo Saxon personality" or the "Aryan nationality" to decipher the truths of the New Testament. Blyden condemned Europeans for not having learned a good deal from what the Bible taught about Christian brotherhood. For this reason Blyden cautioned Africans not against learning Christianity but against learning Christianity from European missionaries. More important for this analysis, Blyden dismissed the idea that Europeans would ever willingly share knowledge of their technology and industry.

Blyden used the idea of providential design. God had allowed the European's greed to lead Europeans to the African coast. On the African coast, Europeans found Africans to carry to the New World as slaves. In the process of exploiting the labor of African slaves, Europeans taught one part of Africa's people what they would never teach the other part. New World Africans learned European technology and the version of Christianity that allowed Europeans to use that technology to conquer the world. To some of those New World Africans, primarily but not exclusively in the United States, God also granted the Christian discipline to master European technology and put it to work fending off European domination. Blyden hoped these chosen few, mostly African Americans, would return to Africa. Once there, African Americans would teach Africans "the various elements and appliances of civilized life," which Europeans refused to share.

As early as 1865, Blyden told U.S. audiences of freed people that they needed to migrate to Africa, bringing with them "the arts of industry and peace."[36] Eighteen years later, he preached to students at Hampton Institute that it was God's providential design for them to get their education and then head to Liberia, where it would be their calling to "build up the nation."[37] Large-scale migrations of African Americans to Africa, however, never occurred. Still, the role that Blyden first envisioned for African Americans as technical experts determined the objective of his second proposal for black American participation in the regeneration of Africa.

In a highly publicized letter to Booker T. Washington in March 1895, important for a number of reasons, Blyden talked about the repatriation movement he had promoted for more than thirty years:

> I believe that while there are and will continue to be intense longings on the
> part of many in the South for Africa, and while there will be now and again

> small emigrations to the Fatherland, the time for a general exodus is far
> distant—perhaps three hundred years off—so that practically the Negro is
> in the United States to stay.[38]

Blyden conceded that the prospects of the success of the back-to-Africa movement were not good.

Of equal, if not greater significance, in Blyden's letter, he congratulated Washington for having demonstrated the path toward the "industrial development" of the "Negro in the South." Blyden explained:

> To me next in importance to the religious development of the Negro in the
> South is his industrial development. But I think the former depends largely
> on the latter. . . . [When the Negro] has attained to that industrial status
> which will enable him to realize to the utmost his great material possibili-
> ties, he will not only . . . command the respect of the white man, but he will
> come nearer to God.[39]

In this, he articulated the racial uplift shared by Ethiopianists across the Atlantic and congratulated Washington for synthesizing at Tuskegee an Africanized version of European industrial civilization. God had already favored African Americans by granting them mastery of European technology. Now he was giving them Booker T. Washington to show them how to forge their own version of that technology. Washington, as an African American Prometheus, had stolen Vulcan's (Europe's) fire and programmed it into the curriculum of his school. Instead of Africa needing African Americans trained in European ways to return to Africa, Blyden was recommending that Africa should follow Washington's lead and build schools like Tuskegee. Blyden himself attempted to do exactly that, moving to Lagos in 1896 and searching there for funding to build the Lagos Literary College and Industrial Training Institute, a school that, though it never got off the ground, locals assumed would be a West African version of Tuskegee.[40]

Africans in West Africa were aware of Washington and his school before reading Blyden's letter. Still, Blyden's letter looks like the best starting point to talk about the turning of African Ethiopianists away from the idea that African Americans would physically come back to Africa and toward the idea that African American culture, as encapsulated by the educational program at Tuskegee, would provide Africans themselves with the knowledge and training they would need to regenerate the peoples of the continent. If a crude measure of the impact of Blyden's letter may be offered, to look at only two of the West African newspapers used in this study, during the first four years of the 1890s, Washington and his school were mentioned four times. During the rest of that decade after 1895, Tuskegee and its principal were cited in the same newspapers seventeen times.[41] In August 1895, five months after Blyden's letter, at the International Exposition in Atlanta, Washington made his Atlanta compromise speech that gave him worldwide attention. Other factors clearly influenced African discussion of Washington. These factors did not take away from but added to Blyden's case that Washington provided Ethiopianists with a pathway they should follow.

Crummell, it may be said, had an indirect (and Blyden a direct) influence on thinking in West Africa. In the first decade of the twentieth century, Orishetukeh Faduma, leader of the second-generation advocates for African repatriation, returned to West Africa a number of times to speak about the value of industrial education. In 1914 Faduma and Chief Sam led a party of African American repatriates to a settlement in Sierra Leone. Faduma wrote a number of articles promoting the project that were published in West African newspapers.[42] These articles illustrate the extent to which Faduma's ideas on the regeneration of Africa may be traced back to those of Crummell and the extent to which Crummell had an indirect impact on the development of Ethiopianist thought in West Africa. Blyden, however, shaped how West Africans viewed Ethiopianism. He published a continuous stream of editorials and articles in West African newspapers, and his articles in American journals were reprinted in West Africa. Without his encouragement, West Africans would not have talked of repatriation or, later, about Booker T. Washington in the ways that they did.

Neither Crummell nor Blyden had an explicit impact on Ethiopianist discourse in South Africa. Alexander Crummell's writings drew no attention in the South African newspapers surveyed for this study. African Christians in South Africa were not receptive to African American settlers, at least not in the last decades of the nineteenth century. They were open to African American missionaries, however, and African American missionaries built their notions of the tasks before them in Africa based upon Crummell's writings. Crummell helped the Ethiopianist cause in the region by offering an answer to the question of how Africans were to learn to live like Christians. Blyden likewise gained scant recognition in South Africa. Only toward the end of his life did an article under his name appear in a South African newspaper.[43] The South African press honored him more in death than in life.[44] The point made about Crummell in South Africa applies to Blyden as well, however. South Africans did not talk much about him by name, but his ideas were implicit in Ethiopianist discourse. During the 1890s, when African American Christians began to talk to South African Christians about establishing African American churches in South Africa, they did so in language first crafted by Blyden.

## CHRISTIAN REGENERATION AND INDUSTRIAL EDUCATION

African American Ethiopianism did not provide Ethiopianist movements in Africa with many recruits. The Christian back-to-Africa movement in the United States resulted in few actual migrations. African American Ethiopianism provided African Ethiopianism with a tool kit of strategies and projects aimed at racial uplift that were not initially conceived as challenges to European subjugation. They were conceived as vehicles of Christian regeneration. African American Christians demonstrated, however, a capacity to advance the interests of the race in the face of virulent white racism. So African Ethiopianists increasingly looked at the strategies and projects they appropriated from across the Atlantic as weapons for the front line in the battle against European domination.

Chief among the projects African Ethiopianists hoped to adapt to their needs was the foundation of industrial education institutes like Tuskegee. Ethiopianists in both West and South Africa proposed schemes for racial regeneration based upon the local production of graduates of such schools. In both regions, efforts to find funding for such schools gave rise to the first collective movements that transcended tribal and denominational affiliations. In both regions, Europeans promoted rival plans based upon the same design. The prospect of building schools like Tuskegee excited blacks, whites, Christians, and some colonial officials, as well. The perceptions generating their excitement merit explanation.

Readers in the early decades of the twenty-first century have difficulty in even attempting to appreciate the historical situation in which the popularity of industrial education as a Christian approach to schooling first developed. Through the early decades of the twentieth century, Christian churches maintained most of the social welfare institutions and services Western societies offered. Churches operated facilities such as schools, hospitals, and orphanages. They did receive some state subsidies. However, most of the institutions that churches maintained and most of the services they provided received financial support through donations, pious bequests, fees, and taxes that Christians imposed on their own communities. All of these voluntary monies came from the charity of benevolent people. In general, these revenues were irregular, and churches found themselves constantly soliciting new funds. Beginning in the nineteenth century, the states in Western societies assumed responsibilities for the social welfare services churches had maintained previously. Today, state-run institutions, all funded by state-imposed taxes, have replaced the public dependency upon church-maintained services that characterized Western societies in earlier times.[45]

Christian advocacy of industrial education emerged, though, during a time when Christian providers of social welfare services, always strapped for cash and constantly alert for new sources of revenue, looked to industrial education as one such source. "If you give a man a fish, you feed him for a day," an old proverb begins; "if you teach a man to fish, you feed him for a lifetime," the maxim concludes. Christians turned to industrial education because they saw it as a Christian way to teach a man how to fish. Poor people, Christian converts, all those who, for whatever reason, attended industrial education schools would learn how to make things for a living. Knowing how to earn an income, they would not become wards of the church. Industrial education was a Christian way to teach a man to fish that also appeared to offer the significant bonus of being capable of paying for itself.[46] The things students learned to make could be sold for a profit, and those profits could pay operating costs. For Christians, industrial education's most basic appeal was its perceived potential to cover its own expense.

Rarely did industrial education schools accomplish this goal. Original funding for building physical plants and purchasing the heavy equipment needed for training purposes remained the obstacles over which most initiatives for building industrial institutes failed to climb. Once up and running, the schools faced the costs of maintenance and teaching supplies. They also had to meet the competitive costs of teachers whose skills had a demand outside the institution. Things made by students were not always up to market standards, if they were salable at all. Industrial education as an educational strategy remained attractive to Christians, however, even when the anticipated monies from the sale of student-made commodities never materialized. Industrial education, in theory at least, appeared to be the perfect way to teach new Christians what they needed to know about their duties to their church and their community. The proverb about teaching a man to fish, as understood by nineteenth-century Protestant Christians, implicitly taught two other lessons beyond that of the value of self-sufficiency. One suggested a moral: once a man learned how to fish, he could go further and learn the lesson of capitalism, which meant that he could sell part of his catch for profit. The other suggested an obligation: if a man had been taught the ways of Christ, after learning the value of capitalism he would have the insight to comprehend an even greater truth, that he had a Christian duty to give some of his profits back to God in the form of financial support for works maintained for the love of God, such as social welfare projects.

During the many centuries when churches took care of social welfare, Christians measured the existence of Christian communities by the existence of Christian social welfare institutions. Thus, through the early twentieth century, Christians considered a Christian community to exist when, beyond a church, Christians were maintaining schools, hospitals, and other service facilities. These types of institutions survived only to the extent that Christians subsidized their costs. The assumption among all nineteenth-century Christians, not just Ethiopianists, was that, for Christian communities to develop, new Christians needed to possess both disposable income and a predisposition toward sharing this income with their churches.

Industrial education was perceived to supply simultaneously both these needs. Industrial education schools would teach their students how to produce goods and services for the market and how to use the market profits to live comfortable, healthy Christian lives. And, since part of a Christian life is recognition of the obligation to give back something to the church, the anticipation existed that students with an industrial education would give back enough to cover the cost of their schooling and, ideally, all the social welfare institutions associated with their church.

However, no record exists of industrial education working in these ways at any Christian school. Hampton Institute and then its daughter institution, Tuskegee, drew notice exactly because they seemed to supply such examples. Neither Hampton nor Tuskegee ever actually covered its expenditures through its revenues, though General Samuel C. Armstrong at Hampton and Booker T. Washington at Tuskegee boasted that their schools did. Still, Hampton and Tuskegee seemed to Christians to come closer to paying their own costs than any comparable institutions. In addition, the schools seemed to be doing a remarkable job of equipping their graduates with the social and economic skills they needed in order to be competitive in the modern market-driven world, and students who graduated from Hampton and Tuskegee drew praise to themselves precisely for their commitment to the Christian regeneration of black communities.

The leadership positions to which Hampton and Tuskegee graduates aspired got them into trouble with the African American clergy, whom both Armstrong and Washington often targeted as ineffectual, if not incompetent, as guides for the movement for racial uplift. The black clergy in turn took exception to the idea of "blacksmiths and truck farmers" as race leaders.[47] Hyperbole without sustainable proof emanated in the claims and counterclaims of Armstrong and Washington on one side and their detractors on the other. These detractors pictured industrial education as an inferior form of education and the Christianity preached at industrial institutes as an inferior form of Christianity.

The shouting match that developed between adversarial groups of black Christians in the United States had little impact in Africa. African newspapers gave sparse notice to the assaults on Washington and his integrity and to the dangers associated with following his path toward racial uplift. The absence of negative press for Washington reflected African Ethiopianists' proclivities. The African Christians discussed in this study illustrate a conservative outlook. They did not want to destroy Western capitalism; they wanted African capitalism to commandeer its markets. They believed that social, political, and economic transformation should be initiated from the top of society by individuals with recognized authority working though established hierarchies. When they wrote in newspapers about examples of peoples other than African Americans upon whom to model their strategies of racial uplift, most regularly they mentioned the Japanese because of their admiration for the role elites played in effecting change in Japanese society.[48]

African Christians identified with Booker T. Washington because they understood his goals and ambitions. They saw him as playing a worse hand of cards in a far less genial card game than they were playing with missionaries and colonial administrators. This image only made his display of skill in winning more impressive and his election by God more clear. African Christian leaders aspired to emulate Washington. This fact is well known about John L. Dube, who founded a school, Ohlange Industrial Institute, that he was proud to have known as the Tuskegee of South Africa. Other African Christians, as well, embraced the movement to create a school like Tuskegee as a benchmark of their battle for racial regeneration. For them, it was to be the first and most important brush stroke painted by the lion.

# 2

## Making People

### *Becoming Educators and Entrepreneurs at Hampton and Tuskegee*

Let us make the teachers and we will make the people.[1]

HAMPTON NORMAL AND AGRICULTURAL INSTITUTE

The idea of industrial education that caught the attention of black Christians in Africa at the end of the nineteenth century had its start across the Atlantic at Hampton Institute in Hampton, Virginia, where Booker T. Washington trained. The school served as the prototype for Tuskegee Institute in Tuskegee, Alabama, which Washington developed. Washington built upon the idea of industrial education promoted at Hampton and made the idea more attractive to black Christians everywhere.

In the nineteenth century, industrial education was used as a generic term to signify any type of schooling that placed some emphasis on manual training. The expression "industrial" had no necessary connection with the factory floor. Manual education was supposed to make people industrious in ways that humanistic training did not, hence the designation.[2] Christian schools across the world made use of the approach. General Samuel C. Armstrong, founder of Hampton, traced his notion of industrial education back to that of his father, who ran a Christian school system based upon the approach for the kingdom of Hawaii during the 1850s.[3] Hampton Institute employed innovations by pairing industrial education with normal school instruction. Armstrong consciously set out to train future teachers to build and maintain schools for freed slaves in the rural American South. Industrial education as taught at Hampton served as a means to this end. Freed people lived in impoverished areas. Most of them had little to no previous exposure to European intellectual skills, even less to notions of academic discipline. Local communities had no money for school buildings and little with which to pay teachers. In addition, local whites retained bitter resentment about the Civil War and held animosity against any action that could be interpreted as advancing the cause of black people.[4]

Armstrong educated his students to survive and advance in these harsh conditions. He taught them to focus above all else on the inculcation of Christian social discipline. They were tutored to concentrate only on the educational rudiments as teachers. He trained them to teach as a vocation, while depending on a secondary, technical competence for their living. This strategy had costs, the most obvious being the limited intellectual horizon Hampton provided for its graduates, and its graduates in turn for their own pupils. Technical training took up a significant amount of the time at Hampton that at a liberal arts institution would have been dedicated to scholarly course work. Poor students, who, like Washington, appeared at the gates of the school penniless, did extra work and spent extra years working their way through school. As a result, Hampton graduates had comparatively weaker academic preparation when they went out on the job market.

Armstrong insisted, however, that they were better prepared than traditionally trained students for their true task: the Christian regeneration of African American freed people. Looking back, Armstrong remembered his father's postulating that Christian regeneration occurred through the agency of teachers or educators, not through the agency of evangelists or preachers. The teachers his father had in mind taught industrial skills. The industrial school, not the mission station, provided the optimum place for converts to learn to live as Christians.[5]

Behind Armstrong's convictions stood a different understanding from that of most Christians of the conversion experience and, by extension, the regeneration process. Armstrong's ideas shaped those of Washington and, through Washington, the ideas of the African Christians who turned toward industrial education as a solution to Africa's problems. Understanding Armstrong's thinking aids in the comprehension of his industrial education philosophy. Armstrong did not articulate a theology, but he said a great deal, over the twenty-five years he served as Hampton's principal, about Christianity and its practice. After his death, his sayings were collected and published in two separate volumes.[6]

Armstrong deemphasized the importance of the act of conversion and, implicitly, the significance of the evangelist in the Christianization process. He emphasized, instead, the obligation of the Christian individual to pursue a faith-inspired mental and social discipline throughout life. For Armstrong, it was not the act of conversion but the life lived after the act that counted:

> Conversion is indeed the starting point for a better life; it is to character what the seed is to the ripe fruit. The choice of God's service is the initial step; the goal is the rounded, perfect, Christian life. To take the step requires the decision, possibly of the moment; to reach the goal is the struggle of a lifetime. Viewed thus, one understands that it is not the planting of the seed which costs, but the wise and vigilant care of the growing crop.
>
> All over the world we find men accepting, with comparative readiness, the theories of Christianity, while its moralities remain beyond their reach; and this must be so until the reconstructive power of a many-sided training is recognized, and systems are adopted which build up men "all round."[7]

Armstrong had doubts about the ability of Christian converts to live a Christian life on their own. These doubts reflected his perception of true Christianity as an internal state articulated through external comportment.

To the extent that one Christian could guide another in the right direction, Armstrong believed that lay Christians guided other lay Christians best in the way toward salvation. They could help each other maintain military discipline, and Christian life demanded such training. Armstrong served as a Union general during the Civil War, and much like Ignatius of Loyola, founder of the Jesuits, another soldier turned spiritual leader, Armstrong's understanding of Christian living reflected a military mind-set at work. Soldiers are trained through repetition and drill to respond in certain ways to various threats. Armstrong sought to apply the same principles to training for life as a Christian.

At Hampton, Armstrong devised an educational program that emphasized the acquisition, through repetition and drill, of the physical and mental habits he associated with Christianity. "The average Negro student," he wrote, "needs a regime which shall control the twenty-four hours of each day."[8] As Armstrong further explained:

> The education needed for the elevation of the colored race is one that touches upon the whole range of life, that aims at a foundation of good habits and sound principles, that considers the details of each day; that

enjoins, in respect to diet, regularity, proper selection, and good cooking; and in respect to habits, suitable clothing, exercise, cleanliness of persons and quarters and ventilation, also industry and thrift; and in respect to all things, intelligent practice and self-restraint.[9]

All of the traits associated with what Max Weber, in *The Protestant Ethic and the Spirit of Capitalism*, would come to label "this world asceticism" Armstrong aspired to instill at his school in his students using his methods.[10]

Armstrong's commitment to the idea that his students offer more of a behavioral than an intellectual bridge between the life lived by African American freedmen and what he recognized as Christian life translated into a focus on mastering every hour of the twenty-four-hour day. All students at Hampton were required to spend part of each day in some sort of manual skill acquisition. But Hampton was best known for its Trade School Course, or Night School, that Armstrong called his former student Booker T. Washington back to campus to run. Students in the Night School spent forty-nine hours a week in Shop Practice, or factory work, for their first three years at the school, along with thirty-two hours a week of other forms of supervised instruction. Only in their fourth year did students cease to spend the majority of their time in one of the workshops and, instead, take regular classes, typically in the Normal Course. These students were Hampton's future rural teachers. Having a dedicated set of worker students allowed the factory workshops associated with Hampton to function efficiently in spite of the necessity of providing work experience for students majoring in other areas. And it was the Night School that permitted indigent students to pay for their education. Despite the benefits that can be recognized for both Hampton and the students in question, the students were obviously among the poorest and probably the least prepared, and arguably were being exploited.[11] Armstrong, however, saw the Night School as the acid test for his scheme for black racial regeneration. He took great pride in the program for not only giving poor boys a chance but also for weeding out all but the most determined of students. For him, the discipline and focus that Night School students had to acquire in order to succeed through their course of study were characteristics that rural black school children needed to learn from their teachers.[12]

Many students did not complete the Hampton program of study. However, Armstrong championed the ones who did as better suited than clergymen to direct black racial uplift. "Let us make the teachers," Armstrong once proclaimed, "and we will make the people."[13] Armstrong intended to take industrial education beyond teaching manual industriousness solely. The social experiment implicit in his maxim postulated that ethnogenesis could be effected through education. Schoolteachers, trained the right way, to the right discipline, could induce collective social transformation. Schools, not churches, could be the vehicles of African American Christian regeneration.

Viewed from the perspective of educational thinking in the first decades of the twenty-first century, Armstrong's educational approach commands attention. His precocious presumptions concerning the effectiveness of immersion education and about the heuristic power of STEM (science, technology, engineering, and mathematics) instruction for shaping social and cultural behavior merit appreciation for the extent to which they look toward future issues and solutions in mass education. Armstrong sought to demonstrate that his vision of education made better people and better Christians. He believed that education should be practical, as opposed to speculative, training; it should be applied, instead of being dominated by humanistic thinking. Students at Hampton received a functional education that included the necessary amount of language and Bible study but more than enough study in social discipline and technical knowledge to grant a position in a classroom. Their training changed the landscape in terms of what black rural schoolteachers could do and might be expected to do.

Contemporaries recognized the revolutionary nature of the Hampton approach to industrial education. They did so in part because of Armstrong's phenomenal abilities at marketing his school and its program. Armstrong pioneered methods of fundraising, "begging" as he called it, that marked him as a media-knowledgeable Christian evangelist well before the time of today's skilled practitioners. Armstrong made Hampton a national Christian social cause, a "unique educational charity."[14] And, during his tenure as principal, a significant portion of the operating revenue for Hampton came from small donations mailed in to Hampton by pious Christians from across the country.

Armstrong achieved this success, however, at the price of manipulating a set of negative images of freed black people that will haunt his memory forever. Louis Harlan characterized Armstrong as "a racist white man, benevolently racist if there is such a thing, but still racist."[15] Yet Armstrong represented more than racism, and that quality impacted his use of racist imagery. Armstrong recognized helping black people to become true Christians as an evangelical cause that received his life's dedication. For those black people who shared his cause, he created an educational experience that introduced them to true Christianity in a rigorous but effective fashion. To those white people who shared his cause, he turned for help to pay for that educational experience, playing upon their racially based emotions to elicit financial support.

Two articles published in popular media, one from early in Armstrong's time at Hampton and the other from the last years of his tenure, illustrate how Armstrong presented Hampton to the white public from whom he drew support. In November 1873, five years after Hampton was founded, *Harper's New Monthly Magazine* published a long illustrated article on the school.[16] Helen Ludlow, Armstrong's "alter ego" and the woman who ran Hampton when Armstrong was away on his many tours to raise funds, wrote the piece, though Armstrong had an obvious role in its composition. The article demonstrated what might be considered Armstrong's signature strategy of appealing to the white sense of charity through a massage of the white sense of race. All the positive white stereotypes about black people are mentioned, with the understanding that they were commonly on display at Hampton. So the institution boasted its own "Uncle Tom," who, Ludlow informs us, was "as much a character in his own way as his famous namesake."[17]

In another example in the article, Ludlow and Armstrong have an extended discussion about John Solomon, General Armstrong's black valet. During the abolition movement in Britain, Josiah Wedgwood, the successful pottery maker, created an iconic image of a kneeling chained black man asking the question, "Am I not a man and brother?" In response to the image, Armstrong was quoted in the article as answering the question of brotherhood in the affirmative. This "man and brother," Armstrong announced about Solomon, would have been worth the extraordinary sum of $3,000 during slavery, though Armstrong assured Ludlow that he would not have sold Solomon, even for that.[18] To Ludlow's comment that she would have helped Solomon escape to freedom, Armstrong chastised her, saying, "Oh, you needn't bring any of your abolition talk down here, it won't go down."[19] This comment came ten years after the Emancipation Proclamation and eight years after a Union victory that Armstrong and the black troops he commanded helped to achieve. The mixed signals conveyed in the exchange demonstrate Armstrong's promotional strategy. They provided something for everybody:

whites, blacks, Southerners, Northerners, advocates of slavery, and abolitionists. All could see what they read as a prompt to support Hampton.

On April 16, 1889, in what seems to have been a paid advertisement in the form of an article in the *New York Times*, Hampton Institute solicited public contributions for the building of a new Science Hall on its campus. Few details are offered about the proposed building. The bulk of the article focuses on the role Hampton aspired to fill in resolving America's problem with its racial minorities. With African Americans, the solution attempted to fit them into the American dream. Thus, "any well-to-do person" who chose to visit the campus would see "low brows, dull faces and uncouth manners," among the black students, but the visitor would also see that "every boy before him shrinks from no bodily toil by day so that by night he might study to reach some remote likeness to white folks standards." Upon viewing boys acting in this way, the well-to-do visitor was assured that he would "feel a throb in his heart, if he has one," and then send a check to the treasurer of Hampton.[20] In the 1870s Native Americans were sent to Hampton by the U.S. government to be educated. The school's principal task lay in creating acceptance of white authority. As the article explained, presumably with the thought of the cost of mounting military expeditions to Indian lands in mind, "Indian boy braves" could be "civilized far more cheaply than the cost of shooting them when full grown."[21]

Most striking about the *New York Times* piece is its determination to tap every possible race-based motivation for inducing contributions to Hampton. So, after offering the carrots of giving in order to see black students strive to emulate white people or Native American students pacified, the article offers the stick of giving to strike a blow against fraudulent Christianity. Thus, those readers who, continued the article, "think the negro exhorters, those blind expounders of religion to blinder hearers, are objects almost as pathetic as ludicrous will be glad to hear that Hampton is doing something to make them less a discredit to Christian enlightenment."[22] The "something" in question was not specified, but readers were assured that the proposed Science Hall "would provide for [it] also."[23]

Derogatory images of black people abounded in white American newspapers in the late nineteenth century, and white Americans maintained a set of stereotypic ideas and assumptions about black people that were constantly reinforced in print media. Armstrong manipulated these stereotypes in pursuit of funding for his school. But these manipulations went both ways, toward confirmation of positive as well as negative assumptions. If some stereotype should be challenged, Armstrong suggested, give to his school. If some stereotype deserved confirmation, give to his school as well.

At one place in the *Harper's New Monthly Magazine* essay, Ludlow characterized the type of black rural schoolteachers Hampton was attempting to produce as akin to the "missionary in Africa." Like the missionary, the rural schoolteacher was to serve as a "little center of civilization," for freed people, providing guidance on how to build better homes and farms, and supplying a role model on how to be a better citizen.[24] The allusions prompt the speculation that Armstrong was aware of Alexander Crummell's proposal for the regeneration of Africa published eight years earlier. Armstrong proposed essentially the same scheme for transforming African Americans into Christians as Crummell did for transforming Africans into Christians. In both schemes, a black Christian entrepreneurial class becomes a bridge between civilization and barbarism, between white and black. Crummell's plan presumed the previous formation of a class of black entrepreneurs whose faith and self-love—that is, desire for profit—would be sufficient to induce them to redirect their lives and energies toward the regeneration of Africa. In the Armstrong scheme, the existence of this class of individuals was not presupposed but, rather, instigated. Industrial education, as taught at Hampton, claimed Armstrong, would create a class of entrepreneurs in the rural American South who would possess the desire and capacity to make money when opportunities presented themselves and also the commitment and discipline to teach, most important of all.

The Armstrong plan placed the genesis of these black schoolteachers/ entrepreneurs in the hands of whites. Sympathetic white Christians would fund the Christian regeneration of African Americans. Armstrong's plan opened the door to the empowerment of black people who were left out of the Crummell plan, either because of poverty or because of a lack of prior education or both. The plan's weakness lay in its leaving black racial uplift at the mercy of white racial sensibilities, which could and did change.

Armstrong appropriated an Ethiopianist approach to black racial uplift and rethought it according to the proclivities of white Christians. In his scheme, black Christians still figured as the agents of social transformation. Yet, in his scheme also, the black Christians in question would have been previously trained by whites to white expectations and their standards. African American Christians, most significantly black clergy-men, pointed to the problems with white expectations and standards; whites took for granted their own superiority. Therefore, they instinc-tively educated black people toward a sense of racial inferiority. Bishop Henry M. Turner made this point in his description of his visit to the Hampton campus. Turner recognized the mixed signals in Hampton's message. He noted, for example, the portraits of various white Southern Protestant luminaries hanging on the walls in the chapel, including the portraits of President Andrew Johnson, the Southern Democrat who fol-lowed Lincoln into office, and General Robert E. Lee, commander of the Confederate army. Turner wondered and asked, "What [have] the two last ever done for the colored people?"[25]

The experience that drew the bishop's greatest ire, however, was a chance encounter with a white woman teacher who rebuffed Turner's query about the courses in mathematics, ancient languages, and sci-ences being taught at Hampton with her return comment that the black students at the school were not ready for such advanced subjects and would not be ready for years to come.[26] Turner went on to assure her that she must mean only the black people living in Virginia since those living in the other states were more than ready for those subjects. He then indicted the white teachers at Hampton, but explicitly not Arm-strong, either as being "ex-slaveholders themselves" or as pandering "to the spirit of slavery" for teaching "negro inferiority . . . by act, if not by word."[27]

Armstrong's standing among black Christians held such significance that Turner attempted to exonerate the general from any responsibil-ity for the "slaveholder" mentality that to Turner's mind pervaded the atmosphere at Hampton. An Ethiopianist audience would have got-ten the message that Hampton was a place to be avoided. As Turner repeated several times, and as other black critics of the school likewise complained, Armstrong and his school took the initiative in the regen-eration of black people out of black hands and placed it in white ones. Hampton taught black people that they were lost souls, people in need of regeneration, not people prepared to save others.[28]

Robert Francis Engs has written against this assessment and has endeavored to show that, in their self-embraced commitment to the Christian regeneration of other black people, Hampton's graduates were among the staunchest Ethiopianists in late nineteenth-century America. They took the uplifting of the race as a "sacred obligation" to be honored not only through their daily labor but also through ancillary activities like teaching Sunday school and adult evening classes and directing YMCA activities and temperance groups.[29] In Engs' thinking, Armstrong and his corps of teachers, most of whom were recruited from New England, should be given credit for inspiring exactly the sense of racial pride that some black Christians accused them of trying to crush.[30]

Still, under Armstrong, Hampton served and was meant to serve as a testament to white Christian paternalism. Paternalism presumes the existence of children to be raised. And on Hampton's campus, African Americans could not escape being designated as children. Black people who saw themselves as leading the battle to uplift the African race could not help but feel diminished by their invisibility in the eyes of Armstrong and his staff.

### Tuskegee Normal and Industrial Institute

In the literature on the Protestant Reformation in early modern Europe, historians often repeat the adage, "Erasmus laid the egg that Luther hatched," meaning that Desiderius Erasmus crafted the blueprint for church reform that Martin Luther then applied as the Protestant Reformation.[31] A similar argument may be made about the educational approach General Armstrong crafted at Hampton and Booker T. Washington applied at Tuskegee. The outline of church reform Erasmus promoted gave greater scope to lay initiative in shaping Christian devotional life. Luther used this outline to assert the authority of Germany's lay nobility over the Christian churches in their territories. In a similar fashion, Armstrong devised the master plan for an institution that equipped black people from the bottom of society to take the initiative in the Christian regeneration of the black race. Washington used this master plan to build an institution whose graduates aspired to shape Christian black society from the bottom up.[32]

The distinction between what Armstrong envisioned and Washington realized had to do with race. Washington saw potential where Armstrong did not, primarily from lack of perception. Armstrong was not, as Harlan insisted, a racist. The audiences to whom he was making his case were primarily well-to-do whites, to use his term. Armstrong developed Hampton to fit their expectations. To change metaphors, the seed of another type of school, a school that could fit, and perhaps articulate, black expectations existed in what Armstrong created. Washington brought this seed to harvest. Washington demonstrated to black audiences, black Christian audiences most powerfully, that what could be perceived as the racist elements to Armstrong's agenda were incidental to the value of the approach to education Armstrong pioneered. Washington made manifest the possibilities for self-initiated racial regeneration inherent in the approach but left mostly untapped by Armstrong.

Washington's Tuskegee Institute copied and enhanced five attributes of the educational experience offered at Hampton. Three of these had to do with organization and structure. The two others had more to do with faith. First, Washington recreated Hampton's institutional apparatus. This included the campus with its academic buildings, dormitories, workshops, and farms; the military-like uniforms students were required to wear and the regimented life students were required to live; the working approach to pay for student fees and the curriculum with its conscious focus on social discipline and the acquisition of applied skills; and the daily chapel services and the Sunday night addresses to the student body by the college president. Washington translated this entire rubric from Virginia to Alabama, right down to the Night School program and the Negro spirituals sung by all at the evening chapel service. Unlike at Hampton, however, which remained a white-run school for black students, at Tuskegee, blacks supervised and maintained every aspect of the institutional apparatus.

Washington added to and accentuated the emphasis on applied skills and agricultural research implicit in Hampton's mission but never brought to the fore during Armstrong's time. Washington never lost sight of the Protestant idea that demonstrated control of the material world could be read as a sign of spiritual election. Washington took as part of his agenda as a black Christian educator, then, the creation of a class of black Christians who owned property. Entrepreneurship involved more than making money as Washington saw it; it involved seeking and claiming God's grace based upon material success. With this goal in mind, though most Tuskegee graduates, just like most Hampton graduates, went into teaching, still systematic training in the skilled trades was incorporated into the curriculum at Tuskegee, and buildings to house these types of training were a defining feature of campus architecture.[33]

Sir Harry Johnston recorded revealing observations on how the differing agendas of Armstrong and Washington shaped the campuses of the two schools. In 1909 he published twin articles comparing Hampton and Tuskegee in the *Times* of London. Johnston celebrated the "orderly beauty" of the Hampton grounds, which he said offered a sight rarely to be seen in the United States. He noted the numerous workshops dedicated to the trades. He also noted, however, that these workshops were located five miles removed from the main campus. The absence of buildings dedicated to the trades on the main campus prompted Johnston to conclude that at Hampton "music is the main discipline," the reference being to the emphasis on the use of black Christian music as a teaching tool on the campus.[34] In contrast, Tuskegee was preoccupied with "industrial education." In a tone of amazement, Johnston spent a significant portion of the article on Tuskegee describing such things as the museum where "specimens of the innumerable vegetable products of the South are preserved" and the Slater-Armstrong Memorial Trades Building, where "mechanical arts are taught in a most effective and practical manner."[35]

At Hampton under Armstrong, industrial education was a means to an end. At Tuskegee, industrial education was an end in itself. Hampton did not offer its first certificate in training in trade until 1895, two years after the death of Armstrong.[36] "Mechanical arts," as Johnston called them, drew Washington's attention from the start. Charles W. Elliot, president of Harvard University, visited Tuskegee a few years before Johnston did and chastised Washington for the "overdevelopment" of the agricultural and industrial shops at the school.[37] Yet in 1900 the German government crowned Washington's concentration on improvement of research in agricultural and technical fields when it sent representatives to Washington seeking Tuskegee's assistance in the development of commercial cotton farming in Togo, the German West African colony.[38] German supplication of African American expertise demonstrated to black people that Tuskegee was taking education in directions that made black people more, not less, competitive with whites.

In an article celebrating the accomplishments of Tuskegee twenty-five years after its establishment, Washington boasted among other things that Tuskegee maintained "the largest school of academic studies among our people in the world."[39] A number of Muslim institutions in Africa might compete for that claim, but in the Christian world Washington's boast had some validity. In making the statement, Washington may have been simply seeking to counteract W. E. B. Du Bois' characterizations of Tuskegee as primarily a manual training and normal school. Then again, the assiduous ways in which Washington sought to recruit for his school Du Bois himself (before 1903) as the preeminent black social scientist, and George Washington Carver as the outstanding black natural scientist, suggest that Washington did aspire to make Tuskegee a center of academic renown.[40]

The second thing that Washington copied from Armstrong may be called, to follow Engs' terminology, Washington's approach to "educational entrepreneurship."[41] Washington may have possessed the skills for making people give in even greater supply than did Armstrong. Certainly, Washington had few peers in soliciting donations for his school. And no other educator could brag of a private endowment like the one that Andrew Carnegie provided Washington for Washington's own personal needs.[42] Washington built upon the success of Armstrong, however. And Armstrong's influence was crucial in terms of the "begging" strategies Washington employed. The American Missionary Association and the U.S. government initially funded most of the schools for freedmen that came into existence. Armstrong moved very early to seek funding for his school outside these channels and by the 1880s had built up a network of private donors that he generously shared with Washington. Thus, as funding from the American Missionary Association and the federal government declined, as it did in the last two decades of the nineteenth century, and other black schools struggled to find alternative sources of revenue, Washington and Tuskegee built on their existing networks of private sector support.[43]

The trade-off for Washington for this private sector support was sufferance of the racism of many of the white donors. Engs suggests that this was a problem for Armstrong too, but obviously not to the same degree.[44] Even a century later, reading some of the racist platitudes through which Washington had to sit and listen to before the checks changed hands remains mind numbing.[45] But from the Christian point of view, it may be argued that it was in these moments that Washington could be seen to display the forbearance that God providentially grants those who are doing his work. What many modern commentators might see as acts illustrative of Washington's subservience to white racism, in other words, many contemporary Christians would have recognized as a display of Christian fortitude.

The third thing that Armstrong did that Washington copied was to use his school as a vehicle of community outreach. Both Armstrong and Washington aspired to embed their schools in their communities, to use the modern term, meaning that both men sought to make the institutional apparatus of their school a resource for the local community. Circumstances and opportunities differed for the two men, however.

The material resources available to Washington had not been present for Armstrong earlier. Tuskegee came into existence during America's Gilded Age, an age of extraordinary individual wealth, with the emergence of the charitable institutions that still dominate the American philanthropic landscape. The Social Gospel movement arose, with Christian charity channeled in the direction of building and maintaining Christian social institutions to help the poor and working classes. Tuskegee was the recipient of significant amounts of philanthropic aid. Washington used these monies to make Tuskegee the center of local, regional, and even national networks of organizations and institutions aimed at helping black people. The bulk of Washington's initiatives were directed toward the eradication of black poverty through the creation of a class of black property holders.[46]

General Armstrong was known for riding his horse across the town of Hampton in the late afternoons seeking freedmen with whom to converse. The conversations were not about Christianity but about capitalism, with Armstrong preaching the importance of the ownership of property as a first step.[47] Knowledge of these excursions perhaps influenced Washington to initiate the Tuskegee Negro Farm Conferences that began in 1892. The conferences represented a second step for people who had already taken the first one recommended by Armstrong. Washington invited seventy-five people to that first conference; more than four hundred people showed up. From that time, attendance at the conferences continued to grow until it reached into the thousands. The topics of these conferences always had something to do with the plight of black farmers and those who struggled with the realities of an economic system set up in such a fashion as not to favor their continued survival. These topics were always approached from the perspective that it was possible for farmers to do more than survive; it was possible for them to prosper. Incongruously, Washington expounded this message when there was so much evidence to the contrary. Always on stage with him, however, Washington included a number of successful black farmers and businessmen, other examples beyond himself of what personal subscription to the Protestant ethic could produce.[48]

The question of the nature of Washington's religious beliefs deserves some attention before consideration of the ways in which Washington built upon at Tuskegee the Christian experience he underwent as a student at Hampton. The harshest of Washington's critics have framed him as a Machiavellian who feigned devotion as the situation demanded.[49]

Even scholars more sympathetic to Washington have seen him as exhibiting only a "practical," "cold-water Christianity."[50] Criticism suggesting the counterfeit nature of Washington's faith or its "coldness" does not describe, however, the practice of religious life at the school he built.[51] The religious activities that took place at Tuskegee on Friday nights provide an example of the nature and focus of Washington's Christian commitment. At that time, the chapel became the venue for what Washington labeled as "prayer meetings." Attendance at these informal sessions was voluntary. Students and faculty met, as Washington described it, "as one large family" at this, "the most home-like of all services." Washington wrote, "At times so much interest is manifested that it often happens that two or more will be on their feet at the same time striving to get a hearing." He described how others would "raise hymns or begin to pray, or speak or repeat verses of Scripture at the same time."[52] Washington approved of the enthusiasm that filled the Tuskegee chapel on these occasions.

"These meetings are productive of much good," Washington concluded. As a matter of fact, he continued, "Many of the students date(d) their conversions from the impulse received at these Friday evening meetings."[53] By conversion, Washington had in mind the pledge cards students signed in January at the culmination of the annual Week of Prayer (actually two weeks) when continuous preaching by invited ministers from across the spectrum of denominations created a revival atmosphere on campus. On the card students pledged to announce to others that they had accepted Christ, that they would pray and read the Bible every day, and that they would join the church of their choice and begin to live a Christian life.[54]

Scholars have mistakenly searched for Washington's faith in the denominational pieties of the nineteenth century. Washington seemed far more at home and comfortable with nondogmatic forms of Christian religious experience. Washington understood, and Tuskegee institutionally pursued, Christian conversion as a prelude to denominational affiliation. Students were invited to become Christians first and then seek a denominational church (if necessary) in which to nurture that faith.[55] Christianity was, as Armstrong taught Washington, about living the faith. Washington noted with gratification about the Week of Prayer that it provided an opportunity for students to return from a period of lapsed faith to try again to live a Christian life.[56] The good thing was that backsliders kept trying. For Washington, that was the goal of faith.

The fourth attribute that Washington copied may be labeled Hampton's nondenominational Christian character. Armstrong conceived of Hampton as a training ground for a Christianity devised for and propagated by laypeople. Armstrong identified the Protestant church establishment in the United States, as represented by the American Missionary Association, as the enemy to be flanked in order for his school to evolve. He publicly promoted the graduates of Hampton as superior Christians in comparison to the ministers appointed by black denominations and insisted that the former were better equipped than the latter to Christianize freedmen.

Here also, Washington followed in Armstrong's footsteps. In 1890 Washington published an article condemning America's black denominational clergy as corrupt and ill trained. In the article, Washington made the controversial claim that "three-fourths of the Baptist ministers and two-thirds of the Methodists [were] unfit" for the pulpit.[57] Washington's attack on the black ministry has been interpreted in various ways, though never as a continuation of the assault on that ministry begun by Armstrong, who had been publishing similar statements for decades. Less than a year before Washington published his critical essay, Armstrong characterized Negro "exhorters" in the *New York Times* as both "pathetic" and "ludicrous." When given the option of providing a remedy for the problem he identified, Washington opted for the same remedy implemented by Armstrong—that is, the creation of a nondenominational Bible training school for ministers.[58]

Armstrong, however, was content to leave his Bible school as an informal set of courses taught on an ad hoc basis by local ministers. Washington moved quickly to formalize his Bible school. He convinced Caroline Phelps of New York to fund the erection of a building, Phelps Hall, and then fund a new certificate program in pastoral training. The Phelps Hall Bible Training School was officially dedicated in 1893. Symbolically, the dedication was the last official event attended by General Armstrong before he died.[59] As with the "Pastor's Class" at Hampton, the curriculum at the training school at Tuskegee aimed at effacing the boundaries between the pastoral training given to aspiring clergy and mission-minded laypeople. Lay Christians from the communities surrounding Tuskegee who were already involved in some form of ministry but who also had hopes of opening their own churches came to the school to take courses on how to preach.[60] Tuskegee students with ambitions to pastor congregations later learned how to do so at the school following a work-study approach. Each week the students had to fill out a form noting the number of pastoral acts they had performed. The information to be provided ranged from "places you have labored" (church, jail, almshouse, and such) to sermons preached to marriages solemnized to "homes secured through your advice and help during the last week."[61]

The fifth and last attribute that Washington took from Armstrong, but altered in ways meaningful to black audiences, was Armstrong's critique of black Christianity. Washington's comments about the black clergy and the response by black clergy to these comments have blinded historians to this development. Washington sought to position Tuskegee in the same spot as Armstrong did Hampton relative to the Christian establishment. Just as Armstrong pushed to make his school independent of the established denominations, so Washington sought to do the same. Just as Armstrong exploited the independence of his school to critique contemporary practices among black Christians, Washington did the same. But Washington challenged and redirected the critique Armstrong made of black Christianity away from any notion of the moral failure of blacks as a race and toward an indictment of the economic exploitation that came between poor blacks and Christian morality.

Armstrong's critique of black Christianity built on his critique of all missionary-inspired Christianity—that is, that while most blacks as converts found Christianity to be easy to accept, Christianity's "moralities remain[ed] beyond their reach." Essentially, Armstrong was arguing that Christianity, as practiced by freedmen, did not stimulate the evolution of what has already been discussed as Max Weber's idea of the Protestant ethic. Key to Armstrong's understanding of this ethic were the internalization of discipline and obligation as attributes of God's grace. Faith inspired one to work, or it was not faith. On the assumption that most Protestant white Americans had been systematically exposed to the Protestant ethic since childhood, Armstrong reasoned that most white Protestant Americans could recognize a morally deficient version of Christianity, both as preached and as practiced. On the assumption that most nonwhite (and non-Protestant) peoples had not been exposed to true Christianity, Armstrong reasoned that they could not do these things. Armstrong gave white missionaries and black preachers credit for the ability to communicate Christian enthusiasm, but he doubted the capacity of Christian evangelists of any stripe to convey true Christian morality. A presumption of superiority prefaced this conclusion, but nothing in it is inherently racist. Still, coming from a man whose concrete expressions involved using negative examples of black Christian practices, racial condescension seemed to appear in what Armstrong was saying.[62]

One of the stories Armstrong told was about an old black "Auntie" who did not allow her willingness to steal poultry to "come between her and her blessed Lord."[63] Perhaps Washington had the story in mind when he, in turn, told the story in *Up from Slavery* about his mother, who was a cook on the plantation where he grew up and who would sometimes wake her children in the middle of the night to feed them chicken she had just secretly fried. How she had come into possession of the chicken Washington insisted he did not know. But Washington went on to argue that while some people might call what his mother had done theft, and while he, given his station in life when writing about the experience, likewise would call it theft, still, with consideration granted to the time and situation when the incidents occurred, he had to say, "No one could ever convince me that my mother was guilty of thieving."[64] Washington's argument was that his mother was a "victim of the system of slavery," meaning that the material deprivations of coerced servitude caused his mother's moral awareness of stealing someone else's property to be overridden by her maternal instincts toward the survival of her offspring.

Washington challenged Armstrong's notion that there was something like a categorical Christian moral imperative that trumped all circumstances. The need to survive, Washington argued, forced black people to think beyond any Christian sense of right or wrong. As Washington explained it:

> During slavery the Colored man reasoned this way: my body belongs to master; and taking master's chickens to feed master's body is not stealing. This practice thus started has to some extent been handed down to this generation, and when pressed and cramped on every side by this horrible mortgage system, even to get food to keep life in his children, you must not be surprised if he breaks the command—Thou shalt not steal.[65]

Armstrong said that black people as a race lacked a true sense of Christ and his teachings. Washington argued to the contrary that any collective moral failings exhibited by black people were an outcome of an economic system that inhibited black people from being true to their faith. With this thought in mind, Washington regularly punctuated his speeches with the refrain, "You cannot make a good Christian out of a hungry man."[66]

Washington's solution to the economic exploitation of the rural black poor was what he called "practical Christianity," which involved "[mixing] in with religion some practical ideas which will bring about material improvement."[67] Because of his identification of economic privation as the ultimate source for the black inability to lead the type of Christian life he himself was trained to lead at Hampton, Washington held that teaching a man the skills that would grant him the capacity to feed himself and his family was as integral to the Christianization process as teaching him the Christian idea of right from wrong. Poverty kept black people from being good Christians, maintained Washington. Therefore, helping black people out of poverty assisted them to become good Christians.

Practical Christianity for Washington was ameliorative Christianity, meaning that it was faith that prompted some effort to improve the circumstances of the individual and, ideally, the community in which the individual lived. In this sense, when Washington used the term, he was thinking in alignment with the Social Gospel movement.[68] But a "practical Christian" for Washington—or, as he described such an individual in another instance, a "helpful follower of Christ"[69]—was more.

An illustration of the type of individuals Washington had in mind when he thought of practical Christians was offered in an article he wrote that was published in the journal the *Outlook* in October 1914, entitled, "A Remarkable Triple Alliance: How a Jew Is Helping the Negro through the YMCA." Ostensibly, the article related the story of Julius Rosenwald's efforts to help urban black communities.[70] In 1910 Rosenwald had promised that he would match with $25,000 any black community that raised $75,000 to build for itself a YMCA building. As of 1914, by Washington's count, ten black communities had collected the needed funds. Washington clearly played with religious and ethnic stereotypes in lauding Rosenwald's commitment as "the wisest and best-paying philanthropic investments of which I have knowledge," made all the more interesting because it was "a gift from a Jew to a Christian religious institution."[71]

This point made toward the beginning of the article, Rosenwald disappeared in what follows as Washington told every backstory that he could discover of the African American donors to the building funds who gave $1,000 or more. These were his practical Christians, individuals with wealth, faith, and race pride in sufficient combination that they could help in the uplifting of the race. The message of the article was clear. God, through Rosenwald, had given African American Christians a chance to be practical—that is, "an opportunity to help themselves."[72] Washington's joy in the individuals who seized the opportunity was evident in the words of praise he lavished on their life stories. Washington drew an important lesson from the success of the initiative. Writing in 1914, Washington was conscious of the fact that not as many white donors were opening their doors to him as had been the case earlier in his career. Yet the response by African Americans to Rosenwald's invitation was a sign to Washington that black people, black Christians, were starting to take control of their own destiny:

> Men and women who had previously taken little or no part in any organized effort to help themselves or the race were drawn into the movement. Men of all classes and all denominations united and pulled together for the common good as they never did before. The result of this was that when the work was over and the finished building came to be dedicated, the people felt that it belonged to them to an extent that they could not have felt if it had cost them any less effort and sacrifice.[73]

Ownership was power for Washington, and the effort of African Americans to own and operate their own social welfare institutions was proof to him of their emergence as a Christian people.

### Ethnogenesis through Education

Washington provided the most successful example of a teacher made by Armstrong. And, just as Armstrong had predicted, Washington, a teacher, played a sponsoring role in the evolution of a people, the practical Christians, who, as Washington talked about in the article, were remaking African American society. The strategy of teachers taking point in the social uplift of the black race, Washington reiterated whenever possible, was working. In the anniversary article about Tuskegee twenty-five years after its establishment, Washington listed six other schools for African Americans that had copied the Tuskegee model and another ten that had been established by Tuskegee graduates. As Washington proudly noted about the schools founded by his students, "There are altogether not less than 4000 young colored men and women being educated in them, and more than 200 graduates of Tuskegee Institute are engaged as teachers in other industrial schools."[74] Washington did not mention the schools in Africa and Europe that he knew through correspondence consciously sought to follow Tuskegee's formula for racial regeneration.[75] By Tuskegee's twenty-fifth anniversary, photography had become an important vehicle for communicating the process of change over time. The anniversary article, and many others published under Washington's direction for popular consumption, was festooned with photographs of Tuskegee featuring black people living and thriving in all the social acts associated with Protestant Christian civilization. They had learned so that they could teach.[76]

Washington's promotion of Tuskegee proved persuasive. The world accepted Tuskegee as the proof of Armstrong's maxim. People traveled from afar to see the educational miracle Tuskegee represented. European thinkers interested in social development, including Max Weber and Sir Harry Johnston, took the week or so required to travel by rail down to Tuskegee and then back to the North. African thinkers interested in the same subject, including Orishetukeh Faduma and John L. Dube, did likewise. Marcus Garvey came to the United States to make the trip to Tuskegee, but Washington died before Garvey saw the campus. Two American presidents, William McKinley and Theodore Roosevelt, traveled from Washington to Tuskegee during their terms in office. At the ceremonies commemorating Tuskegee's twenty-fifth anniversary in 1906, Washington was joined on the stage by Andrew Carnegie (then the richest man in the world), President Elliot of Harvard, and William Howard Taft (a future American president but then secretary of war).[77]

African American critics offered the one great protest against the recognition of Tuskegee as the educational engine that was powering African American social transformation. Washington inherited the Ethiopianist opposition to Armstrong and added to it by using his success at Tuskegee as a springboard into political lobbying on the national level. Black opposition to what was now seen as the Hampton-Tuskegee approach rejected any positive connection between industrial education and African American achievement. Reverend John W. E. Bowen, Methodist minister and professor at Gammon Theological Seminary in Atlanta, offered the characterization mentioned earlier of Tuskegee graduates as blacksmiths and truck farmers. Bowen made the comment in the context of an argument that, as an outcome of the leadership of Washington and his charges, African American society had degenerated since the end of the Civil War. To get back on its feet and moving in the right direction, the race needed an "educated, consecrated, spotless, God-fearing ministry" to take charge.[78] Bowen's willingness to cast African American history since Emancipation as a counternarrative of degeneration reveals the vehemence, but perhaps also the futility, of the clerical opposition to Washington.

With greater impact, Bowen's colleague and friend W. E. B. Du Bois went after Washington from the perspective of the new discipline of sociology. Writing against the notion that Hampton and Tuskegee graduates had made a difference in African American life, Du Bois collected data that indicated that, as of the year 1900, approximately 2,500 black people in the United States held college degrees as distinct from normal school degrees. Analysis of this data revealed that these college graduates supplied not only the bulk of the black doctors, lawyers, and ministers but also the greater part of the elementary schoolteachers in the American South. They even supplied the majority of the instructors at Tuskegee itself. Numbers illustrated then that the "talented tenth"—the term was coined in the context of this discussion—was made up not of the technically trained people Hampton and Tuskegee produced but of college graduates trained in the humanities. Hampton and Tuskegee had made neither the teachers nor the people being used in the example.[79]

Du Bois' argument resonated as an explanation of the past but not as an anticipation of the future. The force of Du Bois' argument was weakened by its glorification of the humanities at a time when technology was clearly dictating global political and social change. Du Bois' ideas of social regeneration gave little thought to the issue of how black people were going to gain a command of technology. Du Bois observed that the value of learning mathematics and technical skills were the intellectual stimulation, not the practical benefits, they provided: "Manual training can and ought to be used in schools, but as a means and not as an end—to quicken intelligence and self-knowledge and not to teach carpentry; just as arithmetic is used to train minds and not skilled accountants."[80] Du Bois' position raised the question that if black people were going to need carpenters and accountants and other individuals with technical proficiencies, where exactly were black students going to acquire those types of training?

Du Bois developed this argument in The Souls of Black Folks, a book celebrated for its brilliance in African newspapers almost immediately after its publication. Yet while Du Bois' argument against industrial education helped shape political and educational developments in the United States, it generated little support among Africans who were critical of European missions and saw only the limitations of the humanistic types of education provided in mission schools. These Africans saw the promise of industrial education as a way toward the African acquisition of the types of technical competence Du Bois dismissed but that they deemed essential for Africans to have any real chance to throw off European domination.

The young Orishetukeh Faduma offered a prescient statement of broader African sensibilities on this point in 1895, years before he visited Tuskegee's campus. Speaking at a conference in Atlanta on African American missions to Africa, a conference arranged by Bowen where industrial education was ignored except in his paper, Faduma insisted that Christian regeneration in Africa demanded industrial education. "By failing to introduce and develop the industries in mission fields," Faduma observed, the church "seems to be unwilling to recognize God in matter." To correct this, he concluded, "the song of the church and of missions for the new century should be *Christ, Tools and Man.*"[81] Faduma got the message Washington was hoping other black Christians would take from his rethinking of Hampton and its approach: black people also could initiate ethnogenesis through education. Tuskegee supplied proof that one could start with nothing and still change the future of the race. Faduma and other African Christians took this message back to Africa with them.

# 3

# The Advancement of the African

*Redefining Ethiopianism and the Challenge
of Adversarial Christianity*

Fifteen out of seventeen of the students [at Fourah Bay College] have, for reasons not yet impartially known to the public, come under the ban of the Principal's displeasure, and have been suspended in consequence. . . . We have no authorized version of the unfortunate *fiasco* at present, so let us hope that it will [not] turn out to be the repressive influence of Salisbury Square on the *advancement* of the African.[1]

## Adversarial Christianity

In the late nineteenth and early twentieth centuries, thanks to European and North American missionaries, innumerable new Christian communities came into existence in Africa. Even where Christianity had already taken root, Christian life was newly invigorated. Thousands of missionaries sailed to coastal ports and spread out across the continent, establishing networks of mission stations, schools, and centers for social services. African evangelists did the bulk of the face-to-face proselytizing. But missionaries introduced and constructed the institutional infrastructure—the schools and churches, the rituals and social practices—of Christian social and cultural life.

Missionaries brought many good things with them to Africa, as well as some bad things. Perhaps the singleness of their purpose blinded white missionaries to their racial presumptions. In contrast to those whites who, in the flush of racial arrogance after European conquest, suggested that Africans be crushed into servitude or perhaps even exterminated, missionaries defended Africans as peoples who potentially could follow in the footsteps of Europeans themselves. Unlike the Europeans who closed the door to any commonality with Africans, missionaries dedicated their lives to keeping the door open. Since they saw the door as providing an opening into their world, however, they dismissed the possibility that Africans might have the capacity to open it.

During this period, 1880–1920, Africans who were already Christian became very wary of the changes they discerned in missionary thinking and actions. The European missionaries pictured in their parents' personal conversion stories were not the same European missionaries now appearing from everywhere and ordering them about. African Christians recognized the presuppositions of racial superiority that informed missionary decisions and policies. They sensed also the greater willingness of missionaries to share with other Europeans a proprietary claim to Christian civilization as an articulation of European racial consciousness. Lastly, African Christians grew increasingly aware of missionary acquiescence, if not overt complicity, in the European conquest of their homelands.

E. Cornelius May of Sierra Leone summed up the doubts many African Christians came to share about the missionaries arriving around the turn of the twentieth century, as distinct from those who came earlier:

> In the beginning the West African Native looked upon the European Missionary as a father in whom he had implicit faith and confidence, whose honesty and purposes he trusted, and whose earnestness in the love he professed for the regeneration and up-lifting of the African race he thoroughly believed in. But that is now past. The African has begun to learn that he need not look on the white Missionary as a friend from whom he may seek advice and counsel. A good number of white Missionaries now-a-day among us are no better than other white men. . . . They are here for what they can make, and the African must take care of himself or the devil take him.[2]

More missionaries lived in Africa at the start of the twentieth century than ever before, but, from one African Christian perspective, the racism the missionaries brought with them made this a bad development.

African Christians responded in different ways to the perceived changes in missionary attitudes. Three general patterns of response may be identified. The majority of Africans reconciled themselves to European leadership of the churches they joined or attended. A minority of Africans, how large is difficult to say, but especially those with high levels of Western-style education, turned toward what has been identified here as Ethiopianism. A second minority, again of unquantifiable size, began experimenting with indigenous conceptualizations of Christian worship untethered from the contemporary European religious experience.

All of these responses involved in some way and to some degree an adversarial challenge to missionary authority. Africans rarely, if ever, completely embraced missionary guidance. And to the extent Africans did accept missionary directives, acceptance resulted in a selective engagement with missionary Christian practices. In many instances, African individuals and communities typically had before them competing missionaries. Thus, from the start, Africans had a choice of to whom to listen, even if some of the choices might entail a much longer walk on Sunday mornings. But beyond choosing a mission and a message to follow, Africans also selectively embraced the strictures that missionaries insisted Christian life required. General Armstrong's point about conversion being a moment's decision, while living a Christian life demands discipline over time, actually called attention to a cultural frontier in the white evangelization of black people, a frontier over which whites and blacks negotiated. Discipline has to do with behavioral transformation, and the questions in the black mind in both the post–Civil War American South and the early twentieth-century Africa always came back to some decision as to whether the social strictures missionaries sought to impose reflected European chauvinism or the commands of Christ. Sincere, committed white Christians could and did make convincing cases to groups of black people of the latter. The degree to which individual missionaries successfully presented Christianity in ways that transcended race need to be acknowledged. These were the people who shaped the European contribution to the Christian evangelization of Africa.

But the larger argument here concerns the reactions of African Christians to perceived missionary racism. The volition Africans retained in determining the Christian imperative inherent in the commandments pronounced by missionaries translated into a mental, a cognitive, protocol through which missionary commandments were screened for racial/cultural content. Commands deemed only to reflect European sensibilities were ignored or circumvented. And, as many a missionary complained in frustration, efforts at disciplining backsliders—those Africans who ignored or circumvented the rules—often resulted in some of their greatest pastoral failures, with backsliders disappearing from the Sunday church rolls only to be reported later as members of a competing mission church.

The ways previous scholarship has represented African reactions to missionary Christianity requires rethinking. From the moment when Bengt Sundkler published his *Bantu Prophets in South Africa*, scholars have viewed African reactions to missionary Christianity from the perspective that African discontent with missionaries created a pastoral vacuum that indigenous Christian movements evolved to fill. The majority of African Christians are assumed to have been at peace with missionary church leadership. Only Africans alienated from missionary authority, in other words, the two minorities identified above, looked outside of mission churches for direction. Focusing on the formation of what have been called African independent, or more recently African-initiated, churches, Sundkler posited the emergence in Africa of two new ideal types of Protestant clergymen, the Ethiopianist minister or pastor and the Zionist prophet or evangelist.[3] The former led congregations of alienated Africans toward some appropriated version of the Christian church life experienced in European or mission churches. The latter took alienated African congregations toward some imagined version of church life during the age of the apostles that resembled contemporary African life and custom. As Sundkler saw it, neither type of clergyman had the training to pastor African Christian communities toward the kind of sustaining balance between enthusiasm and disciplined commitment required for Christian regeneration. The men who mounted the pulpit in African independent churches could create a vision of church life, but they could not lead their members toward a fruitful engagement with the social realities outside church walls.

With due respect for the insight that Sundkler and those who have followed his lead have brought to the topic, the African reaction to changes in missionary attitudes was much broader than has been acknowledged, and African initiative went beyond the evolution of two new types of clergymen. R. Hunt Davis pointed out about South Africa that the bulk of both the "School" people, or Christians of the Cape Province, and the "Kholwa," or Christian population of Natal Province, remained in mission churches.[4] According to Sundkler's definition, neither could be incorporated into his categories of alienated Africans. Yet, as Davis also noted, Christians who stayed in mission churches became aggressively more adversarial about separating what was Christian in missionary directives from what might be dismissed as cultural chauvinism. African Christian reaction in the Cape community to missionary efforts to condemn *ukulobola*, or "bride price," provided one illustration of the point. Even the African pastors most loyal to the missionaries counseled that this was a practice that should be permitted to die out rather than be suppressed.[5]

Sundkler's use of the term "Ethiopianism" offers a sense of the divide between how whites and blacks understood the term. None of the African Christian leaders discussed in this book fit Sundkler's definition, though they all can be recognized as advancing what Africans considered an Ethiopianist agenda. Blyden was ordained as a Presbyterian, Faduma as a Congregationalist. In different generations they spearheaded the African effort to appropriate Western culture and technology in West Africa, yet during the years when they were actively promoting this cause neither pastored a congregation. Dube similarly spearheaded the African effort in South Africa. He was ordained a Congregationalist minister and never left the Congregationalist fold, but he also resigned from the ministry to pursue Christian regeneration on educational and political fronts. May in West Africa and Jabavu in South Africa publicized in their newspapers Ethiopianist initiatives. Both remained committed lay members of Wesleyan (Methodist) churches all their lives.

African independent churches, as Sundkler recognized and other scholars have confirmed, represented something new in the Christian ecclesiastical landscape. Study of these churches as the main thrust of the indigenization of Christianity in Africa, however, has come at the cost of investigation of the much broader African efforts at making forms of worship first preached by missionaries work for Africans. African Christians recognized the racism that suffused missionary Christianity during the period under investigation. Recognition did not necessarily prompt abandonment, however. The majority of African Christians converted by Christian missions stayed in mission churches and struggled through to better times. From their perspective, the importance of independent churches derived from the spectrum of stances toward mission Christianity that independent churches helped create, stances that many African Christians assumed as some point in the progression of their spiritual lives, even if they later moved on to a different view.

At one end of that spectrum stood African Christian clergymen who, whatever their convictions about missionary racism, could not bring themselves to search for or promote salvation as available outside of the denomination to which they belonged. Worth posing as emblematic in this context is Tiyo Soga, the first ordained African Presbyterian minister in South Africa, and James "Holy" Johnson, one of the first ordained Anglican priests in West Africa.[6] Both men had Ethiopianist sensibilities. Both were acutely aware of missionary racism—Johnson once remarked that it was "a natural impossibility of a white man to love a black man."[7] Both men had opportunities to venture out along the path Sundkler argued for Ethiopianists to follow. Yet both remained steadfast leaders, albeit in subordinated roles, in their missionary-dominated denominational churches. At the other end of the spectrum stood the many lay African Christians who voted with their feet and left mission churches for African-led congregations. A story told by Bishop Levi Coppin, the African American missionary sent to South Africa to oversee the planting of the African Methodist Episcopal church there, serves to illustrate their thinking. At one of his stops on one of his early tours in Africa, Coppin encountered an African woman at a meeting concerning the building of an A.M.E. church in her town. As the woman commented in the context of the negotiations, "You may bring your Church here or not, but I will never step my foot inside another white man's church as long as I live."[8]

This study concerns not so much the African Christian stances at the ends of the spectrum as the Ethiopianist stances in the middle. All of the latter positions, whatever their specific complexion, nurtured an optimistic conviction that no matter what was identified as wrong with the Christianity being preached by white missionaries, the excesses could be fixed by black Christian initiative. Ethiopianist criticism rarely ventured in the direction of disputing the doctrines and dogmas preached by missionaries. Rather, Ethiopianists focused on identifying and moving past the obstructions missionaries placed in the way of the advancement of Africans. As May continued in the editorial quoted above, "The white missionary is still a great force in our country. He controls the educational forces . . . and the training of our youth in largely in his hands." May added, "But thoughtful men are not satisfied with the work of the white Missionary teachers who cherish the idea of Race superiority, and to whom the prestige of color of the white man's skin is greater than any and every interest of the Blackman." As May observed, missionaries were looking at Africans "from the racial point of view." The way past the missionaries was for Africans to "give a very attentive ear to Booker T. Washington" and the latter's advice on the "race question."[9]

An article in John L. Dube's newspaper *Ilanga*, from far away in Natal on the other side of the continent, made a similar argument. Editorializing against what was labeled as the "tutelage nation," by which was meant those whites who thought that "native people . . . can never be anything else than minors to be dictated to and kept subservient," the article accepted that a broad group within white society shared such views. What was upsetting, however, was that "those who professedly are working on the basis of Christianity" had joined the "tutelage gentry." Pointing to missionaries, the article queried why "men who lack the insight of charity should have ventured on a path of duty that is not likely to help them to moral success even if it does provide a Bank account for them."[10] The article did not offer any specific solution to the problem of the tutelage nation. Still, two columns over, on the same page ,was the announcement that the school term was about to begin at Ohlange Industrial Institute, Dube's version of Tuskegee.

As the *Ilanga* article hinted, one Ethiopianist explanation of why missionaries were placing roadblocks in the path of African social improvement was that missionaries had fallen prey to Mammon, to greed, and there was more money to be had in helping other white men exploit Africans than in saving African souls. This indictment also stood behind May's comment that missionaries were no better than other white men. An alternate explanation, one perhaps not so morally damning from the Christian point of view, traced the obstacles missionaries placed in the path of African social progress back to issues of racial condescension of the same sort to which Armstrong and his staff were accused at Hampton. Missionaries could not accept that Africans had anything to contribute to the conversation about Africa's regeneration. An article in the *Sierra Leone Times* in 1892, mentioned at the beginning of the chapter, condemned the Church Missionary Society (CMS) for the suspension of fifteen students from Fourah Bay College, the missionary seminary located in Freetown. The article used the term "Salisbury Square," the location in London of the offices of the CMS, to stand for the missionary society. The article made the point that as long as the African had "groveled" in his "reverence" of the "whiteman as a whiteman," Salisbury Square had been content with the situation in Sierra Leone. Yet once the African had "come to discover that the Scriptures were as much his property as the Whiteman's," a discovery that had granted Africans the capacity to argue with missionaries, Salisbury Square decided to intervene through actions like the suspension of the students. The concern of the editorial reflected an Ethiopianist push for the transformation of Fourah Bay College into something more than a theological seminary. The article intimated that the reason the students had been suspended related to their protest against being trained for the clergy "whether they intend to go into the Ministry or not." The article conceded that it might have been that the students had been disciplined because they had not followed proper channels for the communication of their grievances. Still, the public had the right to know whether the suspensions represented missionary reaction against "the advancement of the African."[11]

John Tengo Jabavu pictured the missionary assumption of European cultural superiority as hindering not just those Africans who made it through to the end of the education pipeline but also every African who came into contact with missionaries. As he explained in a paper read at the Universal Races Congress held in London in 1911:

> [M]issionaries . . . have not always been as wise as they were benevolent. Coming with preconceived notions that they were sent to a barbarous society, they began by denouncing and pulling down every organization they found in order to rear Christianity on the ruins thereof. . . . The results have been more or less a breaking up of Bantu society, which now requires earnest and hearty workers to reconstruct it, even from the missionary point of view.[12]

Racial presumption had its pernicious impact both early and globally in the African encounter with mission Christianity. The solution Jabavu proposed was the establishment of an African-led industrial education institute that would train the workers needed to reconstruct African society. Jabavu made his comments as a prelude to a campaign for foreign donations to help build the Native College he hoped would replicate Tuskegee in Cape Province.

Ethiopianists competed for popular attention with proponents at both ends of the spectrum of adversarial Christianity. And beyond Christians, there were African Muslims as well as audiences of Africans who rejected any assimilation of European culture. Ethiopianists endeavored to attract all these people to their projects through appealing to what today is regarded as pan-Africanism. Ethiopianist projects promised to make African society, not just specific tribes or specific denominations, stronger. Ethiopianists sought to appeal to other Africans through affirmation of a conviction that the path forward for Africa and Africans went through, not away from, European civilization. Europeans read the African propensity to pick and choose among the attributes of European civilization as reflecting an African incapacity to apprehend European civilization in the correct (European) way. Contrary to what

Europeans were saying, however, Ethiopianists told other Africans that not only could European civilization be collectively grasped but it also could be used as a stepping-stone to an African civilization.

The conviction that Africans could take what they needed from European civilization to build an African one derived in part from an ongoing Ethiopianist appreciation of the European secular humanistic tradition. This tradition had given rise to a modern way of life African Christians continued to admire and hoped to assimilate. Africans did not concede to this tradition possessing the racial pedigree with which European scientific racism was trying to stamp it. The great human achievements of the past were not for whites only. Thus, in the same way the humanist tradition had served as an inspiration for European minds, Ethiopianists planned to use it to inspire African minds. As an editorial in the Sierra Leone *Weekly News* in March 1903 explained, "We believe that there is nothing peculiar to the European that is alien to us."[13] The editorial in the *Sierra Leone Times* discussed above proclaimed that, as with the Scriptures, not only the ancient Greeks, "Horace, Homer, Euclid," but also the modern Europeans, "Shakespeare, Milton and Voltaire . . . addressed the African as much as they did the Whiteman" and as such could be used as capital to build an African intellectual culture.[14] Blyden made the same point in his lecture "Race and Study," read before the (Sierra Leone) Young Man's Literary Society. The lecture was published with much fanfare both in the *Sierra Leone Times* and the Sierra Leone *Weekly News* in May 1893 and then printed for sale as a pamphlet later that year.[15] As Blyden explained on that occasion, "mental agility and flexibility" were the outcome not of "intellectual stores," meaning memorization, but of "intellectual drill," which for Blyden meant humanistic debate. With that thought in mind, he recommended that young men meet each fortnight and study the classical European writers. They could devote one evening each to William Wilberforce, Sir Thomas Fowell Buxton, Macauley, Livingstone, and such. Moving on to a study of art, they could give an evening to music, paint, and print artists, such as Michelangelo, Raphael, Titian, Mozart, Beethoven, Shakespeare, Milton, Tennyson, and Wordsworth.[16] Blyden, for all of his condemnation of the racial bias in the European Christian tradition, maintained a conviction both in the heuristic value of the European secular humanistic tradition and in the African capacity to tap into that tradition for purposes of intellectual development. His ideal school, as he later described it, would teach both industrial and literary education.

Blyden's affinity for secular humanism reflected broader African Christian sensibilities—readings outside what the missionaries were willing to teach had been, and for many individuals would remain, the road to African intellectual independence. Still, as the regular stream of articles in African newspapers demonstrated, the audience was much larger for the strategies of racial uplift thought to be behind African American success. These strategies all suggested that laypeople—that is, entrepreneurs, farmers, and technical people, not clergymen—supplied the impetus behind African American social regeneration; that industrial training, not humanistic learning, had provided the mental skills that facilitated African American collective achievement. For Ethiopianists, far more important than the evolution of new types of clergymen was the evolution of new types of laypeople and the establishment of new types of schools in Africa. The starting point of the consensus Ethiopianists hoped to build among Africans was a shared understanding that missionaries could not be trusted with the task of Africa's social regeneration. The import of the point was that some group of civilized black people would have to lead Africa and Africans in the right direction. The strategies for the creation of such a group that Ethiopianists promoted and that drew the most enthusiastic responses from African audiences all turned on the foundation of industrial education institutes such as the ones African newspapers said existed in the United States.

## HAMPTON INSTITUTE IN AFRICAN NEWSPAPERS

Ethiopianist confidence about the African ability to absorb European intellectual culture was not matched with a similar confidence about European technology. Reports of African Americans' facility with such technology gave Africans hope, however, that European technology was open to African appropriation. The emergence of Tuskegee Institute bolstered such hope. Before Tuskegee's emergence, Hampton Institute also received favorable press among Africans. As the discussion about Hampton that took place reveals, African Christians were already considering American-style industrial education as a pathway toward the technological proficiency not provided in mission schools before the appearance of Tuskegee made the conclusion obvious.

The missionary newspaper the *Christian Express* (later renamed the *South African Outlook*), published at Lovedale Institute near Cape Town, had an interracial readership. It introduced South African Christians to

Hampton Institute in 1879 in an article about Hampton's experiment with educating Native Americans.[17] Remarkably, the article did not even bother to mention that Hampton's primary mission was the education of African Americans. For missionaries in South Africa, the education of Native Americans was the closest equivalent to what they did and provided the substance of their curiosity. A second article about Hampton, a highly laudatory reprint from the *New York Herald*, appeared in the *Christian Express* in 1884. While spending a good deal of time on Native Americans, the article did address Hampton's achievements with African American students. The article probably also had the distinction of being the first publication to bring Tuskegee to the attentions of African readers. Three years after its foundation, Tuskegee, with a faculty composed of Washington and five other Hampton graduates, was described in the article, obviously with Armstrong's approval, as "a young Hampton of which we are proud."[18]

The first mention of Hampton Institute in West Africa occurred in an Americo-Liberian newspaper. A report and an editorial detailing Edward Blyden's rejection of an offer by General Armstrong to educate three Liberian students at Hampton were published as two separate articles on the same page in the *Observer* in April 1880. The unidentified writer of the report surreptitiously suggested that Blyden had made the wrong decision. Perhaps because the import of the report was so ambiguous, an editorial was also published two columns later to make clear that the newspaper supported Blyden's position. Blyden argued that going to the United States for their education might spoil the boys. He warned that when a student goes overseas for study and then comes home, "he revolts at a return to his former life as he would at putting on discarded garments after being clothed in elegant attire." The article's writer took issue with this argument, suggesting that the "Hampton drill would avert the danger." As the writer went on to say, "Men fitted for the conditions of simple civilization," meaning those who had the "ground work of elementary and industrial training" offered at Hampton, "would succeed." Without explicitly saying so, the writer gave Hampton a chance to defend itself against Blyden's condemnation, covertly appending to the report several paragraphs taken from the *Southern Workman*, the Hampton Institute newspaper. As the paragraphs proclaimed, Hampton "finds itself a school for civilization. It aims to make, not polished scholars, but men." Speaking about the students who came to the school to learn, the paragraphs taken from the Hampton newspaper conceded to Blyden's warning that, as a consequence of a Hampton education, "these youths [do] acquire new tastes and desires." But, as the paragraphs went on to say, thanks to Hampton, the students "also get the ability to gratify them."[19]

In an article published in the Sierra Leone *Weekly News* in January 1890, Hampton was the subject on the table not explicitly by name but implicitly by educational program. In 1889 the British governor of Sierra Leone, George Hay, floated the idea of building a technical training school in the colony. In early 1890 the government arranged a town hall–style meeting on the project in Freetown where an intense debate developed. The article described this meeting. As explained by the unidentified "Correspondent" who wrote the article, on one side of the debate stood those who saw the initiative as an invitation to establish an "evening Technical school pure and simple," where "pupils could be taught the technical part of their trade." As noted by the correspondent, the minority with this understanding included "the European element" present at the meeting. As the correspondent further asserted about this minority, "It appears to be the aim and policy of certain classes of persons to put every hindrance in the way of the development and expansion of the country."[20]

On the other side of the debate stood the majority who took "a large and Comprehensive view of the scheme." For the majority, the desire was for an "industrial institution" where the pupils could be taught handicrafts and agriculture "scientifically." As the correspondent explained, the school would "raise the people of Sierra Leone to a higher form of civilization." The minds of students would develop in such a way that "they would have the facility of being taught various industries theorctically and practically at the same time."[21] Whether Governor Hay had Hampton in mind when the proposal was first made cannot be determined, but the benefits the Ethiopianists at the meeting saw as resulting from the establishment of an industrial institute can be recognized as reflecting Hampton's educational imprint.

A better, more specific signal of Hampton's influence was that the mental development the proposed institute would induce would make Sierra Leone's youth more entrepreneurial. As the correspondent complained, "At present, thousands of acres of virgin soils may be obtained from the government for a mere song" but for the fact that there were no Sierra Leoneans to develop them. "If the young people had the industrial training to have found plantations," he reasoned, then "the crude treasures which are perpetually exposed to our view might be converted to substantial wealth."[22]

An article reprinted in the same newspaper, the *Weekly News*, from an unidentified American newspaper eighteen months later reinforces the conclusion that Hampton was in fact the school Ethiopianists in Sierra Leone were seeking to copy. The article opened with a report on Hampton's twenty-third graduation ceremonies, where "elevation through education, progress through self-help, the debt of the individual to the race, furnished the theme and fired the speakers." The article celebrated Hampton's prowess as an industrial training institute. Further, it mentioned the newly opened Huntington Industrial Works, where sixty-three "colored apprentices" trained for "every description of technical and industrial carpentry," then went on to talk about how, with state funding, Hampton was mounting a new program in "practical and experimental agriculture" to be taught in the newly built Science Building.[23]

The article also insisted upon Hampton's importance as a center for Christian regeneration. It explained that the future teachers at the Hampton normal school trained at the free primary school Hampton maintained on its premises for local students. In like manner, the new charity hospital opened on the Hampton campus trained African American and Native American nurses while simultaneously addressing the medical needs of the surrounding community. Hampton's greatest investment in Christian regeneration, however, was identified to be its establishment of Tuskegee Institute.[24] According to the article, "From the point of view of self-help, and as an illustration of the effort put forth by the Negro for the elevation of his own race, Tuskegee, Hampton's eldest daughter, is even more remarkable that the parent institution."[25]

For some unknown reason, Hampton Institute was on the minds of African Christians in the summer (winter) months of 1891. On July 18, the article above was published in Freetown. Three weeks later, on August 6, in Cape Town, under the headline "Elevating the Negro," *Imvo Zabantsundu* published verbatim a speech given by General Armstrong. In the speech, General Armstrong pictured Hampton as a Christian boot camp where students learned the value of labor "as the most vital thing in Christian civilization."[26] *Imvo Zabantsundu*'s readers no doubt appreciated the moral message Armstrong was conveying, but industrial education schools, as operated primarily by Scottish missionary groups, were very common in South Africa, so the newspaper's readers were probably more intrigued by the extended discussion the speech offered about what an American-style industrial institute was and how it operated. What *Imvo Zabantsundu*'s readers perhaps also appreciated hearing Armstrong say was that Hampton sought, through its training, to empower its students to change the world. Doctor James E. Stewart, the principal of Lovedale, the largest and most successful of South Africa's industrial mission schools, was famous for saying that the goal of industrial education was the training of Africans to assist effectively European entrepreneurs and craftsmen.[27] Thus, it was perhaps thrilling for African Christians to read the words of a white man who occupied a position equivalent to that of Stewart proclaim:

> Last Saturday I gave my final words to our graduating class. I said to them, "How many of you can go out into the world, and if you cannot get a school (to supervise), how many can work in some line of industry and so support yourselves?" There was a roar. Every one said, "I can."[28]

Hampton students sounded like the agents of racial advancement for which Ethiopianists were looking.

African Christians reached the same conclusion. Jabavu communicated in his introduction to Armstrong's speech that he was reprinting it in part because "Hampton is the Institution from which Mr. McAdoo's company of Jubilee Singers hail." Orpheus McAdoo and the Virginia Jubilee Singers troupe were a group of African American singers and performers who were a theatrical phenomenon in South Africa across the early 1890s. McAdoo was an alumnus of Hampton—class of 1875 along with Booker T. Washington—and McAdoo made a point of mentioning Hampton and its program of racial uplift at the start of each of the group's performances. In October 1890, just after McAdoo and his troupe arrived in South Africa, Jabavu reprinted in his newspaper an article that observed about McAdoo and the Jubilee Singers:

> We are naturally drawn to the conclusion that there is an immense possibility of improvement of the aborigines of this part of the world when we see what American life and education have been able to do for the descendants of West African slaves.[29]

McAdoo's troupe's performances made the power of a Hampton education tangible in ways that excited African Christians with the possibilities for change.

Beginning with the reprint of Armstrong's speech, Jabavu published a number of articles extracted from foreign newspapers offering information on industrial education. In an editorial published in April 1892, he pointed out that industrial education could mean either of two different types of schooling. The two different types corresponded to the dichotomy posited in the debate in the town hall meeting in Freetown discussed above. Jabavu voiced the same enthusiasm for American-style industrial education expressed by the Ethiopianist majority at that meeting. As a measure of its modernity, Jabavu noted that "industrial training" had been successfully introduced into the schools in Sweden. Such training, he editorialized, was "important in all circumstances." The type of education described in Freetown as being offered only in "trade schools" Jabavu described in much the same terms for Cape Town. While trade school education supplied European tradesmen with workers, Jabavu acknowledged, echoing Dr. Stewart, still, it did not meet "any immediate want" of the African people. "Of what use would it be to multiply skilled mechanics fourfold," Jabavu asked as he went further to dismiss trade school education, "when there is no effectual demands for all those already in the fold."[30]

The discussion of Hampton as it took place in African newspapers makes clear that African Ethiopianists were aware of industrial education as something quite different from trade school training. It also makes clear that in their advocacy of Hampton, for the most part, African Ethiopianists took no cognizance of the fact that Hampton's administration and faculty were white Christians very much like the ones they were seeking to outflank. The Ethiopianist disinclination to pay attention to race here should be read as an indication of African excitement about industrial education. The educational program was seen to be effective in and for itself, over and above the individuals who implemented it.

Two African Ethiopianists, though, initially could not get past the issue of Hampton and race. The impact of their opposition to Hampton, however, probably only accelerated their own early promotion of industrial education as taught at Tuskegee. As already noted, in 1880 Blyden rejected the idea of Liberian students going to Hampton. The editor of the *Observer* wrote an editorial siding with Blyden. The editorial identified a number of reasons, probably all first suggested by Blyden, that it was not good for Africans to go to the United States to study, the most pertinent being that industrial education was training for jobs at the lowest rung of the society, the most novel being that in the United States "the Negro" was "more or less" a "Caucasian" because he was educated as one.[31] Acting in his capacity as president of Liberia College, in 1882, Blyden traveled to the United States to recruit faculty. The two African American males he recruited to come teach at Liberia College were very vocal in their disappointment about what they found when they arrived in Liberia, and both recommended to the board of the New York Colonization Society, which funded the college, that the curriculum at the college be revised to conform to that at Hampton. Blyden dismissed the suggestion. Perhaps in an attempt to get him to change his mind, Blyden was invited to give the commencement address at Hampton in 1883. He used the occasion to speak to the students about Islam, so as "to correct the mistakes of white travelers." As he explained, Islam, not Christianity, was the greatest force working for social regeneration in Africa.[32] Blyden was dismissed from his position as principal of Liberia College in 1884, with failure to consider the reform of Liberia College along the lines of Hampton among the cited reasons.[33] Yet a little more than a decade later, in 1895, Blyden published the letter praising Washington and Tuskegee discussed in the previous chapter.

In 1887 arrangements were made for John L. Dube, grandson of one of the first Zulu converts to American Congregationalism, and son of the first Zulu Congregationalist minister, to come to the United States, explicitly with a commitment to study at Hampton Institute. Dube reneged on that obligation as soon as he got to the United States, and would not even go look at the campus. Dube chose instead to complete a degree at Oberlin, the impression being that he wanted nothing to do with industrial education.[34] Later, after hearing about Washington's achievements at Tuskegee, Dube, like Blyden before him, had a change of heart. He requested and received an invitation to meet with Washington at Tuskegee in 1897. Four years later, back in Natal, Dube opened Ohlange Industrial Institute, his own version of Tuskegee. Viewing Hampton from the perspective of Tuskegee, Dube got over his qualms with the former.[35] Inspired by Washington, Dube went to visit Hampton. A few years later, Dube sent his nephew, Mandikane Cele, to Hampton to train. Cele then returned to teach at Ohlange Institute.[36] Skepticism about the intentions of the white Christians who ran Hampton has to be considered as a source of both Blyden's and Dube's early antipathy to the school. Here they both were in alignment with African American Ethiopianists. It turned out, however, that their grievance was not against the educational program as much as against the racism they suspected guided the program's implementation. Once Washington reconceptualized the Hampton educational program, they numbered among industrial education's readiest promoters in their respective regions of Africa.

### DENOMINATIONAL CHURCHES AND INDUSTRIAL EDUCATION

In October 1891, a few months after he published the speech by Armstrong, Jabavu published a letter to the editor by an African lay Methodist who declared that Africans in South Africa needed a school like Hampton and then asked why the Methodist mission did not build one. As the letter framed the issue, "Are our Wesleyan Ministers satisfied that our Native lads must go and seek training amongst the other denominations?" Jabavu did not regularly write responses to letters to the editor. On this occasion he wrote, "Seeing that this letter is denominational in purport it would have been suitable for the columns of the . . . Church [newspaper]. . . . The subject is, however, one which interests the public generally and could very well be lifted out of the denominational rut and discussed in a broad liberal spirit."[37] Jabavu saw industrial education as a pan-Africanist, not a denominational, concern—as a solution to the problems caused by the miseducation of Africans in mission schools, not as a reinforcement of the denominational boundaries erected by missions. It would take another decade or more before other African Christians would see things from this perspective.

Ethiopianists recognized cost to be a major obstacle to the building of an industrial institute. The intense debate that took place in Sierra Leone in 1890 over the approach to be taken in the proposed government technical training school drew its energy from the Ethiopianist hope that the colonial government there would step forward and pay the initial costs for building such a school. This dream would be nursed by Ethiopianist groups across British colonized Africa for the next thirty years, until the Phelps Stokes Education Commission reports made clear how removed the hope was from government ambitions. In the meantime, during the 1890s, the only groups to step forward with plans that addressed Ethiopianist ambitions were black denominational churches with foreign connections.

In West Africa the lead in the effort to institute an industrial school was taken by Mojola Agbebi's Native African Baptist Church, which is best appreciated as a West African Baptist denomination affiliated with the Baptist Union of Great Britain and Ireland. Agbebi reserved the right to appoint bishops and deacons and to ordain ministers in his church, so the association with the British Baptist denominational church was never strict.[38] Agbebi established the Agbowa Industrial Mission on the Lagos Lagoon east of Lagos in Nigeria in 1895 and set up the Jamaican missionary J. E. Ricketts as its principal. Agbowa Industrial Mission was an extension of an educational institution known variously as the Congo House Training Institute, the African Training Institute, the African Institute, and, most commonly in the African press, Colwyn Bay, from its location in northern Wales. The Welsh Baptist missionary William Hughes, who spent the years 1882–1885 missionizing in the Congo, founded Colwyn Bay in 1889. Hughes had come back from mission convinced that sending European missionaries to Africa was the wrong way to evangelize the continent. A more effective approach would be to bring Africans to Europe to learn industrial skills before sending them back as missionaries who made their living using their acquired technical skills. In the context of this study, most fascinating about Hughes' school was its endeavor to isolate the learning of European technology from the learning of European culture and then make the communication of Christian civilization contingent upon the diffusion of European technology. Students from his school were supposed to go back to Africa to proselytize their own people in their own language, while using command of European technology as a vehicle to economic prosperity for themselves and the Christian communities they founded. Colwyn Bay functioned for little more than twenty years, from 1889 to 1912. During that time, eighty-seven students passed through the school. At its height, the school—actually a massive Victorian mansion—housed around twenty students, mostly drawn from Africa but with some also from the New World, including the United States.[39]

West African newspapers did not have much to say about Hampton Institute after the publication of the above articles. Perhaps one reason West African Ethiopianists did not further pursue schools like Hampton was because they had become enthralled with Colwyn Bay. An astonishing number of stories were published about the school in African newspapers, almost as many as eventually would be published on Tuskegee. Ethiopianists identified with Hughes' argument that Africans would make the best evangelists for Africa. They wholeheartedly supported his focus on teaching Africans European technology. For West African Ethiopianists, Colwyn Bay, far away in Wales yet accessible thanks to the free passage offered students by Alfred L. Jones, the British shipping magnate, became their industrial education institute. Coordinating committees for soliciting funds for the maintenance of the African Institute were organized in coastal West African cities. Scholarships for boys to attend the school were raised; "ladies branches" were created to assist in the collection of funds for these prizes. Competition committees were established to choose the winners of the scholarships, with the winners proudly announced in the local newspapers.[40]

African newspapers typically did not print requests by Europeans for money. In August 1898, however, E. Cornelius May accorded Hughes the signal honor of printing in the Sierra Leone *Weekly News* Hughes' appeal for funds to buy a printing press. Hughes asked for £500 to purchase a used one. The press would save the African Institute the £200 Hughes spent each year for printing costs. It would also allow him to institute a training program to teach African students printing. Lastly, the press would allow Colwyn Bay to realize Hughes' dream of the publication of a new monthly magazine, the *African Advocate*, which would print the many "interesting letters" Hughes received from "civilized" Africans. As Hughes explained:

> We have heard for some centuries the voice and opinions of white men with regard to this wonderful Continent, but I believe that the time has arrived when we should know the ideas of the civilized Africans about these matters. . . . Europeans may learn a good deal by listening to the African with a view to the civilization and evangelization of his country. . . . The Christian Church should learn the signs of the times in this respect, unfurl her sails, and make use of the breeze and current in order to win Africa for Christ speedily and that through the instrumentality of the natives themselves.[41]

Hughes was preaching to the choir a sermon they had longed to hear.

Hughes got his printing press, though it is impossible to say how much funds from Africa contributed to its purchase. Over the summer of 1899, both the Sierra Leone *Weekly News* and the *Gold Coast Chronicle* reported the publication of the promised journal, the *African Advocate*. In 1902 the *Gold Coast Aborigines* reported that the printing program at the African Institute had become so successful that the students had also taken on the publication of a new local newspaper, the *Colwyn Bay Times*.[42]

Agbowa Industrial Mission served essentially as a feeder school for Colwyn Bay.[43] Hughes had ambitious plans to establish a number of these along the coast of Africa, but only the one in Nigeria was started. The initiative came from Agbebi, who as a member of the Lagos solicitation committee for the African Institute was impressed enough with what he read about the school that he began a correspondence with Hughes. In 1895 Agbebi went to Wales to spend five months based on the Colwyn Bay campus. During the stay, Agbebi and Hughes began a fifteen-year collaboration for the furthering of the establishment of British Baptist churches in West Africa. Agbowa Industrial Mission was among the fruit of this collaboration. When Agbebi came back to Nigeria from his visit to Wales, he brought J. E. Ricketts, an associate of Hughes, with him to set up the school. Little more is known about Agbowa except for the newspaper reports of the "creditable" job Ricketts was doing. Both the *Lagos Weekly Record* and the *Lagos Standard* in November 1908 reported the touching story of how Ricketts, sick and sensing the approach of death, ordered his people to place him on a canoe and row him across the lagoon to Agbebi in Lagos. Ricketts made it but died a few days later in the hospital.[44] After the death of Ricketts, there are no further newspaper reports about Agbowa Industrial Mission.

In Wales, after two decades of success, Hughes began to encounter problems. Jones, the shipping magnate, had been the great patron of the African Institute. Jones died in 1909, leaving Hughes and his African coordinating committees to account for a set of costs they had not had to deal with earlier.[45] Of greatest consequence, Colwyn Bay became the target of the tabloid journalism of the magazine *John Bull*, edited by Horatio Bottemley, who published several articles of innuendo about the sexual involvements of Colwyn Bay students with Welsh women. Hughes took Bottomley to court on a libel charge but lost. In 1912 Hughes was forced to declare bankruptcy. With that event, the African Institute ceased to exist.[46] Hughes tried to find the support to return to Africa as a missionary but never succeeded. He died in poverty in 1924.

For all of the excitement and activity, Colwyn Bay did little to improve African knowledge of European technology. The number of the students who passed through Colwyn Bay and returned to their countries as technically trained missionaries is unknown. Ironically, it appears that the African Institute actually evolved into a de facto feeder school itself for other British institutions of higher learning. A letter in the *Weekly News* thanked Hughes for training one student to be a tailor but happily reported that the student had been accepted into the medical degree program at Edinburgh University.[47] A story in *Imvo Zabantsundu* in 1915 celebrated the appointment of Davidson Don Tengo (D. D. T.) Jabavu, son of John Tengo Jabavu, as a professor at the South African Native College. Davidson had begun his academic career studying printing at Colwyn Bay. The story mentioned two South African "class mates" Davidson had at the school, one of whom had gone on to train at the Inns of Court in London before passing the bar in Cape Town, and the other of whom earned a medical degree at Glasgow.[48] Even if Colwyn Bay had produced the types of technically trained missionaries Hughes had promised and had been an ongoing success, the number trained would have never been large enough to supply the African demand for technical education. Yet the school did a powerful job of channeling Ethiopianist fervor for technical education. African support for the school also illustrated the willingness of Ethiopianists to work with European missionaries who understood their dreams.

In the wake of African excitement about industrial education institutes, West Africans looked north to Wales as a place where some first contingents of Africans might acquire technical skills. South Africans looked west across the Atlantic toward the United States in search of the same thing. For the first half of the 1890s, Hampton Institute remained the industrial education school in the South African Ethiopianist mind. In the second half of that decade, however, Ethiopianists turned their attentions to another idea, the notion that African American Christians would come to South Africa and build an industrial education school for them.

Orpheus McAdoo and the Virginia Jubilee Singers had a potent impact on African Christian consciousness in South Africa. For Christian South Africans, they came to embody what is called here "adversarial Christianity." Minstrel shows composed of musical routines where whites dressed up in blackface (burnt cork) and performed parodies of African behavior and singing were the number-one form of theatrical entertainment for whites in South Africa. The vogue had been started in 1862 by a run of performances in Cape Town by the Christy Minstrels, the most famous white American group of blackface performers. The Virginia Jubilee Singers performed minstrel routines but challenged the stereotypes by pushing the presentation of black behavior in a more Christian direction. As was observed in a review in one white newspaper, the group's shows were "devoid of the vulgarities and forced humor" of the genre. "Christianised Christies," the reviewer suggested, "may be taken as [more] descriptive of these performances."[49] The

Virginia Jubilee Singers illustrated adversarial Christianity in another way that whites found less appealing, but perhaps to black audiences proved their bona fides. Just as was the case in the United States, at that moment the various governments in southern Africa were instituting laws that mandated racial segregation. McAdoo led a legal battle connected to the issue of his racial status and that of his group. McAdoo insisted that, based upon their American citizenship, he and his group were not native and therefore were eligible for all the privileges reserved for whites. South African courts ruled eventually that race did transcend all other attributes and that African Americans were subject to the laws pertaining to natives. Still, McAdoo and his group provided an example of black Christians battling against racial discrimination.[50]

McAdoo traced his adversarial Christianity back to his days at Hampton. Each night before the group's evening shows began, McAdoo came out in front of the curtain and gave the audience a short speech about Hampton and its mission. One African observer heard McAdoo say that Africans in America had taken control of their own destiny through the establishment of their own schools, run by them without the help of whites.[51] McAdoo's advocacy of the idea of education was so strong that in one locale he was called before an angry committee of local whites who demanded to know whether he was "singing to educate Negroes."[52]

Christian Africans were inspired by McAdoo to look toward the United States as a place where they could get the education not available to them in South Africa. In the last part of the 1890s, a number of African congregations broke away from mission churches to form their own African denominations. Since the children of African Christians who participated in Ethiopianist movements found denominational schools closed to them, these students looked elsewhere for an education.[53] Between 1898 and 1908, approximately one hundred African students left the Cape Province alone to study overseas, primarily in black colleges in the United States. A number of them did end up at Tuskegee.[54]

Still, African Christians eagerly embraced the idea, when opportunity brought it to the fore, that African American Christians could and would build an industrial education institute in South Africa itself. Africans were not the only ones inspired by the Virginia Jubilee Singers. In the early 1890s, two white South African musicians decided to replicate that group's success with their own African Jubilee Singers, assembled from a group of young churchgoing Africans. The new group left on tour to Britain, ostensibly with the goal of raising money for the creation of industrial education institutes in South Africa. The tour of Britain ended in disaster with the singers abandoned in London. Charitable contributions got the singers back to South Africa. One of the singers who had gone to London was a young Wesleyan (Methodist) churchwoman, Charlotte Manye. Despite her earlier experience, Manye decided to sign on again when the two white musicians announced a plan to take the African Jubilee Singers on tour to North America. Once again the singers were abandoned, providentially in Cleveland, Ohio, this time. A local A.M.E. church took in the singers, and Charlotte soon found herself enrolled in Wilberforce University, the university associated with the A.M.E. denomination. In 1895 Mayne wrote back to her sister, Kate, in South Africa exulting the wonders of Wilberforce and of the African American denomination that maintained the university. Reverend Mangena Mokone, leader of the Ethiopian Church, a separatist movement from the Wesleyan Church, read the letter. Mokone wrote to the A.M.E. bishop, Henry M. Turner, asking for more information, and thus began the process through which, in 1897, the Ethiopian Church of South Africa became the Fourteenth District of the A.M.E. Church.

James Dwane was the representative of the Ethiopian Church sent to the United States to negotiate the union. The choice of Dwane signaled the central role the promise of schools played in the willingness of the leaders of the Ethiopianist Church to contemplate amalgamation with the American church. "Give us a . . . college or educational institution that will enable us," one member of the Ethiopianist Church wrote to Turner, "to stand on the same platform as the white race."[55] As Dwane confided to Turner, "You have not the least idea, my lord, how much depends upon this question."[56]

The type of school that the leaders of the Ethiopianist Church had in mind was an industrial education institute. As noted in an article published in the A.M.E. church journal, the *Christian Recorder*, in March 1899, the proposed college would be a combination of Wilberforce University and "the Indian school in Carlisle, Pennsylvania."[57] Wilberforce was the A.M.E.'s denominational university, providing training for its clergy. No doubt the Americans wanted to recreate it as a first step toward the establishment of the church in a new land. Carlisle Institute was an industrial institute established specifically for Native Americans. The inclusion of an industrial education school in the plan reflected African desire.

To be fair, there was some support in the American A.M.E. Church for an industrial education school in South Africa. The "Kaffir University" or "Queenstown College," as the A.M.E. bishop Henry Blanton Parks alternately labeled the proposed school in an article in *Voice of Missions*, the A.M.E.'s missionary journal, would be "industrial and religious." Here, as above, indigenous South Africans were analogized to Native Americans. If the African wanted to avoid the "fate of the American Indian," Bishop Parks counseled, he needed to "get his industrial training first, and meet civilization in the right spirit."[58]

The A.M.E. Church stood by the promise to build schools for its adherents in South Africa; however, it never built an industrial institute. Bethel Institute opened for students in 1902.[59] Bishop Coppin and his wife Fanny Jackson Coppin, who lead the A.M.E. mission, had successful experience in building industrial education institutions in the United States. Their understanding of the South African educational situation, however, recognized that the overarching need was for primary, not secondary, education, for getting people into the educational pipeline, not preparing them to exit at the other end. As Coppin explained in a mission report published in the middle of 1901, even though the chant of the African Christians that he met while touring the locations was "We want school! We want school!" meaning industrial education, Bethel Institute needed to focus on primary education. So when the school opened, it had only an "industrial annex."[60] Coppin and his wife sought to overlay the focus on primary subjects at Bethel—and to allay the disappointment of Africans—with some "Tuskegee-style" courses in practical learning. However, the A.M.E. missionary who arrived in Cape Town to develop these courses did not teach them but became entangled in his own entrepreneurial schemes.[61]

The A.M.E Church damaged its reputation and appeal during its first decade in South Africa because of its inability to build the desired industrial institute. Ethiopianists clearly felt betrayed. Samuel Brander was one of the original cohort who followed Mokone into the Ethiopian Church and then into the A.M.E. Church. Brander explained in his letter of resignation from the A.M.E. Church, "They promised that they would give us a school from America with teachers and all, and this they did not do. . . . We thought that as they were our own color they would help us up, but we found that they helped us down."[62] Brander and several of the leaders, disenchanted with the Americans, left to found their own denominational churches. Dwane and his followers found home in the Church of England.[63]

Industrial education schools were understood by Ethiopianists as the ideal tool to counteract the impact of white racism on Christian development in Africa. The first initiatives by African Ethiopianists to address the possibility of nongovernment funding for industrial education schools involved looking for support from foreign Christian denominations perceived as sympathetic to the Ethiopianist cause. These initiatives fueled Ethiopianist expectations that, for various reasons, were never met. Ethiopianist enthusiasm for industrial education ultimately reached the same conclusion Jabavu had reached in 1892, that denominational schools were not the path to follow. Booker T. Washington's fame reached its apogee around the turn of the twentieth century. Like a beacon, Washington's fame drew Ethiopianist attentions toward him and Tuskegee, the school he had founded. Africans from West Africa wrote and visited Washington for guidance. Africans from South Africa did the same. The guidance he gave shaped different movements in the two regions, different movements that evolved in different directions, though in the end, in both regions the results were the same.

# 4

## An Attentive Ear

### *Hearing the Call of Booker T. and the Pathway to Industrial Education in West Africa*

Let us now give an attentive ear to Booker Washington, from across the Atlantic in far away America. His voice sounds strangely familiar to our minds as if we have heard it before. It appeals to kindred mind, and blood, which is thicker than water, replies.[1]

#### BOOKER T. WASHINGTON IN WEST AFRICAN NEWSPAPERS

The educational programs and strategies to help African Americans that Booker T. Washington was pursuing in the United States at Tuskegee drew significant attention in West African newspapers. From 1880 to 1920, in the fifteen newspapers for which some content is available, there are more than two hundred articles that speak in some way about Washington, his school, or the educational approach followed at his school. Most of these articles were about Washington's achievements and Tuskegee's success. Fewer in number, but more influential in terms of shaping public understanding, two other types of articles existed. First were articles that gave Washington himself an opportunity to speak directly to West African audiences via the reprinting of his speeches and other writings. The *Lagos Weekly Record*, for example, published articles with the titles "Professor Booker T. Washington on the Education for the Negro" and "Professor Booker T. Washington on the Negro in the United States," while the *Nigerian Chronicle*, also from Lagos, offered an extended article published over two issues on Tuskegee Institute with Washington's name as the byline.[2] A second type of article offered sympathetic explanations by other recognized race leaders concerning what

Washington was attempting at Tuskegee. One example is "In Defense of the Negro: Why He Should Be Treated Reasonably," by the British African musical composer Samuel Coleridge-Taylor, reprinted from *Reynolds Magazine* in the *Gold Coast Leader*.[3] Another example is "A Visit to Tuskegee," by Kelly Miller, a respected African American mathematician, published in the Sierra Leone *Weekly News*.[4]

Washington and Tuskegee drew mention in a majority of West African newspapers, but they were a regular source of copy in two newspapers more than all others. In 1884 Reverend J. Claudius May, principal of the Methodist Boys High School of Freetown in Sierra Leone, founded in that city the Sierra Leone *Weekly News*. For the next thirty years his brother, E. Cornelius May, served as the newspaper's editor.[5] In 1891 Robert Payne Jackson, another Sierra Leonean, founded in Lagos the *Lagos Weekly Record*. His son, Thomas Horatio Jackson, followed him as editor of the newspaper in 1915. The May brothers' Christian faith was obvious. The Jacksons' sympathies were more explicitly pan-Africanist than Christian.[6] Still, the readership of the *Lagos Weekly Record* was predominantly Christian. The two newspapers may be fairly credited with being the most resolutely anticolonial newspapers on the West African coast throughout the colonial period till the end of World War I. Both E. Cornelius May and Robert Payne Jackson later in life became active in the formation of the National Congress of British West Africa, the regional political organization most involved in the promotion of greater political rights for West Africans within the British Empire.[7] Significantly, these two newspapers gave much space and ink to Washington and the education program followed at Tuskegee. During 1891–1922 the Sierra Leone *Weekly News* published approximately one hundred articles that cited or discussed Washington and his school. The run of issues available for the *Lagos Weekly Record* is not as complete. Still, from 1891 to 1921, with several gaps in print coverage, the newspaper published more than forty articles offering some consideration of Washington and his school.

Both the Sierra Leone *Weekly News* and the *Lagos Weekly Record* lauded Washington as a great man. An article in the *Lagos Weekly Record* from 1901 listed Washington as the most "prominent" of America's "Negro aristocrats."[8] An article in the *Weekly News* from 1911 went further and feted Washington as "The American Negro King."[9] More substantively, both newspapers presented Washington as a race leader worthy of attention on both sides of the Atlantic. E. Cornelius

May's comments to this effect are noted in the quotation mentioned at the beginning of the chapter. Reflecting upon news of Washington's receipt of an honorary master's degree from Harvard University, Robert Payne Jackson, in an editorial in the *Lagos Weekly Record* opined:

> We have been deeply impressed with all the public utterances which we have seen of Mr. Washington's. He has not said a single word on behalf of the race that Africa would not have him say. He has never been in Africa. He seldom says anything about Africa. He does not deem it necessary to parade his interest in the Fatherland or to proclaim the duty of Negro repatriation. He pursues the sensible course suggested by his own illustration. He drops his bucket down where he is and he is doing more for the race, whether in Africa or in America, than all the ranters and agitators who misrepresent Africa by the violent and inexhaustible resources of cant and splash and splutter which they seem to have at command.[10]

Jackson was making an invidious comparison between Washington and the A.M.E. Bishop Henry M. Turner, who was then actively promoting the emigration of African Americans back to Africa. The more important point in Jackson's statement was his willingness to recognize Washington as articulating a message Africans on both side of the Atlantic could embrace.

## WASHINGTON'S MESSAGE

To build on the May quotation, that which attentive readers found so strangely familiar occurred, in part, because African Ethiopianists understood Washington to validate many conclusions they had reached already about education and racial uplift. While Crummell's name never came up, Washington was seen to be advocating a strategy similar to that first offered by Crummell of Christian regeneration through capitalistic development. The major difference between Crummell's and Washington's strategies, as presented in West African newspapers, resulted from Washington's strategy that allowed Africans themselves to become the Christian entrepreneurs. Washington never explicitly placed Africans in this role. Rather, as with so many of Washington's readers, West Africans read Washington and extrapolated a role for themselves in the initiatives he promoted. Thus, when Washington was quoted to say, "With the exception of the Gospel of Christ, there is no work that will contribute more largely to the elevation of the Race . . . than a first-class business enterprise," he was understood to be speaking to Africans in Africa, not Africans in America.[11]

The concern of Christian entrepreneurs to be involved in "industrial development" or more simply "industrialism" meant involvement in production of some commodity for the market. While Washington was recognized for promoting the notion that the first commodity every individual had to put up for sale on the market was personal service or skill, he was also recognized as advocating that the goal behind the sale of this commodity had to be the creation of sufficient capital to produce other nonpersonal commodities with market value.

West Africans did not look to capitalism as an instrument of proletarianization. Industrial development was about the identification and production for profit of commodities that would supply an individual with the wealth necessary to move beyond wage labor. This point was made in a speech before the students of Mfantsipim School in Accra by G. C. Pietersen, vice president of the Gold Coast Aborigines Rights Protection Society in colonial Ghana, and reported in the *Gold Coast Leader*. The boys were told that their goal in life was not to become "useful hewers of wood and drawers of water for the lower middle class English sojourners in Africa." Rather the boys should imitate the strategy of the Germans who "sought the lowest positions in London offices and British manufactories" and by so doing "learned the rudiments of British industries," and so were now "competing with British merchants the wide world over."[12] West Africans did not think they could collectively ship out to London as a race in order to become industrial apprentices. They did think, however, that as a race they could build a number of schools like Tuskegee, which would serve the same purpose.

West African newspapers further represented Washington as affirming the idea that success in business also signaled social and cultural attainment. In other words, in getting rich, a black person would be advancing the race. As Washington was quoted in the Sierra Leone *Weekly News*, his "highest aim" was "to create the highest possible industrial condition that could be among colored people" to underscore his belief that African peoples could cope better "with the white man and command his respect" by reaching "a high state of industrial development."[13] As Washington went on to proclaim, "The black man that has fifty thousand dollars to lend will never want friends and customers among his white neighbors."[14]

Tuskegee's commitment to drilling into its students table manners and habits of personal hygiene has received more attention from scholars than it did in contemporary West African newspapers.[15] The newspapers gave more attention to two other skill sets Tuskegee was identified as providing for students. First was entrepreneurial acumen. Second was technological training. As a result of what they read in African newspaper publications, Africans understood that the Tuskegee system taught students how to make things that commanded market share.

The nature of technological training was rarely characterized in any systematic curricular fashion. Rather, technological instruction was typically framed in some general way as the positive alternative to liberal arts education. The *Lagos Weekly Record* in 1897 reprinted a speech by Washington under the headline "Dr. Booker T. Washington on the Education of the Negro." In the speech, Washington posited that the production of three things was necessary for the growth of civilization, with the term "civilization" signifying racial uplift. These three things were "food, clothing and shelter." According to Washington, however, African Americans were developing or passing on knowledge of these critical building blocks nowhere save for "Hampton and Tuskegee and one or two other schools."[16]

Speaking about agriculture or food production, Washington lamented, "Boys are being taken from the farms to study law, theology, Greek and Hebrew—educated in every thing except the very subject they should know about." Washington contended, "It would have seemed that since self-support, industrial independence, is the first condition for lifting up any race, that education in theoretical and practical agriculture, horticulture, dairying and stock-raising should have occupied first place in our system." Turning to clothing, Washington related an anecdote. Sometime earlier, he had conducted a national search for an individual to direct a program of study in commercial tailoring at Tuskegee only to discover that "it was almost impossible to find in the whole country an educated colored man who could teach the making of clothes." Washington went on to sermonize that he could find educated black men "by the score who could teach astronomy, theology, German or Latin, but almost none who could instruct in the making of clothing, something that has to be used by every one of us every day in the year." Turning last to the construction of shelter, Washington told a poignant tale of the race losing ground by relating a story of a colored man who had been trained as a skilled mechanic when he was a slave. By his skill and work ethic, he became a successful builder, but in his city where thirty-five thousand people of color lived, young men resided who were trained in the arts and literature, but no one was schooled in mechanical and architectural design who could take over the profitable business the ex-slave had created, so it was soon scattered to the wind.[17]

The moral Washington projected from his three examples illustrates a sophisticated one that belies characterizations of Washington himself as uneducated. Washington's point was that a Renaissance humanist education—the ideal for liberal arts colleges—was not adequate for modern times. He claimed, "You cannot graft a fifteenth century civilization onto a twentieth century civilization by the mere performance of mental gymnastics."[18]

In his presentation, Washington highlighted all three of the areas of instruction associated with industrial education at Tuskegee. There was agriculture, where Tuskegee was considered to be a world-class center of research. There were artisanal crafts, where, in those days before mass production (and plastics), there remained economic opportunities. And finally, there were construction and civil engineering. Washington's contrasting of these areas of study with humanistic learning certainly resonated with the people who supported him, most of whom agreed that humanistic education bred economic dependency. But the rhetorical strategy cost him dearly outside this target group. No matter how much he insisted that he had no animus against the liberal arts, his critics were able to repudiate his claims through reference to speeches like this one.

Washington continued with his assaults on humanistic learning because there was such a ready audience for them in Africa as well as in the United States. In West Africa, the liberal arts colleges and seminaries that served as targets for Washington's barbs in the United States were not plentiful. However, mission schools provided an alternative for attack. Many African Christians had already arrived at assessments similar to that of Washington about the value of industrial over humanistic education. "Since the problem of bread-winning is of more importance than that of culture," argued one author in the *Gold Coast Leader*, "it should now be a nominating purpose in all our schools to give the student a chance to help himself or herself to some industry."[19] Another article published in the *Lagos Weekly Record* argued a similar position:

> Whatever any other people need to grow strong the Negro needs, it is not enough to teach our girls a few lessons in sewing, cooking and nursing, and our boys to beat a little iron ore, drive a few nails, make a few badly shaped bricks, etc. . . . [W]e want the Negro to have higher industrial education. We must be taught to melt iron ore, build locomotives, [do] all sorts of mechanical engineering. . . . This kind of high industrial education is the

only kind that he [the Negro] needs now and is essential to his salvation. This kind of industrial education is the only kind that can give a people permanent strength.[20]

Washington's assaults added to the arsenal of arguments used by Ethiopianists to critique mission education as it was then pursued in West Africa. Articles that urged adoption of Washington's formulation of the issue were composed of two reciprocal arguments: one *for* industrial education, one *against* humanistic education. An example of a case where the argument *for* industrial education was highlighted appeared in the Sierra Leone *Weekly News* in 1918. The colonial government's query into the building of a technical institute in 1889 had taken a turn in a different direction, culminating in the establishment in 1906 of the Bo School for the sons of chiefs. In 1918 the government announced plans to build another school like the Bo School. The article in the *Weekly News* directed a protest against these plans. The writer in the article began by indicting schools that maintained a humanistic curriculum, like the Bo School, for producing only "writing clerks or petty hawkers." Government schools, the writer insisted, should be sending graduates back to their homes as "scientifically trained farmers, good and skilled artisans," or any other profession that would make them "valuable assets for the development of the economic resources of the country in which they were born." The writer concluded by saying that Sierra Leone really needed "Technical, Industrial and Agricultural schools." Such schools, claimed the writer, would allow Sierra Leoneans to "remedy our deplorable impotency and cringing dependences."[21]

An example of a case where the argument *against* humanistic education was emphasized was provided in the *Gold Coast Leader* in 1906. Applauding an article about U.S. president Theodore Roosevelt telling graduates of Hampton to "take up Agricultural work, first for others, but ultimately so as to acquire farms of their own," an unidentified commentator posed the rhetorical question, "What is the cause that discourages the coloured or the black man from taking, heart and soul, to industrial occupation?" From this starting point, the commentator went on to complain about the dangers to Africans of training for occupations where the only opportunities for employment were under European control:

The fever to drive the quill, to wear the wig, to mount the pulpit and to do the one and another thing, leaving the most important, is the cause of all the evils attendant upon the social lives to-day in West Africa. With no private incomes to fall back upon as it obtains in most cases in England, what would my friend the *quill-driver* who may stand the chance of being dismissed from the desk at any moment do? To what other field would my friend the *white-tie-man*, to direct his energies when he is forbidden to ascend the pulpit any longer?[22]

Behind the rhetorical flourishes, the commentator was making a case that mission education produced only clerks (quill-drivers) and clergymen (white-tie men). Careers in both these occupations were at the beck and call of Europeans. With this point in mind, the commentator proclaimed that "the Salvation, freedom and independence of the black man lies in nothing but industrialism."[23]

## WASHINGTON AND TUSKEGEE IN WEST AFRICA: BLYDEN, MAY, AND FADUMA

While a number of West Africans had opinions on industrial education, the discourse on this subject in West Africa was shaped primarily by three men: Edward W. Blyden, E. Cornelius May, and Orishatukeh Faduma. They gave others the information and insight used to form proposals in favor of building schools like Tuskegee. Each of these men had something different to say. Blyden's greatest importance lay in shaping the understanding of industrial education. May did more than anyone else to champion Washington as a race leader. Faduma sought to apply his firsthand knowledge of Tuskegee and industrial education to West African circumstances.

Washington and Tuskegee provided Blyden with proof that the African had the capacity to develop an industrial civilization and was in fact doing just that in the United States. Blyden had no real empathy for industrial education and industrial education schools, however. His admiration was for Washington and for Washington's validation of the African's technological capacities. One illustration of this admiration came from Blyden's refusal to grant Washington's proclaimed opposition to black repatriation to Africa any substance. According to Blyden, Washington was saying that the African Americans needed to concentrate on the task at hand of building up their communities in the United States before thinking about migrating those communities back to Africa. Blyden insisted no doubt should exist that, in "casting down his bucket where he stood," Washington was "building for Africa."[24]

Blyden first signaled his support of Washington and Tuskegee in the letter mentioned above, first published in the *New York Age* in January 1895 but then reprinted in the Sierra Leone *Weekly News* and summarized in detail in the *Lagos Weekly Record*. In the letter Blyden appeared to be suggesting to Washington the course Washington followed in his "Atlanta Compromise" speech later that same year. As published in the *Weekly News* under the headline "Keep Out of Politics—That Is What Dr. Blyden Advises the Negro to Do," Blyden argued, "The Negro in the South cannot afford to be a politician. . . . Every thinking African on this side acquainted with the subject entertains the view I have just expressed." He continued, "We believe the interest of both races would be best served if the Negro would eschew politics and political aspirations where every step of the way is hampered and covered with thorns and briars." Blyden concluded that the Negro is called to higher and nobler work, by which he had in mind industrial education as taught at Tuskegee. To arguments that recognized European material culture as proof of both white superiority and black inferiority, Blyden responded that blacks were only now bringing their God-granted genius to the industrialization process and that the material culture that would result from black industrialization would be the first "distinctly" Christian one. For this reason, Blyden thanked Washington in the letter for showing the African that in the "industrial sphere" his "possibilities were unlimited."[25]

In 1896 Blyden moved to Lagos to work as an educational consultant for the governor of the colony, Sir Gilbert Carter.[26] One of the projects that Blyden put forward was a proposal for a "Lagos Literary College and Industrial Training Institute."[27] The school was to have two departments, "industrial and literary." The industrial department would provide instruction in "the usual mechanical trades and sciences and practical agriculture."[28] In addition, every student would be required to perform a certain number of hours each week in "such industrial work, either mechanical or agricultural, as his taste may select." These were the only two stipulations about industrial education in the proposal. Since Blyden was a humanist and language teacher, his plan should not be surprising. He dedicated much of the proposal to justifying his requirement that all students learn Greek and Latin for the secondary intellectual skills these subjects would help improve.[29] Deserving of note, however, is that Blyden did not acknowledge or build upon the dichotomy

Washington and others maintained between humanistic and technical knowledge. Blyden insisted upon the complementary nature of the two.

Blyden sought to locate Tuskegee's technological achievements in the context of the evolution of an African civilization. May sought to fix Washington in the African mind as the progenitor of economic Ethiopianism, pointing to Tuskegee as the solution to the economic problems British imperialism was posing for the Christian regeneration of Africa. Scant biographical material is available on E. Cornelius. His brother, J. Claudius, was much better known and left a legacy both as a minister and as an educator.[30] E. Cornelius, however, was responsible for keeping the name of Washington alive before his newspaper's reading public. The one hundred or so articles on Washington and Tuskegee published in the *Weekly News* were the fruit of his editorial decision-making. In addition, E. Cornelius published more than fifty articles by or about Blyden. And, over the years, he also published more pieces by Faduma than did any other West African newspaper editor. Though unsung, he played a critical role in the development of Ethiopianism on Africa's west coast.

May regularly celebrated Washington's achievements in the pages of his newspaper but distinguished himself in the way he honored Washington's passing. A number of African writers wrote obituaries upon hearing of the death of Washington. May went much further and wrote a series of editorials identifying the lessons African Christians should take from Washington's pronouncements. He routinely wrote an editorial column entitled Familiar Talks on Familiar Subjects. Under the title, May offered his opinions on various subjects he felt of importance to "the (Negro) Race." Seemingly prescient, May began his series of editorials on Washington just two days before the latter's death.

May typically structured his editorials around a review of some book or article that came across his desk. The authors and topics of these items were wide ranging, but in May's opinion all in some way said something pertinent to the Ethiopianist struggle for Africa's regeneration. The article May reviewed in the first of his series of pieces on Washington presented a vehement attack on missions and missionaries. It was the springboard for May's case, discussed in the previous chapter, why "thoughtful" African Christians should not be satisfied with the guidance offered by missionaries but look instead to the teachings of Washington.[31] The next issue of the *Weekly News* brought the announcement of Washington's sudden death. So, in his second piece, May set himself the task of passing on to his readers, for the "well-being of our Common Race," apothegms culled primarily from the collection of Washington's sayings published in 1898 as *Black Belt Diamonds*.[32] For three months, from mid-November 1915 through the end of February, he closed each column with the injunction that his readers "think, think, think!" about the message Washington was attempting to convey to African peoples across the Atlantic. He stopped doing this not because "the mine" he had been working was "exhausted" but because "even diamonds lose their value to eyes accustomed to gaze on nothing else but diamonds."[33]

If Washington was an apostle of the Protestant ethic, May was his disciple. May was a firm believer that capitalism was the way forward for the African race. He quoted Washington saying:

> Aside from the direct good to the individual or individuals, a business success cuts like a two-edged sword, bringing the white man confidence and respect, giving to the Negro faith in the fidelity and ability of his people, and creating at the same time an inspiration that will lead to a higher mental development of the whole race.[34]

Capitalism brought the individual African wealth. Capitalism improved race relations between Africans and Europeans. Capitalism made the African race stronger.

Washington made his case for industrial education by posing humanistic education as the "other." May went in a different direction and created a new "other": Europeans who came to West Africa to trade on their race with colonial governments and expatriate businesses. Europeans as a group were in Africa for purposes of economic exploitation because of the imperial and colonial enterprises of their home countries. In making this point, May was not condemning capitalism. Capitalism was to be the vehicle of Africa's transformation. May's indictment stressed that European sojourners in Africa were not adding to capitalism's positive impact but detracting from it because all they had to trade was their skin color.

May spent most of one editorial complaining about a group of white railway workers in Sierra Leone who decided to go out on strike in protest against using the same latrines as African workers. He characterized the strikers in the editorial by saying, "Here are men, not drawn from the higher walks of life in their own country. They were evidently delighted at the chance of earning for their livelihood a salary which in their wildest dreams they dare not hope to receive in England."[35] For

May, the Europeans flooding the West African coast were poor white opportunists. The railway company refused to build separate accommodations, which broke the strike. What infuriated May the most was that the white workers were "so eaten up with prejudice against the black man in his [the black man's] own country."[36] May saluted the European capitalists who owned the railway for allowing capitalism to work as it should work, that is, as a barrier against racism. But his point was that imperialism made this example an exception rather than the rule. May complained repeatedly about the appearance in West Africa of "lofty Englishmen." These were Britons who claimed privilege and economic opportunity based upon race.[37] In making such complaints, May was implying that African owners and operators would be impervious to whites using the race card in such a fashion to gain an advantage. African owners and operators would allow capitalism to work as capitalism should and thus facilitate Africa's regeneration. For May, this was Washington's message. Imperialism, through the willingness of white capitalists to coddle white supremacists, was getting in the way of capitalism. The solution was the production of black capitalists, which was what Washington was doing at Tuskegee.

E. Cornelius May was a man extremely conscious of the mental shackles of racial subjugation. From the perspective of someone seeking to get Africans to the point of thinking independently as free participants in the civilized (Western) world, May advised Africans in editorial after editorial to look to Washington's words for direction. Washington had lived and worked in the American South "in the center of color prejudice." In this, the harshest of climates, where white racism had corrupted everything, Washington had shown African Americans how to pursue capitalism successfully as a vehicle of racial uplift. Washington had taught African Americans to "lean more" on their own efforts and to "limit" their aspirations and ambitions to what they could accomplish on their own. One of the first of Washington's "diamonds" that May passed on to his readers was Washington's observation, "The fact that a man who goes into the world conscious that he has within himself the power to create a wagon or a house gives him a certain moral back-bone and independence in the world that he could not possess without it."[38] May argued that mental discipline validated by task completion should be remembered as Washington's most vital insight. The militancy behind May's commentaries needs to be highlighted. Following Washington's teachings, May insisted, African Americans had not just survived but also advanced. The one historical figure of African descent that May compared favorably to Washington was Toussaint Louverture.[39] And to May's mind, Washington, like Louverture, appreciated that "a judicious general . . . would remember that discretion is the better part of valour, and would wisely reserve himself and men for the moment in his secret mind when he hopes to bring his opponent at bay and compel him to accept battle or defeat."[40]

Blyden lauded Washington and Washington's demonstration of the technical proficiencies of people of African descent. May posed Washington as a race leader with a plan for racial regeneration. Neither of these men, however, could offer West African Ethiopianists any practical instruction on the implementation of an industrial education program. As an African guide on this topic, West Africans listened to Orishatukeh Faduma. In the obituary of Washington that he wrote, Faduma mentioned that he had met Washington several times and that, before he immigrated back to Africa in 1914, he wrote Washington with a request to tour Tuskegee's campus. Washington generously acquiesced to his request. Faduma was thus one of the few African advocates of industrial education in West Africa who had actually been to Tuskegee.

Perhaps no individual, in his life, ideas, career, and faith, better encapsulated the black Christian Atlantic than Faduma. Born in British Guyana to Yoruba parents who had been freed from a slave ship by a British squadron, at an early age Faduma returned to Africa with his parents to settle in Sierra Leone. Because his intellectual skills were obvious to all, he was sent as a boy to live in the household of the Reverend J. Claudius May, E. Cornelius' older brother. Faduma attended Methodist Boys High School in Freetown, where J. Claudius was principal. Faduma's academic ambitions prompted him first to leave Africa to study in Britain, where he earned a bachelor's degree from the University of London. Faduma returned to Freetown to teach, but intellectual restlessness once again took him across the Atlantic, this time to the United States. In the United States, Faduma entered the Divinity School at Yale, where he earned a bachelor of divinity degree in 1894.

Though Faduma spent long periods of his life associated with the A.M.E. Church, he was ordained as a Congregationalist minister in 1895. He applied to the American Missionary Association for funding to return to Africa as a missionary, but the financial straits of that organization led him in 1897 to accept a dual position as the principal of Peabody Academy in Troy, North Carolina, and as pastor to the black

Congregational Church in that community. At Peabody, Faduma introduced an industrial education curriculum. He remained in Troy for seventeen years, gaining an American family and American citizenship. In 1914 Faduma and his family immigrated back to Africa, as part of Chief Sam's Back-to-Africa movement.

The years running Peabody Academy in the United States made him, in African eyes, an expert on industrial education. Faduma presumed to play this role even before returning to Africa to settle in 1914. He visited Sierra Leone in 1908. During that time, he gave a lecture in Freetown on industrial education. Announcing the lecture, the *Weekly News* noted that, at Peabody Academy, Faduma had instituted an "industrial" program of study to go along with the school's "literary" coursework. In order to run the industrial program, Faduma had earned a certificate at the State Agricultural and Mechanical College. Based upon this training, Faduma maintained a forty-acre farm at his school.[41] As summed up in the *Weekly News*, during his visit, Faduma discussed the three "aspects" of industrial education: the "domestic," the "mechanical," and the "agricultural." The presentation on the domestic aspect was about cooking and how many "domestic feuds" could be averted if a "labouring man" had a "tasty and easily digestible meal" waiting for him in the evening. Faduma's presentation on the mechanical aspect attacked the animus against "manual labor" among lettered people. "Consumption without production tendeth to bankruptcy," Faduma warned. Upon the agricultural aspects of industrial education, Faduma was assumed to have the most to say. He identified agriculture as the "department of labour" most likely to "bring us [Africans] to competence and independence if pursued on the right lines." As the article admonished, "Clerkships may fail us when they can only be obtained at the expense of our manhood. But the soil is inalienable."[42]

Historians have investigated the German effort to use Tuskegee's proficiency in cotton growing to help develop the German colony of Togo. From 1900 to 1909, graduates of Tuskegee led experimental cotton growing plantations in the territory for the German government. The perspective taken in existing scholarship has been to emphasize the connection between the plantations and colonial exploitation.[43] As noted in the previous chapter, Africans did not see the experiments in that light. For Africans the venture validated the agricultural/technological achievement of Tuskegee and, more broadly, the agricultural know-how of African Americans. Faduma in his visit to Africa in 1908, in his various presentations on industrial education, was taken to represent this expertise. The *Gold Coast Leader* from neighboring Ghana also published an article on Faduma's lecture in Freetown and commented that "the Professor" was "preaching the gospel of self reliance." The *Gold Coast Leader*, like the *Weekly News*, saw Faduma as making the case for industrial education as a pathway via agriculture to economic nationalism. The newspaper used its understanding of Faduma to ridicule as inconsequential government recommendations about agricultural development. In a later editorial, after snidely contrasting the insights offered by Faduma on how to use maize to feed both humans and animals with the insights offered by a British colonial official on how to prepare a "delicious beverage from pine apple," the *Gold Coast Leader* concluded, "We think much can be taught about our food supply to our lasting benefit by those who come from America."[44] Several months later, an editorial in the *Weekly News* made the same point in a much more explicit fashion. Having noted first that after the German government in Togo had hired agricultural advisors from Tuskegee to train its farmers, with the result that exports of maize from that country had increased fivefold, from 660 to 3,000 tons, and having noted second the failures of the agricultural advisors dispatched to Sierra Leone from Kew Gardens in Britain, the editorial ended with the plea for a group of agricultural advisors from Tuskegee for Ghana as well:

> What we as Africans and black men want, are black men like ourselves or coloured men with the requisite scientific training to teach our people **tropical agriculture**. . . . We are sure that should the Government make such an experiment now, there is nothing to prevent such magnificent results as have been achieved by the German Government in Togoland.[45]

Tuskegee expertise was what Africa needed.

In October 1914, upon his return to Africa as part of the Chief Sam party, Faduma published in both the *Weekly News* and the *Gold Coast Leader* a long exposition on the principles of the Back-to-Africa movement.[46] One of the ambitions of the movement was to facilitate the industrial development of Africa. Having made the case that economic opportunities in the United States were "closed" for members of the "Ethiopian" race, specifically members of the race who had graduated from Hampton and Tuskegee, Faduma rhetorically posed the question, was the "industrial training" of these young men and women to be "wasted?" No, was his answer:

> The African (Back-to-Africa) movement . . . takes the initiative to welcome our industrially trained men and women of African ancestry to become pioneers and cross the Atlantic to Africa, their ancestral land. . . . The African movement believes in business in religion and religion in business. It is an appeal to the business men and business instincts of the race to expand their horizon and organize to exploit the land of their ancestors and not allow the foreigners to take it all. . . . It is voicing the cry of Ethiopia's sons and daughters in Africa to those in the United States to come over and help develop the land for Africa and the world.[47]

Faduma agreed with Washington that Hampton and Tuskegee graduates possessed the understanding of the Protestant ethic needed for the regeneration of African peoples. These graduates had no outlets for their talents in Jim Crow America, but they could make all the difference in colonial Africa. Of note in Faduma's exposition is its return to Crummell's original scheme for the regeneration of Africa. African American entrepreneurs were asked to come develop Africa for profit, with the assumption that their economic expertise would diffuse to indigenous peoples. The difference between Crummell's original proposal from 1865 and Faduma's later scheme from 1914 illustrated that, in the intervening half century, Hampton and Tuskegee had emerged to define African American entrepreneurship.

After Washington's death in November 1915, Faduma made a bid to become the leader of the industrial education movement in West Africa. In pursuit of this goal, he published a proposal on the subject in the *Weekly News* in July 1916. In the second chapter of the present study, mention is made of Faduma's paper he gave in Atlanta in 1895 at the Congress on Africa entitled, "Drawbacks and Successes of Missionary Work in Africa." He came back to that title, though interestingly enough with the terms inverted, in the 1916 article and presented modern times as the age of industrial missions prophesized by Isaiah in the Hebrew Testament. Taking as his text Isaiah 29:17-19, Faduma looked upon his time as one when the songs of war and greed that had captivated humankind in the past would give way to the song of "Christ, tools and man."[48] In his obituary of Washington, published in November 1915, Faduma credited Washington with using the "selfish materialism" of the United States to help his race.[49] Eight months later, Faduma returned to the theme, writing about the "materialist spirit of the twentieth century" that was prompting Europeans to carve up Africa. Yet, Faduma proclaimed, "the God of Nations" was "working through this materialism and preparing the way for [Africa's] civilization and regeneration." Industrial education, Faduma argued, supplied African Christians with a vehicle toward self-respect, a vehicle toward "manhood." Faduma identified "foreign missionaries," by which he meant European as distinct from African American missionaries, as the individuals most prone to "crush" the African Christian's spirit and initiative. Industrial education missions, ideally undertaken by Hampton and Tuskegee graduates, teaching the Tuskegee program, promised a better way to regenerate Africa. Gaining some technical competency would provide African Christians with a means to make a living independent of foreign missions and thus allow Africans to stand on their own legs.[50]

The problem centered on funding. As with every other scheme for the regeneration of Africa, Faduma's came back to the issue of revenues and expenditures. However, Faduma appealed to European missions to fund Ethiopianist industrial education schools. He made his appeal indirectly. First, Faduma complained about "old baby missions," that is, mature mission stations that still depended upon funding from outside sources. These missions would already be self-supporting, according to Faduma, "if only proper care [had been taken] at their inception to teach the natives industrial training." An industrial education program not only would have covered the cost of maintaining the mission station but would also have provided better pay for "school-teachers, catechists and evangelists," for the station's African personnel. Second, Faduma argued that existing missions should be reformed so that they functioned based upon the principles of "industrial" agriculture. Teaching pupils at mission station schools "the cultivation of corn, rice, peas," the "preparation of food," and the "rearing of cattle and poultry," Faduma suggested, "was as necessary to their education as the study of books." In light of these two suggestions, Faduma thirdly proposed that there should be a "missionary industrial leader," meaning a person of African descent, associated with every mission station. The leader would be "acquainted with the methods of modern industrialism" and would teach these to the pupils in the station school. Missionaries would remain in charge of the station. They would concentrate their energies, however, on "evangelical" endeavors. As Faduma summed up in his final paragraph:

> If the native convert must be honest and independent, if the native church must be self-supporting . . . industrial missions are a necessity. Africa needs a Christianity which is practical, a Christianity which will respond to the yearnings of her spiritual and physical life, a Christianity which does not antagonize the two natures but brings both in complete harmony with the law of Christ.[51]

In exchange for turning existing mission stations into miniature versions of Tuskegee, mission organizations would gain uncontested hegemony over Christian evangelization. Mission stations would remain under the jurisdiction of missionaries who could then preoccupy themselves with full-time proselytization. The social regeneration of African converts to Christianity would be placed in the hands of Ethiopianists. The latter would both teach the converts the true nature of a Christian life and provide the convert with the industrial training needed to maintain that Christian life.

From the perspective of the challenge Ethiopianists had been mounting to missionaries since the 1880s, Faduma's proposal might be appreciated as an effort at rapprochement between the two groups initiated from the African side. By 1916 Ethiopianists knew that colonial governments were not their allies in a battle against missions. Rather, colonial governments were committed to building schools that neutralized the influence of mission-educated Africans over the rest of the African population. Ethiopianism needed allies to go forward. May must have had some sympathy for Faduma's proposal; otherwise, he would not have published Faduma's plan in the *Weekly News*. What other Ethiopianists thought about it cannot be said, and no evidence exists to show that Faduma ever got a positive reaction to his proposal from Ethiopianists or missionaries. Perhaps the clearest indication of the overall reception to the proposal is that Faduma wrote nothing more on the topic in African newspapers.[52]

### ETHIOPIANISTS AND INDUSTRIAL EDUCATION INITIATIVES

Ethiopianists conceived of industrial institutes as building blocks for African independence. That conclusion did not escape the administrations of colonial governments who actually had some interest in industrial education schools, but only for African collaborators whose loyalties governments believed they could guarantee. So although Ethiopianists continuously lobbied colonial governments to build Tuskegee-style schools, government-sponsored school building in West Africa went in the direction of training academies for the children of elites.

Sir Leslie Probyn, who began a seven-year tenure as governor of Sierra Leone in 1904, made the establishment of an industrial education school a priority of his administration, and in 1906 the Bo School came into existence. To the chagrin of Ethiopianists, admission to the school was reserved exclusively for the sons of chiefs. Even more problematic from the Ethiopianist perspective, most of the students were Muslims, and, even though the first principal was a missionary and the first teachers were African Christians, the governor prohibited Christian evangelization on the campus. The guidelines Governor Probyn announced for the development of the school reveal the colonial state's understanding of industrial education as a prophylactic against Africans undergoing what the state labeled as "denationalization," a negative way of describing the evolution of an Ethiopianist or pan-Africanist consciousness. Three instincts, all identified as outcomes of Western education, required obstruction. Book learning bred an antipathy toward manual endeavor, so the Bo School emphasized farming, carpentry, bridge building, road making, and surveying as the main subjects of instruction. Book learning likewise generated disdain for village society and traditional authority. To correct for this instinct, Probyn originally mandated that students live together in makeshift versions of tribal villages, though this was soon abandoned and replaced with a version of the English public school residential house tradition, with students boarded and taught according to tribal affiliations. Command of English was deemed necessary for future collaboration with the colonial government. Still, Europeans feared that knowledge of English brought out in Africans the worst instincts toward self-actualization. So students at the Bo School spent two years being vetted in writing and speaking English before being taught to read from English language textbooks. And, to steer the students away from any ambition to use their English-language skills for comparatively lucrative employment as clerks, Probyn made clear that the government would not employ any of the students as clerks (though it did as teachers).[53]

British administrators contended that the Bo School followed in the tradition of Hampton and Tuskegee, but with its curriculum adapted to the government's needs for chiefs trained to serve as local agents of the colonial state. Ethiopianists disagreed. They complained that the Bo School was an institution for Muslim elites subsidized by the state and that the government should establish schools of equal caliber for other students.[54] The determination to claim state funding prompted Ethiopianists in Sierra Leone to challenge the financial support colonial governments were providing to "religious," in this case Muslim, schools. An editorial published in the *Weekly News* in October 1909 made three points. In the past "the Church" had provided all education, including industrial education. In present times, however, "the State" had taken the lead in education from the church, prompting the emergence of a distinction between "Religious Education" and "Secular Education." Since religion was more important than anything in secular life, the church should focus its energies on building up religious instruction, and the state should concentrate its energies on building up secular instruction. Industrial education was a form of secular education. Therefore, the state should concentrate its energies on building up industrial education schools. The editorial concluded, "The activities of the State should be confined to material and business Education—Industrial, Technical Education and chiefly at this state in our development to Agricultural Education."[55] The arguments of the Ethiopianists were to no avail. The Bo School became the model for government schools.

In 1896 Edward Blyden put forward a proposal in Nigeria for a Lagos Literary College and Industrial Training Institute. He secured approval from the colonial governor, Sir Gilbert Carter, to back his proposal with an offer to contribute £2,000 if the local community could come up with £1,000.[56] Carter wanted to establish an institution of higher learning that would provide West Africans with an alternative to traveling to Europe to complete their education.[57] Blyden added the industrial track. Robert Payne Jackson, editor of the *Lagos Weekly Record*, took the lead in lobbying West Africans to contribute the £1,000 needed to get the project off the ground. The funds were never collected, however.[58]

In 1907 Captain C. H. Elgee, resident administrator of Ibadan in Nigeria's Southern Province, proposed to the Colonial Office in London, based upon a visit to Tuskegee, that the colonial government build a version of Tuskegee between the towns of Ibadan and Oyo in Yoruba territory. Key to the proposal for Elgee was the sending of Yoruba schoolteachers to Tuskegee for three years of training at the expense of government. The men would then return to Nigeria to teach, in Yoruba, what they had learned. Replicating Tuskegee, as Elgee saw it, would facilitate the introduction of modern technology to a loyal group of Africans without the threat of denationalization. A summary of Elgee's proposal was printed, along with an accompanying editorial, in E. D. Morel's newspaper, the *West African Mail*, in February 1907.[59] In the editorial, Morel thought that building a version of Tuskegee in Yorubaland was a good idea but took issue with the idea of sending schoolteachers to train in the United States, because if the concern was denationalization, then "it must be remembered that the American Negro has lost a good deal more of his African nationality than . . . West Africans."[60] A measure of the excitement the idea of a government-supported version of Tuskegee generated among Ethiopianists, even those who were not Yoruba, can be illustrated by the fact that within a month copies of Morel's editorial had been reprinted in the Sierra Leone *Weekly News* and the *Lagos Weekly Record*, while the *Lagos Standard* published a rephrased version of the summary first printed in the *West African Mail*.[61] May, in a separate editorial in the *Weekly News*, specifically endorsed Elgee's proposal as amended by Morel, labeling it "progress."[62] But the excitement does not appear to have had any result. In articles published in its April 29 and May 13, 1908, issues, the *Lagos Standard* reported that the governor of the Gold Coast, Sir John Rogers, "a firm believer in industrial education," had traveled to the United States to visit Hampton and Tuskegee. The latter article expressed the hope that Rogers would bring back to London with him an appreciation of how important schools like Tuskegee were for the future of the African race and for the prosperity of the British Empire. There were no follow-ups to these reports.[63]

The Nigerian appeal for a government-sponsored industrial institute became progressively more plaintive. Under the headline "A Moribund Scheme," the *Lagos Standard* in 1911 dedicated a long article to describing a government plan launched in 1905 to train Africans to replace European technicians in government works. The "Technical Scholarships" would have permitted young men who had completed Standard VI to apprentice at government expense for three years in the Government Railway, Public Works, and Marine Departments, after which qualified students could apply to go to Britain for further training. Six years later, however, at the time when the article was published, only two of the twenty or so students who had qualified to be sent to Britain had actually been sent. The newspaper article questioned what "sinister influence" had been at work to "retard" the progress of the program. Whatever it was, the newspaper speculated, it was the same influence that had worked to send back home the large number of technically trained West Indians who had come to Lagos a few years back to replace European technicians. The *Lagos Standard* article revealed a

growing sense among Ethiopianists that not only were colonial governments unsympathetic to new schemes for the development of industrial
education schools but also the governments were reneging on previous
commitments. The newspaper promised to publish more on the story,
but this did not happen.[64]

More and more, however, over the last decade or so under consideration in this study, Ethiopianists looked to private sources in hopes
of funding for industrial education institutes. An article in the *Lagos
Standard*, in January 1910, announced that Alfred L. Jones, shipping
magnate and patron of the African Institute, had left a bequest of over
£200,000 for the establishment of an industrial institute on Africa's
west coast.[65] The *Lagos Weekly Record*, in June 1910, published a proposal by the scholar G. Rome Hall that the Jones money be used for the
creation of an "intermediate college"—something between a grammar
school and a university—which would have two tracks, "scholarly" and
"scientific." As Hall conceived of his college, it would be a preparatory
academy for readying young men to head to Britain for university education. In July, the newspaper followed with a letter to the editor that
rejected the Hall proposal, pointing out that Jones meant the money
to be dedicated to technical, not humanistic, education.[66] The debate
over the money became moot when, as announced in the *Lagos Standard* on April 23, 1913, the estate executors made the decision that the
Jones bequest would be kept in Britain to found the Liverpool School
of Tropical Medicine. Twenty thousand pounds was reserved from the
bequest toward the original goal, the promotion of industrial education in Africa.[67] In 1917, as reported in the *Weekly News*, the governor
of Sierra Leone announced that this money would be used to found a
trade school.[68]

In an article published on September 25, 1907, entitled "Native
Energy," the *Lagos Standard* celebrated the success of the "Technological Institute," established and directed by a Mr. Isaac A. Cole, who was
introducing Lagosians to knowledge "along the same lines" as "the
great and good work that is going on by Prof. Booker T. Washington in
his Institute at Tuskegee."[69] The energetic Mr. Cole regularly advertised
his services in the *Lagos Standard* and the *Lagos Weekly Record* as a
"builder and contractor also funeral undertaker." In 1907 the Technological Institute had sixty-five students.[70] Based upon Cole's advertise-
ments, evidence shows the school continued for at least another decade.
Cole's school illustrates that West Africans did take some initiative in

seeking to supply privately the technical training colonial governments declined to provide.

After Blyden died in February 1912, the *Lagos Standard* reported that a "Blyden Memorial" fund had been established, one of its projects being the establishment of a "Blyden Memorial School where industrial and technical knowledge will be imparted, combined with the most liberal intellectual equipment, such as the deceased patriot advocated all of his life."[71] The project was an effort to revive as a private initiative, without government support, Blyden's proposal for the Lagos Literary College and Industrial Training Institute. No records survive to determine what happened to the drive other than it ended without any concrete plan to open a school.

In 1918 a group of Ghanaians tried a different tack in an effort to generate funding for industrial education. Led by the nationalist, lawyer, and scholar J. E. Casely-Hayford and calling themselves the "Founders of Gold Coast National Schools," the group began renting advertising space in the *Gold Coast Nation* on a weekly basis. The advertisement they placed was always the same. It announced that the group was looking for two hundred "patriotic, educated, well-to-do and influential sons of the soil," each willing to give fifty pounds toward an "Education Scheme." One objective of the scheme was to set up a series of secondary schools in Ghana. The curriculum in these schools was to be "industrial" as well as "scientific." Seeking to stave off any accusation that the planned schools were intended to compete with denominational schools, the advertisement emphasized that the scheme was not meant to "rival" any "existing educational machinery." Rather, "the Promoters of the Scheme are convinced that Education is the greatest asset of any nation and the time has arrived for the people to take up education seriously." The advertisement ran off and on for about two years, but again without a positive outcome.[72]

An event held in Sierra Leone in 1921 reveals one last direction in which Ethiopianist initiative flowed. The A.M.E. Church mission launched in Freetown that year a new school, the Girls Industrial and Literary Institute.[73] At the "Great Public Meeting" held in Freetown to kick off a funding campaign for the school, the past, present, and future of Ethiopianist promotion of industrial education all came together. Orishatukeh Faduma was one of the featured speakers, representing the past. Adelaide Casely-Hayford, wife of J. E. Casely-Hayford, was the other featured speaker, representing the present. The cosponsors of the event signaled the future. The women's branch of the Universal Negro Improvement Agency (UNIA), the local chapter of the Garvey movement, helped organize the event.[74]

The event caused quite a "misunderstanding" in government circles in Sierra Leone, however, because the governor took exception to the inclusion of the UNIA in the meeting. As explained in an article in the *Weekly News*, Mrs. Casely-Hayford defended her involvement in the event with the argument that the idea for the meeting had come originally from the UNIA, and she was just assisting in a worthy cause. Meanwhile, the women's branch of the UNIA was offended by the "cavalier" treatment they were receiving and requested the return of the fifteen pounds they had helped raise.[75] A second fundraiser for the school, an "Oriental Concert," was quickly arranged. This one, held in June, was also under the auspices of Mrs. Casely-Hayford, but not the ladies from the UNIA. At this event, the governor and his party graced the performance by staying "until the close." The fundraiser was characterized as a great success in the *Weekly News*, the concert netting more than ninety pounds for the girls' school.[76] Still, the women's chapter of the UNIA may have had the last word. As a proud member of the chapter wrote later to the *Weekly News* to report, an article with the UNIA version of the events was published in the Garvey newspaper, the *Negro World*, in New York.[77]

Booker T. Washington insisted that practical Christianity involved "mixing" faith with material improvement.[78] The benchmark he set for practical Christianity was the capacity of black people to generate among themselves the funds for social welfare projects like the YMCA buildings in American cities about which he wrote. The attentive ears of Ethiopianists in Africa made them conscious of Washington's ideal—practical Christians were often mentioned in articles about Tuskegee. A sense that Africans were not living up to Washington's ideal is perhaps one explanation for the self-condemnation discernible in African commentary about the failure of the industrial education movement in Africa.

In 1921 a blistering editorial in the *Lagos Weekly Record*, by Thomas Horatio Jackson, the new editor of the newspaper, indicted contemporary Nigerians for their failure to fund industrial institutes. These private schools, according to Jackson, could have been "living protests against the low standards of education set by Government."[79] As an example of the sort of private school he had in mind, Jackson referred his readers to

Blyden's proposal from 1896, which he argued would have established a school "along the lines of Tuskegee" that might have served as the nucleus of a West African University.[80] In one paragraph, the editorial told the story of the rebuff of colonial interference in India, where it argued, when Lord Curzon attempted to do to the Indian education system what Lord Lugard had done to the Nigerian education system, an Indian "solicitor" spent £500,000 of his own money to endow a "College of Science and Technology." In another paragraph, the editorial illustrated how the Japanese paid foreign technologists to come to Japan to live for five to seven years and train Japanese students. As a result, the editorial argued, when it was time for the foreigner to leave, there were always Japanese "graduates" to fill the vacancies. In comparison, the editorial lamented, when, in 1896, Nigerians were asked to put forward just £1,000 for a similar investment in economic freedom, the funds could not be found, so the scheme had to die a natural death. The editorial concluded that it was time for Nigerians to stop talking "patriotic gas," that is, to stop complaining about the refusal of government to sponsor industrial education schools.[81]

Nigerians and other West Africans did not follow his suggestion. In 1920 industrial training remained on the list of ongoing "problems" with the Nigerian education system about which Henry Carr, director of education for the Southern Province, spoke at a dinner held for the Phelps Stokes Education Commission.[82] In a list of desired governmental reforms submitted to Governor Hugh Clifford via the *Nigerian Pioneer* in 1922, a request signed by many of the chiefs and most influential men in the Southern Province proposed that "for purposes of developing our (Nigeria's) natural resources . . . a technical and industrial institute along the lines of Tuskegee Institute" be established.[83] The National Congress of British West Africa, the confederation of African nationalists concerned with the position of West Africa in the British Empire, resolved in 1926 that "National Schools" modeled specifically on "Booker T. Washington's Tuskegee Institute" should be built in all of Britain's West African colonies.[84]

As these last pronouncements suggest, by the 1920s industrial education had become primarily a political issue, promoted by men with political agendas. During that decade colonial governments asserted their right to license all schools and the things the schools taught. Thanks to the recommendations of the Phelps Stokes Education Commission, governments came up with their own idea of industrial education, which they sought to implement in schools that they built. The fight over all types of Christian education now took place in government offices, mostly between political officers and missionaries. Educated Africans were rarely consulted. With few opportunities to pursue Ethiopianist goals, African Christianity began to evolve in other directions, leaving behind the evangelical campaign for social regeneration. African independent churches became more and more prominent during the decade, and they did not give much attention to any sort of Western education.

West African Ethiopianists attentively listened across the Atlantic to the words Booker T. Washington spoke about industrial education in the United States. It was not just that they recognized Washington as an African American who embraced his African ancestry and who wanted to help his African kin. It was also because Washington validated their convictions about capitalism and about its potential as a vehicle for economic Ethiopianism. They did not question whether the Tuskegee approach worked as advertised—most of the things they heard and read said that it did. The question with which West Africans struggled was whether funds could be found to facilitate Tuskegee's replication in West Africa. African hopes rose and then faded as affirmative answers to this last question dwindled.

# 5

# On the Same Lines as Tuskegee

*Contesting Tuskegee and Government Intervention in South Africa*

A considerable amount of enthusiasm has been evoked by the movement that was initiated some months ago by Mr. [John] Tengo Jabavu . . . with the object of creating an Inter-State Native College. . . . We have already in these columns drawn attention to the excellent and instructive programme carried out by Mr. Booker T. Washington, at the Tuskegee Institute, in America. It is proposed to develop the work to be undertaken by the new College on the same lines of industrial training as in the American Institute.[1]

### WASHINGTON AND TUSKEGEE IN THE SOUTH AFRICAN PRESS

In the lands that ultimately united to form the Union of South Africa, the treatment of Booker T. Washington and Tuskegee was both more widespread and more complex than it was in West Africa. A number of African newspapers regularly featured articles about the man and his school, all of which could be recognized as advancing some version of an Ethiopianist agenda. South African Ethiopianists promoted images of Washington and Tuskegee very similar to those promoted in West Africa, though with an added awareness of the obstacles to the realization of an Ethiopianist agenda posed not just by European colonial governments but by European settlers as well. And South African Ethiopianists were not in agreement on the stature and importance of Washington. In addition, in South Africa, the missionary press, and the liberal white thinkers who used that source as a vehicle for communicating their ideas on race relations, maintained images of Washington and his school that ran counter to Ethiopianist depictions. Missionary images challenged notions that Washington and Tuskegee provided evidence of black agency. These images cast doubt on whether Washington himself should even be considered black. Tuskegee, from this last perspective, remained a preeminent vehicle for the Christianization of the African, but always under white tutelage.

During the last two decades of the nineteenth century, John Tengo Jabavu was the most influential African politician in South Africa. During the first two decades of the twentieth century, John L. Dube became the most influential African politician in South Africa. The political influence of both Jabavu and Dube can be traced back to their control of public media. Both men owned and edited their own newspapers; Jabavu owned *Imvo Zabantsundu* (Native opinion), while Dube owned *Ilanga lase Natal* (The sun of Natal). Both used their newspapers to shape debate and discussion among their fellow literate Christian Africans. Using this sway, both in turn sought to negotiate as the representative of African public opinion with whites in power. Their success in being accepted in such roles was the key to their wider influence.[2] Over the first two decades of the twentieth century, on different coasts of the country, both men expended much of that influence in efforts to build educational institutions like Tuskegee.

*Imvo* and *Ilanga* offered very different types of coverage of Washington and Tuskegee. Before 1906 Jabavu's approach to the presentation of Washington emerged out of his appreciation of General Armstrong and Hampton Institute.[3] Starting in 1906, however, once Jabavu became the "traveling secretary" for the movement to establish the Inter-State Native College, articles about Washington and his school became associated with the promotion of the college.[4] *Imvo* did not regularly mention Washington and Tuskegee from any other perspective again until 1911, when it announced Washington's planned "International Conference on the Negro." Once that event was over in 1912, *Imvo* returned to reporting on Tuskegee as a model for the proposed Native College, coverage culminating in a series of stories on Jabavu's son Davidson's two-month visit to Tuskegee in 1913.

*Ilanga*'s coverage more typically connected with the report of some honor or award received by Washington as a statesman, such as the report in 1909 that Washington was receiving the Order of Redemption from the Republic of Liberia for his help in resolving that nation's financial difficulties.[5] Stories in *Ilanga* about Tuskegee similarly reflected positively on Washington's leadership, such as the somewhat envious report in 1911 that Tuskegee had received a bequest of £100,000 (pounds, not dollars, as the newspaper noted) from the estate of a wealthy New Yorker.[6] Dube respected and to an extent idolized Washington. He saw Washington as an American, however, and thought that only an African could do for the African people what Washington had done for African Americans. Dube's coverage in *Ilanga* of what Washington had done at Tuskegee was meant to serve as background for what he, Dube, was trying to do at Ohlange.[7]

Ethiopianists did not universally celebrate Washington in the South African press. *Izwi Labantu* was founded in 1897, primarily with funding from Cecil Rhodes. One of its coeditors was A. Kirkland Soga, son of Tiyo Soga.[8] *Izwi* positioned itself as opposed to *Imvo* and against institutions such as Lovedale and eventually the Native College. This animus helps explain its grief against Washington.[9] *Izwi* had positive things to say about Washington as an educator, but it excoriated him as a politician, listing Washington as chief among "Negro Philistines."[10] The newspaper pictured Washington's interactions with the Republican Party as the source behind the sufferings of African Americans. As one article explained, "intellectual slavery" was the price of Washington's leadership, and "Negro Republicanism" was the "broad road" that had led to this state of servitude. "All roads" in African American political life "lead to Tuskegee," the article continued, much in the same way that all roads in black South African political life once "led to Lovedale."[11]

The South African missionary press, best represented by the *Christian Express*, possessed both a readership and leadership among African Christians. Over the period between 1895 and 1915, the number of articles or comments about Washington and Tuskegee in the *Christian Express* probably equaled the total number of such stories in all of the African-edited newspapers combined. The principal of Lovedale set the editorial tone for the newspaper. Through the first half of the period under discussion, Doctor James Stewart served as principal. After Stewart's death in 1905, Reverend James Henderson assumed that office. Under Stewart, the newspaper did not treat Tuskegee as a black school. Stewart refused to concede Washington to the African race. As he observed in some form on more than one occasion, "Mr. Washington is not a pure African either by race or birth. . . . [H]is mother was a slave woman," Stewart affirmed, "but his father was a white man." He concluded, "Therefore, Mr. Washington's success must not be unduly attributed to his African blood. History and experience throw the emphasis the other way."[12] During Stewart's tenure, Tuskegee was identified in the *Christian Express* not as a black but as an evangelical Christian school. Few of the newspaper's articles failed to mention the Christian transformation Tuskegee demanded of its students. From his appreciation for this last trait, in 1906 Stewart worried whether Washington's success with finding financial support would not lead Tuskegee to lose its evangelical character and become *"unduly secularized."*[13] Under Henderson, the way Washington and Tuskegee were presented changed. Washington did not become black, but he did become biracial. Different from Stewart, Henderson called little attention to Tuskegee as a vehicle of evangelization. Primarily, he let Washington speak for himself, printing long speeches like Washington's address before the Brooklyn Institute of Arts and Sciences entitled "The Educational and Industrial Emancipation of the Negro"[14] or, more typically, short pieces of commentary on contemporary issues, such as "Booker Washington on the Country School" or "Dr. Booker T. Washington on the Negro Problem."[15]

South African newspapers in general reveal a point about the discussion of industrial education at the turn of the twentieth century that will seem counterintuitive to readers a century later. When advocates discussed industrial education, "industrial" meant not the factory floor but the planted field. In 1901 *Izwi* contrasted "the science of practical agriculture" against the "classical" idea of industrial education being offered at Lovedale, the thrust of the argument being that it was only "the specter of the American Negro on the brain" that led Lovedale to place itself "athwart the wheels of progress" by not teaching agriculture. Washington and Tuskegee were closely identified with agriculture in South African newspapers. Pursuing its indictment of Washington for political cronyism, in this same column *Izwi* passed on the rumor, taken from a British tabloid, that in the United States, President Teddy Roosevelt was about to make Washington his secretary of agriculture.[16] In 1907 Henderson, in the *Christian Express*, in an article on technical education, wrote about Washington laying "great stress on the importance of industrial ownership of land by the Native" as a means for the "Native" to "introduce improved agricultural methods."[17] Sir Harry Johnston took the connection among Washington, Tuskegee, and agriculture for granted in his book, *The Negro in America*, published in a serialized form in the *Christian Express*.[18]

Industrial education was pursued as an educational strategy in South Africa before the arrival of American ideas. Curricula for training

Africans to assist white shop owners working in metal (blacksmithing) and in wood (carpentry) were already in place in most mission schools. What these schools lacked was a program of study on scientific or practical agriculture aimed at training students in the production of crops, ideally for the world market. Tuskegee was understood to offer the prototype for such a program. The *Christian Express* made the connection between Tuskegee and commercial agriculture on a regular basis in articles published between 1900 and 1915. Ironically, *Izwi* made the same point in its diatribe against Lovedale. Ohlange, Dube's school, was premised on the assumption that Washington's approach to agriculture could be replicated in Africa. In 1909, in the context of describing in *Ilanga* the programs of study taught at Ohlange, Dube talked about "the agricultural section"—that is, the farms maintained by the school—as "the final feature of the industrial side of the school."[19] The original scheme for the Inter-State Native College proposed that all students be required to take "a progressive and educative program in industrial training" in order to make them of greater use to their people.[20] "Industrial training" here was implicitly agricultural training.[21]

## THE AFRICAN AMERICAN CONNECTION

The European reaction to that which Europeans identified as Ethiopianism shaped the debate about Tuskegee and industrial education in South Africa. In a foreshadowing of what would happen later with the Phelps Stokes Education Commissions reports, white notions of Tuskegee and the social and political potential of its educational program were posed as an antidote to black notions of the same. The battle in South Africa was not, as it was in West Africa, about whether a school like Tuskegee should be founded; rather, the struggle involved which version of Tuskegee should be made real, the one dreamed of by Europeans or the one dreamed of by Africans.

That which was identified by whites in South Africa as "Ethiopianism" had to do with white reactions to two overlapping but different developments whose common denominator was Christian African outreach toward Christian African Americans. A previous chapter considered one of the developments, the push by African Christians to recruit African American denominations to establish themselves in South Africa. The expansion of the A.M.E. Church into South Africa, especially the visit by Bishop Henry M. Turner to South Africa in 1898 to finalize the amalgamation of the Ethiopian Church into the A.M.E. Church, drew a remarkable response of negative press in the *Christian Express*. The missionaries sent to South Africa by the National Baptist Convention, the largest African American Baptist denomination, were censured at the same time, for the same thing—the alacrity with which Africans joined their churches. For white missionaries, the phenomenon could be understood only as a function of the Americans' willingness to appeal to race, though for white missionaries race had to do primarily with an accommodation with African culture that the American churches never made but that later became a feature of African independent churches. Still, white missionaries condemned African Americans for opening the doors of the church to the "corruption of paganism," doors they had kept firmly shut.[22]

The other development involved Ethiopianist churches sending students to the United States to study. During the 1890s a number of African ministers, trained and ordained by European denominations, and leading denominational churches, left denomination-controlled churches, taking large portions of their congregations with them. The new churches these ministers set up maintained the same denominational doctrines and rites as the older churches. Yet they were under African control. The new churches offered their adherents freedom from the rhetoric of racial domination preached in mission churches. This freedom came at the cost of access to mission social welfare institutions, however, most importantly schools. Ethiopianists seeking affiliation with African American denominations wrote across the Atlantic asking African American Christians to come set up churches. Ethiopianists building black versions of white denominations also sent letters across the Atlantic but, in their case, to ask African American schools to help train their children. In 1898 P. K. Mzimba, pastor at the Scottish Presbyterian African church associated with Lovedale Institute, angry about the racism he discerned in the actions of Stewart and other missionaries, decided to lead his congregation out of affiliation with the Scottish mission. With a number of fellow African Presbyterian ministers, he founded the Presbyterian Church of Africa.[23] In 1901 Mzimba, seeking education for students shut out of Lovedale Institute, wrote to Booker T. Washington, saying, "The sons of Africa are crying to the Africans in America, 'Come over and help us' for we have about twelve young men and six women anxious to go at once [to Tuskegee if the necessary funds are found]."[24] A few months later, Mzimba himself, along with another elder from the Presbyterian Church of Africa, were on their way across the Atlantic, with ten of the students in tow. Mzimba left some of the students at Lincoln University in Pennsylvania, a college with a Presbyterian affiliation. The others he took to Tuskegee.[25]

One missionary summed up with brutal brevity white opinion of this last development:

> Each year an increasing number of young men and women are being sent from Africa . . . to study in the Negro universities of the United States. There they obtain a superficial veneer of knowledge, while breathing the atmosphere of race hatred which pervades these so-called seats of learning.
>
> After the attainment of a more or less worthless degree, these students return to their own country to preach, with all the enthusiasm of youth and obstinate conviction of the half-taught mind.[26]

For white missionaries in South Africa, the arrival of African American missionaries was bad, but the departure of African students for study among African Americans was even worse. In part, such condemnation stemmed from a British chauvinism that rejected the notion that American schools were on the same level as British schools.[27] In part also, however, it came from a fear that an American education would "practically ruin" young black South Africans.[28] As one settler newspaper observed, echoing the missionary above, after returning from study in the United States, young South Africans "resume life here to propagate sedition and incipient rebellion."[29]

Dr. Stewart traveled to the United States in 1903 to evaluate the educational situation, traveling to a number of African American colleges. As Stewart told the story, while visiting "Booker Washington's place," he received a rude shock. The students taken to Tuskegee by Mzimba a few years earlier came to greet him. They previously had been students at Lovedale. When asked by Stewart why they were completing their studies in the United States, the students' simple answer was Mzimba.[30] Stewart told the story before the South African Native Affairs Commission (SANAC; 1903–1905), a government commission set up explicitly to investigate the dangers posed to Britain's southern African colonies of "Ethiopianism" and African American missions.[31] The audience at SANAC meetings would have known about the stormy past relations between Stewart and Mzimba. Thus, the pathos of the encounter in Alabama would not have been lost to the people listening to Stewart's account in Cape Town. Therefore, the Christian moral Stewart would have whites in South Africa draw from his story was the need for whites to turn the other cheek collectively and to establish a South African version of Tuskegee in order to "remove the sense of injustice which black students feel and leads to their going to America and bringing back wrong ideas, political and social."[32]

Stewart's assessments were in line with those of many whites in South Africa, that, in the interest of "self defense," the government needed to offer Africans an alternative to going to the United States for education.[33] Thus, the SANAC recommendations in its report published in 1905 included that the South African government create an "Inter-State Native College" and direct African students there from all parts of southern Africa.[34] Dr. Stewart made his plea for the college his dying wish, and many Christians in South Africa thought the proposed Native College was to be his legacy.[35] Stewart saw Washington as white and Tuskegee as a missionary school. For him a South African Tuskegee would have operated under white missionary supervision, very similar to, if not an extension of, Lovedale. His dying wish envisioned the establishment of an institution that would allow missions to re-establish their control over African education.

### John Tengo Jabavu and the Inter-State Native College

Ethiopianism, as a type of adversarial Christianity, promoted a conviction that whatever was wrong with the civilization being introduced in Africa by Europeans could be repaired through African initiative. No South African pursued this conviction with greater commitment than did John Tengo Jabavu, who was committed to identifying and appropriating the forms and institutions of modern Western civilization of potential benefit to the African race.[36] He was further dedicated to inserting his voice, as representing African opinion, into all public discourse in South Africa concerned with charting the future of indigenous peoples. His consistent goal remained the creation of sufficient space for Africans, ideally under African Christian guidance, to advance collectively. Jabavu dubbed this dedication "practical Christianity," reflecting the impact on his thinking of the news of Washington's achievements in the United States.[37] Just as his initiative in founding a newspaper, *Imvo Zabantsundu*, had provided Christian Africans with a vehicle for the articulation of "native opinion," so too, going back to his first comments about Hampton Institute in 1892, African initiative in establishing an American-style industrial education could provide Christian African society with a vehicle for the transformation of indigenous people into competitive participants in the modern world. In London, in his presentation before the Universal Races Congress, after indicting missionaries for "breaking up" Bantu societies, Jabavu offered his explanation for how a school like Tuskegee, in this case the Inter-State Native College, would facilitate the advancement of black South Africans. Seeming to take a page from the individual who followed him a few minutes later to the podium, W. E. B. Du Bois, Jabavu advocated the creation of a "talented tenth" in South Africa. Instead of using that term, Jabavu repeated what he described as a favorite "apothegm" of his former mentor, Dr. Stewart, that "light comes from above."[38] The "masses" in South Africa, Jabavu explained, should be educated in the "vernacular," meaning existing schools. The proposed "Native College" would educate "leaders and uplifters," who would then educate the masses. Jabavu's "uplifters" were Washington's "practical Christians." He used the term "uplift" in the same way that Washington did to signal race-conscious acts of social welfare paid for by black people. The capacity to provide "uplift" presumed wealth, and wealth presumed some sort of economic success. By using the word "uplifters," he had in mind successful black capitalists and entrepreneurs. As Jabavu ended his argument in the speech, he claimed that the existing examples of such men proved "without a shadow of a doubt that if a Native College . . . were established to provide a hundred or two well-educated instructors of their people, what looked like an insoluble problem would disappear."[39]

Jabavu stayed generally on the sidelines during the battles between Ethiopianists and Europeans. The one article he published in English on Bishop Turner's visit was a reprint from the *Christian Express* and revealed much about his ideas.[40] Jabavu stood on the sidelines because, for him, African Americans were outsiders and he was not in favor of South Africans letting outsiders do what they needed to do themselves. In his view, African Americans were the descendants of West Africans, not South Africans.[41] While he admired African Americans and hoped to replicate their achievements in South Africa, he did not look at them with the sense of racial identification Ethiopianists such as Mzimba expressed.[42]

The proposal for an Inter-State Native College prompted Jabavu to join the fight about education. Whites in South Africa did not anticipate the enthusiasm the idea of a Native College generated among Africans.

This enthusiasm should not have been surprising. African desire for an industrial school had been a driving force behind the amalgamation of the Ethiopianist Church with the A.M.E. Church. The desire had not disappeared once it became apparent that Bethel Institute was going to be focused on A.M.E. denominational needs. The desire just lost steam. The government's announcement of its scheme to build a school based upon the Tuskegee model gave the desire a new object and helped it regain momentum. Very quickly, African Christians appropriated the proposed college as a project of their own initiative.[43] Leading the African charge was Jabavu, who managed to have himself appointed "traveling secretary" for the campaign to fund the college. In this capacity, he traveled across South Africa, firing up interest among South Africa's black population.[44] *Imvo* was the key to this marketing promotion. As described by André Odendaal, conventions and meetings were arranged across South Africa where Africans spoke their minds about the design of the college and the nature of the programs it should offer. *Imvo*, through its articles, gave these supporters a sense that they were participating in a collective endeavor. The South African government required that African communities raise £50,000 toward the establishment of the college.[45] Jabavu approached the raising of this money as a nationwide church fund drive, citing local collection efforts and individual gifts and regularly publishing a tally of the accumulated funds. The longer title, "The Inter-State Native College," soon was shortened to "The Native College" and became a regular headline in *Imvo*, allowing interested readers to turn quickly to news of the latest developments connected with the college.[46] Mahatma Gandhi lived in South Africa during this time and edited his own newspaper. Looking at the Native College movement from the outside, after noting the plan to build a school modeled on Tuskegee, Gandhi observed of the African school movement:

> All this can do nothing but good, and it is not to be wondered at that an awakening people, like the great native races of South Africa, are moved by something that has been described as being very much akin to religious fervour. To them undoubtedly the work must be sanctified and hallowed, for it opens up a means to advancement of thought and gives a great impetus to spiritual development.[47]

Gandhi viewed the Native College movement as precipitating the development of an African nationalism.

For South African whites, both missionaries and settlers, there was something wrong with this picture. White support for the idea of a South African Tuskegee evaporated. Historians have put forward two possible explanations as to why whites abandoned the idea. James T. Campbell suggested that the "self-help" characteristic of Tuskegee-style industrial education became a stumbling block for whites in South Africa, who distrusted any idea that communicated to Africans the possibility of freedom from white control.[48] Odendaal's work provides some support for this line of explanation.[49] The conventions Odendaal described were presumably among the reasons why provincial white governments opposed the funding of the college.[50] Once whites peeled away the rhetoric of racial accommodation associated with Tuskegee, they recognized the potential for African nationalism, or what they would condemn as Ethiopianism, inherent in the Tuskegee approach. And, once they perceived the Ethiopianism, they abandoned the Tuskegee idea. Paul Rich offered a very different explanation. According to Rich, the Native College itself and, by extension, the idea of making it a South African Tuskegee were victims of the push by Lovedale to reassert its hegemony over African education. After Stewart died in 1905, his replacement, Reverend Henderson, made a renewed case for the need of missionary oversight over African education. By 1908 Henderson had taken control of the planning committee for the Native College. In 1911 he took the preemptive step of establishing at Lovedale an "agricultural institute" that was the signature educational innovation associated with the Tuskegee model. Henderson obtained funding for the institute from the monies collected for the Native College and the South African government.[51]

Reading through the evolving presentation of the Native College movement in the pages of *Imvo*, evidence sustains both of these explanations. By 1908 the various South African governments began to treat the Native College project with "benign neglect." The scheme for the Native College melted into the politics involved in the movement of South Africa's four settler colonies toward what became the Union of South Africa. For three years, from 1908 to 1911, when reporting on the Native College, all Jabavu could do was assure his readers that the question of the college was being discussed favorably in the various negotiations taking place.[52] Only in 1911 could he report that consideration of the Native College project had reached the floor of the new Parliament of the Union of South Africa. But then all he could say was that it had been sent to committee.[53]

By 1913 the coalition of African groups that Jabavu had lobbied into existence began to disaggregate. The crowning glory of the earlier fund drive had been the grant of £10,000 from the Transkei Executive Council (the Transkei Bunga) in 1907. For Jabavu the gift had been the validation of the power of practical Christianity. It was proof that "the Natives as a whole will show themselves as possessing the commonsense . . . that will enable a man, a tribe, a race to throw their influence on the side of what is for their highest good."[54] In 1913, however, citing the decline in African support and labeling the national convention called to reignite the movement a "fiasco," the Transkei Executive Council withdrew the grant. Jabavu lambasted the decision as an act of "hari-kari," though much worse than the physical suicide of an individual since it involved the killing of the "life and progress of the Native people."[55]

Meanwhile, in 1911, as announced in the *Christian Express*, Lovedale introduced a new program or "Course in Agriculture," funded by a grant from the Executive Committee for the Native College, of which Henderson was chair.[56] According to Rich, the Scotsman hired as an "agricultural demonstrator," H. Alexander Shaw, sought to teach Lovedale students how to compete with Europeans in the agricultural marketplace but was fired for his effort. Henderson tried to recruit a new agricultural demonstrator in the American South.[57] Jabavu does not appear to have grasped the significance for the Native College of the inauguration of the agriculture program at Lovedale. Other Africans did, however. Rich made a strong case for anger over Lovedale's appropriation of monies for the Native College as the motivation for the Transkei Executive Council's decision to withdraw its support.[58] Perhaps a last big push to regain control of the direction in which plans for the Native College were evolving was the force behind the publicity Jabavu gave to his son Davidson's visit to Tuskegee in 1913.

Davidson Jabavu spent eleven years, between 1903 and 1914, studying in Britain. After beginning at Colwyn Bay, he took a degree from the University of London. He moved from there to enroll in courses at a business college and at a journalism school, clearly signals that he planned to take over the family newspaper. But he changed his educational direction and began a teaching degree program at Kingsmead College, a Quaker missionary training school in Birmingham, England. His studies at this stage were being subsidized by the London congregation, or "Meeting," of the Quakers. In preparation for his teaching certificate, Kingsmead administrators arranged for Davidson to go to Tuskegee to study Washington's teaching methods. Back in South Africa, his father used his connections at the South African Native Affairs Department to get Davidson a fifty-pound bursary to help cover the cost of his trip. In exchange, Davidson was required to write a report identifying the features of Tuskegee that might usefully be included in the design of the proposed Native College.[59] From July through November 1913, *Imvo* published eight articles on Davidson's visit to Tuskegee. As explained in the second of these articles, "the Union Minister of Native Affairs" had asked Davidson to "furnish a full report of his impressions of Mr. Washington's educational methods and their suitableness to the Native conditions of this country." The article closed by stating, "Let us hope the Government will see its way to reduce [the report's] suggestions to practice."[60] Davidson's trip to Tuskegee remained front-page news in *Imvo* for most of the rest of the year, and he composed a detailed report that remains an underappreciated source on Tuskegee and its practices late in the Washington era. Yet, for all the publicity, Davidson's report and, indeed, his trip to Tuskegee were never mentioned again in his father's newspaper. However, the good news came in 1915 that Davidson had been appointed to a faculty position at the Native College.

Finally, in January 1915, the South African Parliament authorized the establishment of the Native College. Plans indicated that the college was to be built on a gift of land from Lovedale. It was to be located at Fort Hare, an abandoned military fortification, across the river from Lovedale. In Britain, Alexander Kerr applied and was accepted for the position of the first principal for the new school. In his memoir about his time in South Africa, Kerr made no reference to the idea that the Native College was ever envisioned to be a South African Tuskegee, though he must have known this since he was met upon his arrival by Jabavu and his one colleague on the teaching staff during his first years was Davidson Jabavu. Reflecting on his beginning as principal, Kerr remembered his charge from the first to be the establishment of a college that at some future time would provide Africans with academic training equal to that available for whites in South Africa.[61] He knew nothing about Tuskegee except what he learned during a trip in 1922 to Tuskegee, Hampton, and other African American schools paid for by the American philanthropy the Phelps Stokes Fund. Kerr seemed unimpressed by the lessons he extracted from the experience.[62] He noted the pressure placed upon him for the Native College to "raise the economic standards of the

African people." Kerr pleaded lack of staff as the reason this concern had not been pursued.

Perhaps Kerr's reluctance to mention any connection to Tuskegee was a reflection of past battles. John Tengo Jabavu did not passively accept the turning of Fort Hare away from the industrial education idea. Though Kerr did not acknowledge it in his memoir, he and Jabavu fought. Some glimmer of the acrimony comes through in the contents of a letter from Jabavu to Kerr. He wrote, "It seems to me as a Native, the fatal colour prejudice which is the bane of much of the mission work in this country, and is the fountain and origin of the Ethiopian sect—the colour prejudice is being introduced by the thin end."[63] He was convinced that white racism was shaping the decisions being made about the Native College.

Jabavu lost the battle over the use of Tuskegee as a model for the proposed Native College, and the price of defeat seems to have a prohibition on ever publically promoting the idea again. Further comment on Davidson Jabavu's trip to Tuskegee appears to have been part of the same agreement. When the South African Native College at Fort Hare opened in 1916, the campus consisted of four small, all-purpose buildings, the bungalows that remained from the old fort. It had a faculty of two—Kerr and Davidson Jabavu. Kerr taught courses on English, mathematics, and physical science; Davidson taught courses on African languages, European history, and Latin. The industrial training component of the students' education consisted of the students providing the physical labor for the construction of new buildings, most notably Stewart Hall, opened in 1918. If John Tengo Jabavu experienced feelings about his defeat, he did not articulate them publicly. In *Imvo* he played the good soldier and defended Kerr's announcement that a first priority of the new college would be preseminary training for the "Christian ministry," an objective of the missions then supplying the bulk of the nongovernment funding for the school. The *Cape Times*, commenting on Kerr's announcement about the priority to be given preseminary training from the perspective of "the ruling races of South Africa," wondered why a greater precedence had not been given to the training of teachers. In response, Jabavu sought to fit clergymen into the schema he had advanced seven years earlier at the Universal Races Congress in London:

> The problem of the uplift of the Natives is a three-cornered problem. Given in a Native location a well-balanced Native Minister; a highly trained and

intelligent teacher; and a headman or leading man well primed in agricultural and business methods—the Administration has at once a local potent Committee that is bound to move the Native inertia that is at present the despair of every Native reformer.[64]

In London in 1911, Jabavu had identified missions and ministers as part of the problem to be solved. In South Africa in 1918, missions and ministers had become an integral part of the solution. Jabavu concluded his editorial comment by saying that "the influence of a gentleman of the cloth on a people of the Native's degree of enlightenment is incalculable."[65]

Still, in the next issue of *Imvo*, in an unsigned editorial that reflected Jabavu's true feelings, disappointment was voiced that the course of the new college was to be "slavishly set according to the conservative English or Scotch pattern." The editorial continued, "One of the great lessons of history" was that "the Nation of Shop-keepers, Traders, Manufacturers, in short of Business had invariably led the van. . . . What is greatly needed amongst our Native people is a School of Business Training on absolutely Modern Lines." The editorial concluded with the question, "Will the S.A. Native College supply this, or must America be looked to again?"[66]

The South African government took the option of sending students to the United States off the table, however. The Native College might not have lived up to African expectations, but it did serve the purposes of the government. Now that there was a college for African students, there was no need for students to go away for an education. The opening of the Native College provided an excuse for the government to step in and regulate African travel to the United States for purposes of study. Students seeking to travel to the United States had to fill out passport forms and, significantly, to supply character reference letters from whites. Perhaps even more imposing, they had to pay a fifty-pound fee (later one hundred pounds), ostensibly to cover the potential cost of their repatriation. These regulations had the intended effect of cutting down on the number of South African students going abroad to American schools.[67]

The idea of establishing an industrial education school open to students from across South Africa provided African Christians with the concrete goal around which they organized as a movement for the first time in history. The mind behind the movement belonged to John Tengo Jabavu, although it is not so clear how well he understood industrial education as an educational strategy. The expectations for the Native College were not met, and Lovedale, with government assistance, used its course in agriculture to reassert its hegemony over African education in the Cape Province. But, as was the case with Blyden, Jabavu was far more interested in what Washington had done with industrial education than with industrial education itself. Washington had generated an economic power that could not be denied. The Native Land Act approved by the South African Parliament in 1913 stripped Africans of the right to own land outside the "homelands," the areas that the government designated as belonging to African tribes. Africans saw their country being taken from them by colonial settlers through legislative fiat. In May 1915, when African anger and disillusionment over the passage of the legislation was at a height, *Imvo* published a short article, under fifty words in length, with the simple headline "Land in U.S.A." The article announced that Washington had purchased for Tuskegee "10,000 acres of land in the vicinity of Cheechaw, Alabama." A lumber mill had already been started on the land, and a railway connecting the property to Tuskegee was in process.[68] The economic power represented in that article spoke volumes to a people searching for a response to dispossession.

## DUBE AND OHLANGE

Some similarities exist in the ways that John Tengo Jabavu and John L. Dube attempted to introduce American-style industrial education in their respective regions of South Africa.[69] The differences, however, were more significant, even though in the end both men discovered themselves, and the Ethiopianist ambitions they represented, shut out of any direct influence over the schools they either helped to found or founded. Both Jabavu and Dube envisioned industrial education as having its greatest regenerative impact through the training of a class of agrarian entrepreneurs. Since Jabavu never had a clear understanding of what the development of commercial agriculture entailed, he let Lovedale Institute introduce in Cape Province Tuskegee's innovative approach to the study of agricultural production. However, in his biography of his father published in 1922, Davidson Jabavu announced, with a sense of triumph, that the "lectureship" in agriculture his father had been instrumental in setting up at Lovedale in 1911 had been recently transferred to the Native College.[70] Dube, who visited Tuskegee, had his eye on rural transformation from the start. In an article published in the *Washington Post* in 1899, announcing that Dube and his wife were on their way back to Natal to bring the "producing and developing power of Christian civilization" to the Zulu people, Dube explained, "The religion that I shall introduce into Zululand will be one that will teach the natives how to build a two-roomed house, manage a plow, make a wagon and raise sugar cane, tea and coffee."[71] Eight years later, in an article published in the *Missionary Review of the World*, under the headline "Practical Christianity among the Zulu," Dube wrote that the goal of his now-flourishing school was the "turning out" of "first-class Christian agriculturalists."[72] As proof, he celebrated the fact that male students had already learned how to plant lemons, oranges, peaches, and pineapples. This promised to be a "very useful industry for young Zulus," according to Dube, because of "particularly good markets for Natal and Zulu land fruit" in Cape Colony and Johannesburg.[73]

Another great similarity between Jabavu and Dube was their resistance to the idea of African American involvement in the establishment of schools like Tuskegee in South Africa. The distance that Jabavu put between himself and the Ethiopianists who brought the A.M.E. Church to South Africa, ostensibly to build a school, has already been noted. In 1903 *Ilanga* reported that a group of colonial officials and businessmen lead by Earl Grey publicly extended an offer to Booker T. Washington to come to southern Africa to help adjudicate race relations between blacks and whites. The article continued by reporting that Washington declined the offer, citing the unwillingness of Teddy Roosevelt to release him from his obligations in the United States.[74] Few Africans admired Booker T. Washington more than did John L. Dube, yet two weeks later, in an editorial entitled "The Salvation of the Native," Dube commented:

> Some prominent men in England approached Booker T. Washington to come here and preach to us the Gospel of Work. But we are of the opinion that had he consented, it would have been the waste of money. Dr. Washington does not understand the Zulus or any other people in South Africa. This is our question right here. If it is to be solved, it will be solved by the whites and blacks of this country.[75]

For Jabavu, as well as for Dube, African Americans were role models to be copied, not followed.

A marked contrast existed in the ways the two men sought to fund and maintain the two respective schools. Jabavu looked toward public funding. He certainly canvassed missions and philanthropies for donations, such as he did during his visit to London in 1911. But he looked to the various African polities and communities for the start-up costs mandated by the government and expected ongoing subventions from the same groups to maintain the school. Dube focused on private funding. As Dube acknowledged in the interview published in the *Review of Reviews* in 1909, almost all the money he had used to establish Ohlange had come from American donors. Dube constantly lobbied the Natal provincial government for financial support and local patrons like Marshall Campbell for help to cover the costs of the school. Still, the initial success of Ohlange was a function of Dube's ability to keep the money coming in from the United States.

A second major difference between the approaches taken by the two men rested in the population choice each targeted for social regeneration via industrial education. The Inter-State Native College, as initially conceived by Jabavu, represented an effort to bring together and mobilize the various African peoples of South Africa to create an educational institution from which they would all benefit. The Zulu Christian Industrial School, later known as Ohlange Institute, intended only to bring about the religious transformation of the Zulu, who would then serve as missionaries to the surrounding African peoples. As Dube explained, through their military might the Zulus had conquered territories of South Africa in the same way as the Anglo-Saxons once dominated much of Europe. After the Zulus had been Christianized via his school, as Dube envisioned, they would again conquer their African neighbors, but this time with and for Christianity, he promised.[76] Dube would later broaden his understanding of the mission before him to reflect a more pan-Africanist perspective. But in the beginning he pitched his school to white audiences outside of Africa as an instrument of Zulu ethnogenesis.

Lastly, Jabavu and Dube had very different skills as promoters. His many years as an editor creating a market for his newspaper gave Jabavu insight into how to make funding the Native College a challenge Christian Africans were eager to accept. His many years of living and lecturing in the United States gave Dube a similar set of instincts but tailored to a white overseas Christian audience. Dube had "begging" skills of which General Armstrong would have approved. As Dube explained to William Thomas Shead in an interview in the British journal *Review of Reviews*, if "a number of well-to-do boys and girls in England" would each offer six pounds a year to cover the cost of sending one Zulu boy or girl to Ohlange for the school term, then "the cash nexus would be the basis of a genuine human interest between Bantu and Briton."[77]

Between 1896 and 1899, Dube attended Union Theological Seminary in New York City, where he studied for the ministry. During this time, Dube and his wife lived in Brooklyn and made their church home at the Lewis Avenue Congregational Church, where Dube first began to speak about his meeting with Booker T. Washington and about his idea for building a version of Tuskegee in Natal. Using the Lewis Avenue Church as a hub, Dube preached and lectured across a significant portion of the United States looking for funds for his school.[78] Reverend David Kent, pastor at Lewis Avenue, volunteered to establish a committee of support for Dube's school. The American Committee, as it was called, supplied most of the capital that allowed Dube to open the school he envisioned, Ohlange.[79] Dube wrote a number of articles detailing the progress of Ohlange for American and British consumption. A feature of these articles was Dube's recognition of the role of white individuals or churches in funding what Dube identified as an Ethiopianist charge. The *Missionary Review of the World* article from 1907 described the grist mills built on campus for grinding grain supplied by Park Congregational Church of Grand Rapids, Michigan. An article in *Outlook*, another American journal, in 1910 mentioned the completion of the June Memorial Building, the largest building on campus, which presumably housed the industrial shops. An unidentified American friend from Chicago supplied the $6,000 to pay for this building.[80] Dube invariably followed the recitation of progress he had made with the monies received with an itemization of further needs. As Dube explained to William Thomas Stead in the *Review of Reviews* interview, so far Ohlange had collected about £3,000 (approximately $18,000) from donors from the United States. "Do you think that 5000 pounds would be too much," he rhetorically queried Stead, "to ask from wealthy John Bull for his Zulu boys?"[81] The "Practical Christianity among the Zulu" article published in the *Missionary Review of the World* offered an extended discussion of the need of money for a dormitory for girls. At that stage, girls could attend Ohlange only as day students. Yet, as Dube observed:

> Woman has from time immemorial been looked upon as inferior to man, and in order to destroy this mischievous idea we desire to have girls as regular boarders and to give them work with young Zulu men and boys.

The latter will then get an idea of the intellectual strength of womankind and lose his erroneous ideas of his own mental superiority.[82]

With these comments, Dube was voicing surprisingly progressive ideas for 1907, but his argument still can be looked upon as a clue to the church circles in the United States and Britain to which he was tailoring his petitions for funds.

Thanks to its American benefactors, Ohlange probably went further in replicating the educational program at Tuskegee than did any other school in Africa. The curriculum was partially the same as that at existing South African mission industrial schools with training in ironwork and woodwork.[83] The great innovation was the program in commercial agriculture, modeled on the one Dube had observed at Tuskegee.[84] The American Committee shipped a good deal of agricultural hardware Ohlange's way, and Dube put it to work as much as he could without the aid of expert instructors.[85] Dube was careful, however. As the SANAC report made clear, white workers and farmers feared any education that might make Africans economically competitive with them.[86] In *Ilanga* Dube sought to defuse the concerns of white workers with the argument that educated Africans would maintain the same patterns of consumption as Europeans and would consume all the produce of African skilled labor, thereby neutralizing the impact of African produced goods on the market.[87] Dube used a variation on this argument to describe the agricultural program at Ohlange. Boys were being trained in commercial agriculture with the goal of selling their crops for export to Britain, thereby creating new markets for South Africa.[88]

As for Christian instruction at Ohlange, almost seeming to channel General Armstrong's antipathies, Dube made it clear that his school suffered no dependency on missions. In an article in *Ilanga* in 1909, Dube observed, "though the Christian religion is not neglected [at Ohlange] any more than in an English school, the curriculum is of a severely practical nature," meaning that it focused on technological as opposed to theological training.[89] Dube demanded that students at Ohlange observe a strict Christian routine, but there was no denominational orientation to campus life. Dube left proselytization on campus to visiting evangelists and preachers from all denominations.[90] Reflecting the impression on African Christian life made by the Virginia Jubilee Singers, Ohlange pioneered in the development of vocal and instrumental music education in the tradition of Hampton and Tuskegee. The school fielded a brass band and two chorale groups: the Inanda Native Singers and the Ohlange Choir. An article in *Ilanga* in 1909, reprinted from the settler newspaper the *Transvaal Leader*, referred to the student brass band Dube brought with him to Johannesburg for a visit. The band had scheduled performances at some of the local African churches and compounds. Dube expressed the hope that some of the city's "leading white citizens" would also invite the students to play.[91] Noketula, Dube's wife, had spent her time in New York studying music. Together the Dubes created a book of songs in Zulu for the chorales to sing. Among the songs was one that evolved into the South African national anthem.[92]

Ohlange Institute was Dube's dream, his proof of himself as a leader. In assessing the development of Ohlange beyond the initial years, it is difficult to separate the history of the school from the biography of Dube, who is remembered primarily for his political achievements. His foremost biographer, Heather Hughes, noted, because of Dube's service as the first president of the South African Native National Congress, which later became the African National Congress (ANC) political party, Nelson Mandela symbolically chose Ohlange, Dube's school, as the place to record his first vote as a South African citizen. After his own election as South Africa's first black president, Mandela kneeled at Dube's gravesite and memorably announced, "Mr. President, South Africa is now free."[93]

Yet, during the first part of his career, Dube did not aspire to leave his mark as a politician. He thought first to serve as an evangelist, then as a minister, and then as an educator. Upon his first arrival in the United States in 1887, Dube's decision not to attend Hampton as had been planned was related in an earlier chapter. During the following five years, Dube stayed in the United States, primarily enrolling in courses at Oberlin College in Ohio. After he returned to South Africa in 1892, Dube took a teaching job at Amanzimtotzi, the school maintained by the American Zulu Mission, the Congregationalist mission in which he was raised. Dube assumed a teaching role for a while but did not find it rewarding. In 1894 Dube and his new wife, Nokutela, decided to become Christian evangelists in the South African interior. But Dube remained unfulfilled. In 1895 Dube resolved to campaign for election for the pastorate of Inanda Congregational Church, the position his father once held. Dube's announcement of his candidacy was a direct challenge to the American Zulu Mission, which was accustomed to choosing Africans for all church positions. Dube won the vote, but the missionaries disqualified Dube because he was not ordained. Dube decided to return to the United States to be ordained. In 1900 the Reverend John L. Dube did in fact become the pastor of the Inanda Congregational Church.

Eight years later, Dube resigned from the pastoral position. He had gone to the United States determined to become a minister, but he came back to South Africa determined to be an educator in the mold of Washington. During his time in New York, Dube heard about Booker T. Washington and became so enthusiastic about what he heard that he wrote to Washington asking whether he might go to Alabama to see the campus for himself. After visiting and speaking at Tuskegee, Dube and his wife traveled to Hampton, where Dube also gave a lecture. Based upon these visits, Dube concluded that his life's calling was to build and maintain an industrial education school like Tuskegee. A year after taking over the ministry of Inanda Congregationalist Church in 1901, Dube founded Ohlange. Two years later, he established his newspaper, *Ilanga*, at his school. By 1907 the school and newspaper were taking so much time from his ministry that Dube decided to resign from his pastoral obligations. Bowing to pressure from his congregation, Dube agreed to remain as pastor another year. However, in August 1907 Dube gave a long speech to the graduating class at Inanda Teachers Institute. In the speech, Dube gave evidence that he had already moved on from any notion he may have once maintained of the ministry as a vehicle for racial uplift. Dube identified teachers, not missionaries or pastors, as the "formulators of the thought and spirit of the rising generation of the Bantu people." Characterizing himself as an educator, not a minister, and then speaking about the children he and the new graduates would together shape, Dube tasked the future teachers with "up-lifting their students to the state of civilization."[94] A few years later in 1912, Dube went even further along this line and rethought the argument of providential design itself, with educators and entrepreneurs replacing missionaries and evangelists as the agents of Africa's regeneration.[95]

In 1915 Dube printed in *Ilanga* a letter sent to him by a committee representing the Mbabane Native Community thanking Dube for visiting their homeland, Swaziland. "Dear Mafukuzela," the letter began, addressing Dube by his Zulu praise name, which translates as "He who stirs things up." "We would like to express out highest appreciation," the letter went on, "for all the good works that you have continuously done for the uplift and protection of the Black Races of the Fatherland." First among the good works listed was the Ohlange Native Boys Training and Industrial Institution, which was described as an "institution for educating and uplifting young men of your Black Races." Another good work the letter mentioned was Dube's role in ending the "strong racial ill-feeling that had existed for centuries among the Black Tribes of South Africa."[96] Clearly, the letter writers were repeating to Dube what he had described during his visit with them as his greatest accomplishments. Dube, by that time, was president of African National Congress. The thank-you for ending tribal conflict probably reflected Dube's work acting in this capacity. Still, at that moment in Dube's mind ,what he had done at Ohlange stood above this last achievement. But perhaps what was most remarkable about the letter was the absence of any mention of Dube's accomplishments as a Christian. By 1915 Dube had even ceased to add the title "Reverend" before his name.

Dube's evolution did not stop with his embrace of the role of educator. The second part of his life was spent in politics, mostly as a lobbyist for African rights against the ever-increasing bureaucratic edifice of repressive settler government. In 1912 Dube was asked to serve as first president of the African National Congress. The ANC aimed to unite all the African peoples that Europeans insisted were separate tribes, having no claim to political rights outside their "homelands" to bring pressure on white governments. Dube understood his charge as requiring leadership on two fronts. Africans needed to transform themselves into a civilized people and through achievement on this social/cultural front to prepare themselves for what Dube anticipated would be a centuries-long battle on the political front to claim civil rights. In 1912 "the whole body of educated Nativedom throughout South Africa," to use Dube's words, chose him to be the president of the ANC. In his acceptance speech, Dube talked about Christianity and civilization, and he argued that if Africans acquired both these things, they would have the capacity to win their struggle for political rights. When he talked about Christianity and civilization, Dube reprised his arguments for the preeminence of educators and entrepreneurs as the agents of racial uplift. From this point of view, Dube acknowledged Booker T. Washington as his "patron saint" in his acceptance speech and explained his plan to expand nationwide the education program he had developed at Ohlange.

To fight settler domination, Africans in South Africa hoped to mobilize public opinion in Britain and the United States for their cause, and Dube's skills at appealing to overseas white audiences must have played some role in his election. Between 1898 and 1917, the American Christian monthly the *Missionary Review of the World* published a piece either by or about Dube almost every year. He was published or mentioned in other Christian publications more than once, as well, during the same time period, and this publicity was key to Dube's funding strategy. Presidency of the ANC and the Native Land Act of 1913, the piece of settler legislation the ANC was most determined to fight, drew Dube almost full time into politics, at the cost of his canvassing for funds for Ohlange. Revealing here are the last articles connected with Dube in the *Missionary Review of the World*. An August 1914 article leads with news that Rev. Dube of the Zulu Christian Industrial School was now the president of the ANC, the organization that represented the interest of the ten million natives of South Africa in their fight against the Native Land Act, an act that "reduced" Africans down to "serfdom." Only secondarily did the article mention Ohlange and the educational activities going on there.[97] In the March 1916 issue, the journal published a long piece by Dube entitled "The Black Problem in South Africa." In the article, Dube lays out his case against the Native Land Act. Ohlange is not discussed.[98] Even in *Ilanga*, Ohlange was meriting less and given less attention. Issues for *Ilanga* are available for the period 1903–1909 and for the period 1913–1919. In the earlier period, the school was mentioned in the newspaper approximately ninety times, but during the later period the school was named only approximately thirty times.

Many of the later reports signaled the financial distress with which the school then contended because the external funding had dried up. The Lewis Avenue Congregational Church stopped sending monies in 1915. The greatest local patron of Ohlange, Marshall Campbell, died in 1917. School fees, no matter how high Dube made them, could not cover expenditures.[99] In *Ilanga* in January 1921, Dube announced that because of high costs, female students would not be accepted for the coming school term. Male students would be accepted only through Standard VI.[100]

Dube went to London in 1921 to participate in the Pan-African Congress organized by W. E. B. Du Bois. During his time in Britain, Dube consulted a number of potential donors in hopes of finding further funding for his school. In October of that year, he arranged an appointment with John Harris of the British Anti-Slavery and Aboriginal Rights Society. Dube petitioned Harris to help him save his school. The following June, back in South Africa, Dube received a letter from Harris outlining the conditions for financial support. Most pertinent, the Department of Native Education in Natal agreed to take over the school and its finances if Dube agreed to give up his authority over the school and place that authority in the hands of the chief native commissioner of Natal and a governing committee; relocate himself, his family, and his newspaper (*Ilanga*) off school grounds; and recognize the appointment of a white principal at Ohlange, and possibly other white teachers. To save the school, Dube had no choice but to accept.[101]

Dube expressed his bitterness and frustration over the loss of his school in a short treatise remarkably similar in tone and indictment to the editorial written by Thomas Horatio Jackson and published in the *Lagos Weekly Record* the year before. The treatise was given its title and theme by the Zulu proverb, "a person is his own worst enemy." In the treatise, Dube indicts his fellow South Africans for refusing to unite in the cause of emancipation, for not holding down regular employment, for lacking in entrepreneurial spirit, for shunning their own craftspeople and artisans, and for failing to help Ohlange stay financially independent of the government and the missions. Dube's repeated refrain in the treatise was the question: "Who is one's enemy?" to which the response was, one's enemy "is one's own self."[102]

While he expressed frustrations similar to those expressed by Jackson in Nigeria, Dube's mind-set on the issue of race and industrial education was more akin to that of E. Cornelius May. Both Dube and May saw the acquisition of the ability to make things as a doorway to sentience. "Think, think, think," May forever counseled Africans, the point being that social transformation, in keeping with the Protestant ethos, was a process of incremental change and that Africans needed to be able to discern such increments. Industrial education would train African minds to see the needed calibrations. What historians have condemned as Washington's gradualism, his African supporters recognized as being among his greatest gifts. To be able to see and cultivate change in the material plane, to see Christ in the man-made world, that was the key for Ethiopianists. Jabavu used the promise of such a key to galvanize Africans toward the subsidization of a school along the lines of Tuskegee in the Cape Province. In the end, white governments and Christian missions made sure the promise was never realized. Dube used American funding to build a school that demonstrated the promise of Tuskegee. However, then he had to confront the never-ending task of keeping such a school operating as an industrial institute. In the end, Ohlange likewise failed to live up to its promise.

# 6

## Men Who Can Build Bridges
### Retrieving Washington's Influence in the Work of Marcus Garvey and Thomas Jesse Jones

Whole-heartedly the writer wishes that it were possible to transplant either or both [Hampton and Tuskegee] to West Africa, or at least to create their fellow there. Our present educational system is too bookish, too little practical. . . . Our colleges should not be satisfied with their current output of men destined only for the pulpit, the surgery and the bar. . . . We want men who can build bridges, construct harbours, light cities, survey countries—men to whom the skilled handling of the dynamo or motor or aeroplane is a matter of everyday concern. West Africa is developing by leaps and bounds: we want her own sons to have a share in that development.[1]

### THE INTERNATIONAL CONFERENCE ON THE NEGRO

African Ethiopianists initially conceptualized opposition to their ambitions as coming primarily from Christian missions. By the 1910s events and developments such as described in the two previous chapters had made it obvious even to them that white governments in Africa posed a greater roadblock to the realization of their aspirations. The battle with missionaries, however, remained unresolved. Booker T. Washington was well aware of the contest between Ethiopianists and missionaries in Africa. A number of West Africans wrote him on the subject, and Mzimba and Stewart, as well as Dube from South Africa, all visited Tuskegee's campus. Washington made an effort to intervene in the battle. He announced a conference to be held on the campus of Tuskegee in April 1912. Entitled the International Conference on the Negro, he invited to the conference anyone seeking to use a school like Tuskegee as a platform for black racial uplift. He hoped that Ethiopianists and missionaries would come and iron out their differences.

Washington's strategy for intervention presumed that the tension between Ethiopianists and missionaries could be traced back to the question of African oversight of Christian social institutions, primarily schools. Missionaries, motivated by a number of reasons, among them racism but perhaps also a fear that Africans did not understand the difficulties inherent in keeping Christian social institutions operational, blocked the promotion of Africans into positions of control. Ethiopianists, in response, undertook to establish their own social institutions, challenging in the process mission church hegemony over the Christian religious experience. Yet, as Washington believed and preached, and much of the world then agreed, Tuskegee was the greatest example to be found of black people successfully overseeing a Christian social institution. Thus, Washington was confident that being at Tuskegee while it was in session, seeing the students earnestly learning with the twin goals of racial uplift and Christian advance, would inspire both Ethiopianists and missionaries to find a common way forward. In his letter of invitation to newspaper editors in Africa, Washington said that the goal of the conference was a "general interchange of ideas about organizing and systematizing the work of education of the native peoples in Africa," his assumption being that "wider knowledge" of Tuskegee, among Ethiopianists and missionaries, would "open means of co-operation that do not now exist."[2]

Louis Harlan characterized the conference held at Tuskegee in 1912 as an articulation of Washington's political ambitions. The original idea for the conference, according to Harlan, came from the white sociologist Robert E. Park, who began his career as Washington's advance man, ghostwriter, and advisor. In Harlan's version of the story, Park recommended that Washington arrange a conference where, along with missionaries and educators, "the Powers in Africa" could work out the details of the extension of industrial education and, by implication, Washington's influence to Africa. Harlan went further to suggest that Washington asked the U.S. State Department to use its prestige to "publicize" the conference among European governments. Based upon the way the conference was promoted, Harlan concluded that it was not surprising that "most of the delegates were white" and that "very few black Africans" attended.[3]

Contrary to what Harlan suggested, the article where the idea of the conference was first broached was not addressed to the "Powers in Africa." The article in question, "Industrial Education in Africa," published in 1906, was framed as Washington's response to a published request by an "enlightened" young West African "prince," Momolu Massaquoi, for advice on how to adapt industrial education to the needs of his people by calling for a conference of Africa's "friends"; Washington presented himself as seconding the idea.[4] He identified missionaries as chief among the "friends" of Africa who should respond to Massaquoi's request. As for the focus of the conference on industrial education, Washington concluded, on the basis of what missionaries reported to him about the situation in Africa, that "no single measure would do more to improve the character and condition of the native peoples and prepare the way for the permanent establishment of Christian religion and Christian civilization than the introduction and wide extension of industrial schools."[5] Washington was highlighting the area of agreement between the goals of Ethiopianists and those of missionaries.

"Industrial Education in Africa," however, was aimed foremost at missionaries. The "Powers in Africa" were mentioned in the article but as a group whose domination needed to be constrained. Washington proposed that an international society of "scientists, explorers and missionaries" be established as watchdogs to protect the peoples of Africa from the predations of colonial regimes.[6] In the article, Washington returned the compliment offered by Dr. Stewart in the *Christian Express* that Lovedale Institute was the Tuskegee of South Africa by giving Lovedale pride of place as an industrial education institution even older and more venerable than Hampton. Washington traced all other industrial education schools in Africa back to Lovedale.[7] His praise was not gratuitous, however. He was making a case that the expertise in industrial education the continent of Africa needed was already there. Washington was not grabbing for power in Africa; rather, he was trying to redirect the desire expressed by African Ethiopianists that Tuskegee provide African schools with industrial education instructors. Washington argued that missions should take charge of industrial education in Africa and urged colonial governments to fund mission efforts in that direction. He intimated that the alternative to putting missions in charge of industrial education was something more sinister. Washington had recently completed his first foray into international relations, taking a leading role in lobbying the U.S. government to bring its influence to bear on the government of Belgium to reform exploitative colonial practices in the Belgian Congo. Probably with the Congo example in mind, Washington warned against the ambitions of an unidentified group of Europeans who advocated the teaching of industrial education to Africans by "force" or "enlightened self-interest."[8] Washington insisted that these strategies would not work and that Africans would respond only to Christian instruction.

Washington was not taking the missionaries' side in the battle. He could conceive of Christian progress along the lines of the Protestant Christian civilization in Europe and North America only as a consequence of affluence, as an outcome of the application of Andrew Carnegie's "gospel of wealth." He did not see acknowledgement of this economic reality by Christian Africans as an inhibition to their Ethiopianist ambitions. Rather, recognition of the relationship between affluence and institution building would allow African Christian entrepreneurs to focus their energies on capital accumulation; prosperity would, in turn, facilitate the funding of African-led social welfare projects. Here again the collaboration between Julius Rosenwald and middle-class African Americans to build YMCA campuses in American cities serves as illustration of what Washington had in mind. As Washington interpreted matters, leaving schools under the control of Christian missions would give what he labeled practical Christianity a running start in Africa.

"Industrial Education in Africa" appeared in print in 1906. Only five years later did plans for the proposed conference, the International Conference on the Negro, materialize. Early in February 1911, the South African newspaper *Tsala Ea Becoana* (Friend of the Bechuana) published in Kimberly in the Northern Cape Province, reported that Washington was planning to hold a conference at Tuskegee, tentatively the following January, for all those who sought "to build up Africa by educating and improving the character and condition of the native peoples."[9] An official announcement inviting interested parties to come to Tuskegee for an "international conference on the Negro" to be held in April 1912 was not mailed until July of that year. Over the last half of 1911 and first months of 1912, six African-edited newspapers, along with the *Christian Express*, publicized the conference primarily by printing verbatim the circular letter sent out by Washington describing the conference and its aims.[10]

By 1912 Washington had successfully experimented with the conference format in two areas. First was the aforementioned annual Tuskegee Farmers' Conference. That conference grew to be a two-day event that attracted thousands.[11] In 1900, perhaps taking hold of an idea first advanced by W. E. B. Du Bois, Washington attempted to replicate the success he had with farmers by pursuing a similar approach with a conference for black businessmen. In that year, Washington held the first meeting of the National Negro Business League in Boston, with the response resulting in making that conference also an annual event.[12] The format of the two conferences was basically the same: a forum for a discussion of best practices as expressed in short speeches by the practitioners themselves. At each, beyond his welcoming keynote, Washington delivered a major presentation in which he surveyed the development over the previous year of subjects of interest to participants. Mostly, though, Washington listened with the rest of the audience as chosen speakers explained their successes and used the conference as a bully pulpit to express their views on the relationship among Christianity, financial success, and racial uplift.

Washington sought to apply the same format to the discussion of industrial education by missionaries and Christian educators. The call for participants that Washington sent out was for people with some expertise in managing industrial education schools or people with some demonstrated commitment to building industrial education schools. Those people were invited to attend the conference at Tuskegee and share their experiences with others like themselves. The letter did express a desire that governments send their representatives, but it only invited "missionaries and other workers" in industrial education "to take an active part in the deliberations."[13] Those who came to the conference "properly accredited"—that is, possessing a record of past work as a missionary, Christian leader, or educator—would be "under no expense during their stay."[14]

Newspapers in West Africa read the invitation as being directed toward Africans and the conference as an occasion for black people to come together. The *Lagos Weekly Record* called the attention of its readers to the conference and to Washington's invitation, and then commented that "there cannot be any doubt that the gathering together of Negroes from every part of the world, and an exchange of views between them must help not a little to a better understanding of the position of the race, and lend stimulus to any effort intended to benefit the race."[15]

The newspaper took for granted that the conference would pursue pan-Africanist agendas.

The *Gold Coast Leader* approached the invitation as a call for local African elites to get involved with education. It used the report of the invitation as an opportunity to offer a variation on the proposal advanced a few years earlier by Captain Elgee, district officer to the Yoruba in Ibadan, that Yoruba students be selected to train at Tuskegee and then return to Nigeria to teach. Elgee's proposal asked the colonial government in Nigeria's Southern Province to pay for the program. His request disappeared into a bureaucratic void, never to be talked about again, at least in African newspapers. In reprising the proposal, the *Gold Coast Leader* wanted local tribal governments in the Gold Coast to cover the costs Elgee had asked the colonial government in Nigeria to pay. The newspaper recommended that each *Omanhene* (traditional chief or ruler) select boys from their districts and finance their education at Tuskegee for a commitment of their determination to return and teach in their district. More narrowly connected to the conference, the newspaper suggested that the Gold Coast Aborigines Rights Protection Society, an African rights organization, recognize as a matter of "national concern" the need to send delegates to the conference.[16]

In South Africa, in contrast, African newspapers treated the conference as an invitation to whites to discuss educational policy pertinent to Africans. At the time the conference was announced, African Christians were coming to grips with the results of the political union of the four settler colonies the previous year. In addition, the two Africans who might have been expected to shape the African understanding of the event, John Tengo Jabavu and John L. Dube, were both effectively out of the conversation. At the time the Tuskegee conference was announced, Jabavu was presenting his paper at the Universal Races Congress in London. He was also still waiting to hear whether the new government of the Union of South Africa would provide funding for the proposed Native College. Dube was also away from Africa, in the last weeks of a twenty-month tour of Britain and the United States in search of funds for Ohlange. He, too, was waiting to hear whether the government of Natal Province would respond to his request for financial support of his school.

African newspapers in South Africa pictured the conference as a near-providential opportunity for local whites with some control over educational funding to be (re)exposed to notions of African education as a vehicle of African advance. The unknown author of the comment on the invitation in *Ilanga* observed that there would be "people of note and talent" at the conference, and that these people would make clear that "no nation," that is, the new Union of South Africa, had a right to control the "great economic factor," that is, education, that was "intimately connected to the African people as a whole."[17] Whoever was editing *Imvo* in Jabavu's absence likewise took for granted that Africans would not be attending the conference. The invitation was understood to be directed to "Government and Mission Societies," not to Africans. The article went on to offer a prayer to God that the "wisest and sanest officials" from both government and missions would be chosen as delegates to attend the conference, and that the delegates would formulate a "wise and statesmanlike . . . Native Affairs policy" for the new Union of South Africa.[18]

No representatives of European imperial governments, the "Powers in Africa" to which Harlan alluded, attended the conference. The government officials in attendance listed in surviving documents were connected to fledgling government education agencies, an example being P. P. Claxton, commissioner of education at the U.S. Bureau of Education in Washington, D.C., the highest-ranking American official.[19] The other government representatives present came predominantly from British West Indian colonies. Harlan erred in suggesting that the majority of participants in the conference were white. According to A. W. Baker, a white South African evangelist who wrote the report on the conference published in the *Missionary Review of the World*, only twenty of a hundred and twenty participants could be categorized as Europeans.[20] Harlan observed that few black Africans attended the conference. The majority of the participants in the conference, however, were of African descent, either American or from the West Indies. The preponderance of the speakers and the conference audience were ministers, missionaries, and other church people.[21]

A number of articles published in the United States, Britain, and Africa provided eyewitness descriptions of the conference.[22] The most influential summation of the conference was the official press release, composed by Robert E. Park, Washington's assistant.[23] Demonstrating the transatlantic nature of the conference, the press release enjoyed distinction by being published in six different newspapers in four different versions on three different continents.[24] The press release also found secondary life as the source for published editorials on the conference. The widespread use of the official press release gave a positive spin to a conference that, according to most other reports, was a chaotic disappointment. A. W. Baker observed, "Many addresses were cut short. There was no room for discussion and no provision for a committee to digest the proceedings; no delegate could carry away more than a hazy generalization of the multitudinous subjects treated."[25] Baker concluded that the conference program was "too full to be effective."[26] He was being polite. An early draft of the official press release, one that was not circulated, noted that by the evening of the first night the printed program had been scrapped. As Emmett Scott, Washington's secretary, explained in his opening remarks, several of the individuals listed on the program did not come, while several individuals not listed on the program arrived and asked to speak.[27] Many of the presentations were too long and off topic. Mark Hayford, Baptist minister and brother of the Gold Coast nationalist J. E. Casely-Hayford, gave a paper on the "antiquity and past grandeur" of some of the peoples of the Gold Coast that was "so learned and so long that Mr. Hayford did not succeed in completing it."[28] Nor do records note clearly when the conference officially concluded. According to Baker, the conference "closed abruptly" on Friday at noon, when Washington announced that he had to leave to catch a train to New York.[29] The Reverend A. M. Pinanko, however, the representative sent by the Gold Coast Aborigines Protection Society, wrote in his report to that society, later published in the *Gold Coast Nation*, that he gave his paper and entertained questions on Friday afternoon.[30]

A conference format that worked well for black American farmers and businessmen proved to be a liability for an international event. Maurice Evans was a white South African attending the conference as the official representative of the (later Royal) African Society of Great Britain. As Evans complained in his report to the African Society, instead of the session structure being maintained, "the Conference resolved into one continuous meeting of all of the delegates."[31] Pushing the organizational chaos was the fact that most of the participants, spontaneously inspired by the chemistry at the meeting, became preoccupied with agendas only secondarily concerned with industrial education. Only one of these agendas had import for this discussion. On the second afternoon, African, African American, and European clergymen took time off from the conference for an improvised meeting about race and Christian proselytization in Africa. The concern that brought the clergymen together related to the obstacles being placed in the way of African American missionaries by colonial governments in Africa. The missionaries were having difficulty gaining the visas necessary to travel to and from the continent. On the third morning of the conference, members of the group issued an ad hoc resolution requesting that "some important American Negro" go to South Africa "and place before the white people of that land the true spirit of the Negro missionaries," which was "to uplift their people and not to incite sedition."[32] Of course, the "important American Negro" the group had in mind to send to Africa was Washington. As characterized in the press release, Washington would be charged with seeking "some working basis by which the colored missionary societies could have their part in the redemption of the Dark Continent."[33]

The official press release sought to save face for Washington and the conference by showing how the pursuit of the various unanticipated agendas culminated in new mandates that recognized Washington's influence and Tuskegee's achievements. As for industrial education, which had received so little hearing at the conference, the press release implied that its discussion had simply been postponed until a later occasion. In a set of resolutions voted at the end of the conference and included in its entirety in the press release, conference participants as a body recognized the importance of Tuskegee as a "great experimental station in racial education" and the need for meetings, such as the one that had just ended, on a triennial basis. To this last effect, a central committee composed of an ecumenical cross section of the participants was elected and listed at the end of the press release. The committee was charged with preparing for a second International Conference on the Negro to be held in 1915.[34]

Washington made mistakes in conceptualizing and promoting the Tuskegee conference. Inadequate analysis of how the conference should have been organized in order to realize his goal of passing on industrial education as a legacy compromised the intended impact of the meeting. Attendees with their own agendas steered the conference away from the subject of industrial education. Their ability to do this, however, was a result of the absence of any important issues connected with industrial education to stimulate debate, which reflected the paucity of attendees with any firsthand experience actually running industrial education institutes. Washington celebrated self-help and self-reliance, and these ideas were behind his promise that if an individual could get to Tuskegee for the conference, Washington would cover the cost of their stay. Washington and his advisors failed to appreciate that, for the people with the expertise they wanted to tap, travel costs would be a prohibiting factor. African Ethiopianists struggling to get the money together to found a school would not have the money for transoceanic voyages. Neither, for that matter, would most of the missionaries engaged in similar endeavors. Washington should have called upon one of his wealthy benefactors to provide travel funds for missionaries or other Christian workers actively engaged in running industrial education schools in Africa. These people would have kept industrial education on the table.

## The Aftermath of the Tuskegee Conference in Africa

With the results of the International Conference on the Negro, Booker T. Washington missed an opportunity to ensure that the people in Africa battling over industrial education could come together at Tuskegee, at the school whose program they hoped to emulate, to at least talk about their differences. Still, as unfruitful as the conference seems to have been on the American side of the Atlantic, it had promising outcomes on the African side. One of the missionaries in attendance at the conference put forward a proposal for an industrial education institution in West Africa that drew praise from Ethiopianists. And, in both West and South Africa, Ethiopianists signaled some softening of the adversarial relationship they had previously held against missionaries.

One of the missionaries in Africa who attended the Tuskegee conference was Reverend James Denton from the Church Missionary Society, acting principal of Fourah Bay College in Sierra Leone. Denton wrote a long article on his visit to Tuskegee, then Hampton, that was first published in the CMS *Church Missionary Review* in November 1912, before reappearing in the Sierra Leone *Weekly News* a month later.[35] The overarching lesson that Denton recommended the CMS and other denominational missions take from the examples of Hampton and Tuskegee was that, as mentioned in the quotation at the start of the chapter, the two schools, and their approach to education, should be replicated by West Africa. In the article, Denton seemed to enjoin missionaries to find a way to work with Ethiopianists. May reprinted it with that understanding. Yet, when identifying how this fellow school to Hampton and Tuskegee was to come about, Denton incorporated neither Ethiopianists nor their ideas into his proposal. With the network of mission secondary schools available in Freetown in mind, Denton proposed that each mission secondary school should develop a course of instruction in one specific area of industrial education, and then all the schools should pool these offerings, in this way creating their own version of the Hampton/Tuskegee program. In Denton's scheme, missions asserted control over industrial education initiatives in Sierra Leone. All industrial training would be under denominational auspices. All the students would be adherents of one of the denominations and, at the end of their training, return to those churches.

Denton's plan proposed structures similar to the scheme Reverend James Henderson of Lovedale was bringing to fruition in South Africa as head of the committee overseeing the establishment of the South African Native College. Both schemes proposed that missions move beyond their previous competition among themselves for African converts toward future cooperation in maintaining a school not primarily concerned with the production of evangelists and ministers. Relevant to this point, the most-discussed matter among the missions concerned with the opening of the Native College in South Africa was whether at Fort Hare they wanted to come together to build one dormitory for housing African students or build separate denominational hostels. For economic reasons, all agreed to the proposal to build one dormitory and name it in honor of Doctor Stewart.[36] After the International Conference on the Negro, missions across Africa showed their determination to retain their control over African adherents regardless of changes in education the future brought.

Africans in South Africa deeply resented the movement of Reverend Henderson to commandeer the Native College at Fort Hare in the name of the missions. The afterglow of the Tuskegee Conference, however, allowed Africans in West Africa to see Denton's plan in a more positive light. In the editorial May published as a preface to the reprint of Denton's article, he exempted Denton from his general condemnation of white missionaries. According to May, implementation of Denton's "delightful" proposal would be "a great gain to us [Africans], it would widen our outlook, make firm for us the foundations, and put us in line with Providence." May did not display optimism, however, about the colonial government granting Denton's scheme a chance to move forward. "Suppose Tuskegee should be transplanted here," May speculated. "What would be the attitude of the Colonial Government to it," and the men the school would produce? The "present attitude of the local Government to the general welfare of the people of Sierra Leone,"

May concluded, did not give "confidence" that men trained in a West African Tuskegee "would be assisted to realize themselves."[37]

May published Denton's article and his editorial in December 1912. The following March, Denton's proposal received a second endorsement in the pages of the *Weekly News*. In a running series of editorials on the needs of Sierra Leone, a writer known only as "Ahguyahvee" made a different case for the implementation of Denton's idea. Having observed that "a generation of clerks is the pronouncement on the results of our past system of education" and that "a generation of clerks means perpetual dependence," the writer went on to argue that "except our future system of education be worked upon the lines of Tuskegee Institute, we are doomed to failure." With this goal in mind, the writer endorsed Denton's scheme as a means of improving education in Sierra Leone through a unified system of schools maintained by the missions. Denton's plan would aid mission schools to adopt "uniform standards" and to operate under "one executive," though they would retain their denominational independence.[38] Both May and Ahguyahvee identified government, not the missions, as the obstacle to African advancement. May could be accused of inconsistency here—he was soon back to blasting missionaries for their racism. Still, his comments, in conjunction with those of Ahguyahvee, reflect a developing trend in West Africa. Ethiopianists began to speak of racism as expressed by political authorities as the adversary in the African Christian effort to use industrial education as a vehicle for the Christian regeneration of Africa.

A number of South African newspapers also published versions of the official press release. *Imvo* offered a summary in Xhosa. *Ilanga* used the press release as the basis for a comparison of white attitudes toward black education in the United States versus white attitudes on the same subject in South Africa.[39] *Imvo* had nothing to say in English about the conference, but, during the second half of 1913, readers of the newspaper were entertained with news of John Tengo Jabavu's son, Davidson Jabavu's visit to Tuskegee. The *Christian Express* printed a selective version of Park's report that it announced came from the Tuskegee student newspaper. The *Christian Express* felt compelled to comment on the section about clergymen asking Washington to travel to South Africa to make the African American missionary case before the South African government. The newspaper welcomed Washington's visit but insisted that what he would discover was the damage done in the past by Bishop

Turner's visit, combined with the ongoing damage being done by African American missionaries stealing converts from European missions.[40]

Still, in what can be considered as the spirit of conciliation engendered by the Tuskegee conference, the *Christian Express* did give one African American mission a chance to state its case. A General Mission Conference was held annually in South Africa. The September 2, 1912, issue of the *Christian Express* reported that a letter had been received by the missionary conference just after it had closed its meeting. The newspaper opted to print the letter so that it might be more broadly known. As the letter explained, it was under Washington's aegis that the "Coloured Baptists" of the United States, that is, the National Baptist Convention (NBC), were writing to the missionaries in South Africa to make clear that they were not associated, "by voice, pen or finance," with the movement toward independent denominations among African Christians. The NBC wanted missionaries in South Africa to appreciate that it strove to keep a "conservative Christian brother" as the superintendent of its work in South Africa and that it aspired to work "in perfect harmony" with the English Baptist mission. The NBC requested that South African missionaries and, by extension, the South African government not hold the NBC responsible for any "unlawful acts" by "natives claiming to be Baptists." The NBC promised in return to discipline any of its missionaries found guilty of "over-lapping or bringing undue influence to proselytize."[41]

One last bit of reaction to the Tuskegee conference merits attention. In the South African newspaper *Tsala ea Batho* (Friend of the people), published in Kimberly, on May 22, 1915, a report appeared about a new tradition then starting at Tuskegee. Each year in March, the English Department at Tuskegee held a program to raise funds for the Tuskegee Chapel at Monrovia in Liberia. Called the Rhetoricals, the program consisted of "declarations, stories and poems on Africa." In the past, presentations had been given by "representatives of all the classes in the school." Beginning in 1914, however, the program had been taken over by "African students who have been coming to the school in increasing numbers since the International Conference on the Negro." At the event in 1915, none but students of Africa, or people working on the "Dark Continent," performed.[42]

WASHINGTON'S LEGACY AS AFRICANS SAW IT

The death of Booker T. Washington on November 14, 1915, at the age of fifty-seven, was widely covered in African newspapers. "A prince and a great man has fallen in Israel," was the lead article in the *Lagos Standard* on November 24, 1915. The article continued, "The Wizard of Tuskegee, the man whose magic touch transmuted everything, not into gold, but into something more useful than gold, has passed away."[43] The obituaries of Washington composed by African writers made some effort to place Washington and his work in the context of the African fight against European domination. As expressed in these obituaries, Africans were quite conscious that, as was said in the Sierra Leone *Weekly News*, someone important to the "13 million Negroes in America" but also "the 200 millions of the black skinned children of Africa" had been lost.[44] Significantly, placing Washington in historical perspective for African writers involved a comparison of Washington's strategies for facilitating racial uplift with those advocated by W. E. B. Du Bois. Washington represented industrial education, understood to challenge domination gradually through economic development. Du Bois' name was already associated with political activism aimed at immediate results. Not surprisingly, the obituaries mostly sided with Washington. Only those sympathetic to Washington would write at his death of his memory. But the ways in which African writers framed their endorsement of Washington and his legacy suggest that while there was some awareness of the limitations of Washington's approach, there was broad agreement about the value of industrial education as a vehicle for racial regeneration and about the ongoing utility of Tuskegee as a model for future schools.

West African newspapers published a mix of obituaries of Washington, some taken from American and British newspapers, with others produced by local African writers. Few of the obituaries written by West Africans touched on Washington's Christianity. They were more concerned with Washington's approach to racial uplift. Two obituaries can be taken as representative of West African comment. Orishetukeh Faduma published the earliest and most informed obituary in the *Weekly News* only five days after Washington's death. One year before, in preparation for his departure from the United States as a member of the Chief Sam Back-to-Africa party, Faduma had spent three days at Tuskegee studying its industrial plant. As Faduma noted with admiration in the obituary, Tuskegee was "a beehive of industry, a town in itself. There were students from Cuba, the West Indies, West and South Africa, taking such industrial course as best needed in their different countries." In regard to Ethiopianism, Faduma recognized Tuskegee as something of a Geneva, the Swiss city that John Calvin turned into an international city for the study of Reformed Christianity. Yet Faduma voiced ambivalence about Washington as a race leader and chided Washington for dismissing the issue of higher education for African Americans. He wrote, "What is to become of the Negro without Negro doctors, lawyers, teachers and preachers? In a land full of race prejudice, who is to take care of the Negro's health, his property, his race aspirations, his spiritual needs?" Faduma clearly was voicing a critique influenced by Du Bois. Faduma further criticized Washington for his "opportunism" yet lack of nerve before white racism in the United States. Faduma established and maintained Peabody Academy, his own industrial education school, in North Carolina before he repatriated to Africa in 1914. Perhaps reflecting upon his own knowledge and experience as a school principal in the United States, Faduma condemned Washington for "crippling" the growth of several schools, though on this last point Faduma offered no details. In the end, however, Faduma came down on the side of those who recognized Washington's greatness by saying, "He used the selfish materialis[m] of the country to help his race. . . . His weakness was his strength. By refusing to talk back to the South in order to prevent opposition to his work, he showed the wisdom of Solomon, 'Answer not a fool according to his folly.' "[45] Faduma could see the direction behind Washington's actions, even though he declined to follow the same path.

A similarly equivocal characterization of Washington, though couched in much less biblical language, can be found in the obituary of Washington written by A. O. Delo-Dosumu and published in the *Lagos Standard* on December 1, 1912.[46] Delo-Dosumu was a recent graduate from the University of London, then serving as vice principal in Eko High School in Lagos. For Delo-Dosumu what Africans needed to remember about Washington first was Washington's life story of overcoming "gigantic forces of depression and hatred" that would have "doomed" an "average man," and second, even more importantly, Washington's achievement in "raising others from filth, degradation and ignorance." For Delo-Dosumu, Tuskegee was the "embodiment" of Washington's "devotion, love of race and passion to uplift fellow men" and as such stood as "one of the greatest romantic creations of human genius." Still, in Delo-Dosumu's vision, for Washington, "theoretical (meaning liberal arts) education was a waste on the Negro." Washington failed to draw a line "between expediency and utility, between what is and what ought to be." As such, according to Delo-Dosumu, Washington advocated that the "best practical thing" was for black people to "benefit themselves" as "hewers of wood and stone." Delo-Dosumu contrasted Washington with W. E. B. Du Bois, a "scholar and litterateur" who had emerged to lead "a strong party" that saw Washington's position as "entirely repugnant." Du Bois and his followers promoted as an "antithesis" to Washington's ideas "a scheme of training in which theory and practice take their proper place" as the best means of uplifting the Negro. However, this argument made, Delo-Dosumu appeared to backtrack in his assessment of Washington. The approaches of Washington and Du Bois, he suggested, should be recognized as strategies to be followed at different stages of (racial) development, the strategy put forward by Du Bois presumably coming later. Defending Washington's "success," Delo-Dosumu concluded that Washington had found the South "teeming with a mass of purposeless Negroes" yet made of it "a country full of enterprise for the Negro."[47]

South African newspapers took a different tack on communicating Washington's death. Les Switzer made the case that, beginning in the 1930s with the appearance of the newspaper *Bantu World*, it is valid to talk about a "captive" African press in South Africa, meaning a self-policing African press that did not challenge political domination out of fear of government reprisals.[48] The African press during the 1910s was perhaps not so repressed, but there does appear to have been some self-policing, particularly in regard to reportage on African American life and activities and, most pertinent here, Booker T. Washington and Tuskegee. For example, John Tengo Jabavu in his newspaper *Imvo* spotlighted his son Davidson's trip to the United States in 1913 to visit Tuskegee before dropping the story, never to reprise it. Rather than write about Washington and his strategy for racial uplift, the focus that had dominated African coverage before the Native Land Act, African-edited newspapers in South Africa concentrated instead on details of Washington's death and funeral.

Showing the speed with which the news traveled to Africa, *Imvo* reported Washington's death in a short article in Xhosa on November 16, a day after the event. *Imvo* followed with a short article in English the next week and then an obituary written in English by Davidson

Jabavu on November 30. The November 23, 1915, article in *Imvo* about Washington's death was surprisingly brief, only a paragraph long and tucked at the bottom of a column where the main story related to the latest battles between John Tengo Jabavu and the Native College Council headed by Henderson. No mention was made of the connection between Tuskegee and the South African Native College. *Imvo* simply commented that Tuskegee had "introduced and developed new and startling factors into the solution of the problem of the Coloured races."[49] The sense that the senior Jabavu was trying to circumvent some type of gag order is reinforced in the obituary *Imvo* published the following week. The obituary, written by Davidson Jabavu, was presented in the form of a "character sketch." Davidson did not take up the question of the value of Washington's educational program for the regeneration of Africa. But he did defend Washington from two unfair indictments by giving Washington credit for teaching African Americans the importance of material improvement. He conceded that the emphasis Washington placed on the acquisition of "chickens and pigs, bank accounts and property" allowed Washington to appear "materialistic, and if not irreligious [then] morally indifferent." Davidson insisted to the contrary, however, that Washington was "a sincere and exemplary Christian" who took the Bible as his guide. As for Washington's attacks on the black clergy, citing Washington's maxim about the difficulties of making a good Christian out of a hungry man, he argued that Washington was trying to get clergymen to "devise a correlation between religious ideals and practical life." Unlike West African writers who held Washington up to censure based upon a critique that originated with Du Bois, Davidson Jabavu sought to defend Washington from the attack of Du Bois and a group that he labeled as "advanced Negroes" hailing from the "American North." He characterized the group as being more self-interested than concerned for the race, as being antagonistic to Washington because his politics "compromis[ed] their Northern circumstances." Avoiding any direct discussion of politics, Davidson framed the debate between Washington and Du Bois as a contest of oratorical styles. Du Bois' "classical, mellifluous and learned eloquence" may have appealed to the "advanced Negroes," he observed. But if "merely academic rhetoric" could be put aside, he believed that Washington had no peer in speaking to and for the race save for Frederick Douglass.[50]

The *Christian Express* announced the news next, stating in its December 1, 1912, issue that Washington's passing had created "a feeling of dismay and sense of deep loss" "in hearts set upon the uplift of Africa's backward races." Demonstrating the extent to which in death as in life Washington remained a contested symbol between whites and blacks in South Africa, the obituary remembered Washington primarily for the work regime he instituted at Tuskegee. The article reviewed how students at Tuskegee did three days of labor in factories and three days of study in the classroom each week before concluding, "it will be a great day for South Africa when [Washington's] ideals and methods find a larger place in the Native educational system of South Africa."[51]

*Ilanga* did not report Washington's death until its January 14, 1916, issue, two months after the fact. *Ilanga*, like *Imvo*, avoided any explicit editorializing on Washington and what he had achieved at Tuskegee. The January 14 story in *Ilanga* that served as an obituary Dube copied from an American newspaper, the *Public Ledger*, published in Philadelphia.[52] *Ilanga* did not mention Washington again until the end of February, when Dube reprinted, from an unidentified source, the description of Washington's funeral written by Lyman Ward, president of the Southern Industrial Institute, a small industrial education school for white students near Tuskegee, and pastor of the congregation of the Universalist (Christian) Church that maintained the school. Seeking to memorialize Washington, Ward, through his reflections upon the event, wrote:

> Booker Washington is not dead and some way no one there seemed to feel he was gone. He lives in the lives of millions of his race. He was yesterday and is to-day in countless homes where he had taught his people a new life and living, and into the old homes he has given a new grace and tenantry. Booker Washington lives in the hearts, not only of those who know the English tongue, but in the lives of those who do not know our language and its meanings. Booker T. Washington lives as Christ lives. He is alive as Paul is yet alive. His voice is the voice of Lincoln—that Lincoln who cast off the shackles. Call Booker T. Washington educator, orator, statesman, patriot, if you will, but above them all, call Booker T. Washington the real emancipator of his race.[53]

Ward's paean to Washington clearly resonated with Dube's insistence, similar to that of Davidson Jabavu, that Washington be remembered as both a race leader and a Christian.

In 1922 a commemorative piece of public art was introduced on the Tuskegee campus. Entitled *Lifting the Veil of Ignorance*, the cast bronze sculpture featured the figure of Booker T. Washington with a cloth in his hand standing above the head of a kneeling young African American. Thirty years later, in 1952, Ralph Ellison published his novel *Invisible Man*. In it Ellison, a former Tuskegee student, commented that from the time of the artwork's installation, students and others had pondered whether Washington was lifting up the cloth from the kneeling figure's head or lowering it down. The same question had dogged discussions of Washington and his program since Du Bois first framed the issue in 1904. As shown here, Africans seeking to assess Washington's legacy in the months after his death made the question the focus of their assessments. For the most part, they came down on the side that Washington was lifting the veil up.

### Industrial Education and the Christian Black Atlantic

Washington's death signaled a change of direction in the history of industrial education as an educational approach on the African continent. During the heyday of Washington's international prestige, especially the decade between 1900 and 1910, industrial education had been an offensive tool, used by Ethiopianists as the basis for their claims to leadership of the movement to Christianize Africa. Washington's death forced Ethiopianists back into a defensive posture, looking to maintain the validity of their version of the educational approach in the face of mounting European condemnation and growing division among themselves. Industrial education had an appeal to Africans before Washington achieved renown for perfecting the approach at Tuskegee. Washington's success had boosted the prestige of the approach even further in African eyes and had provided Ethiopianists with new strategies for building industrial education institutions. Washington's death, however, left Ethiopianists without a sense of direction for industrial education's future, most importantly in the area of funding.

Efforts at establishing an industrial institute continued in West Africa after the death of Washington. Faduma sought to rethink industrial education, as a joint project of Ethiopianists and missionaries and a group of Gold Coast nationalists, led by J. E. Casely-Hayford, promoted an education fund that would build industrial institutes. Neither effort made much headway. In South Africa, Ohlange continued to enroll students, though, beginning in 1915, with no money with which to maintain industrial shops or to pay instructors, Dube dropped the practice of advertising the school as Ohlange Industrial.

In 1920 two developments revitalized the Ethiopianist debate over the establishment of industrial education schools. Early that year, newspaper articles signaled the arrival in Africa of the ideas of Marcus Garvey.[54] Later in the year and on into 1921, newspaper articles detailed the travels of the first Phelps Stokes Education Commission. Though Garvey was a West Indian, for Africans, Garveyism still represented the latest articulation of African American thought. For some West Africans, this was a good development. The *Lagos Weekly Record* saw the emergence of the Universal Negro Improvement Agency as evidence that "the American Negro has caught the spirit of the age and is successfully organizing himself into a formidable force with which the world will have to reckon."[55] For other West Africans, it was not so auspicious. The *Gold Coast Leader* was "amused" by Garvey's "presumption" that, because he was "a Negro from America," he was "the best man to direct the African today."[56]

Garveyism appropriated industrial education as part of its appeal. Garvey first came to the United States with the ambition to go to Tuskegee to see how it operated in order to duplicate Tuskegee back in Jamaica, his home country. Garvey was not an educator, however. More than anything else, he was a political organizer of genius. Garvey grasped that, after two generations of listening to sermons on the virtues of industrial education and attending schools that taught some idea of industrial education, African Americans collectively saw themselves as knowing what there was to know about the subject. Garvey's scheme for a steamship line and for an industrial corporation presumed that African peoples in the New World already possessed the knowledge needed to construct an industrial civilization. The one thing they required was the space to do so. Taking Africa back from its European colonizers would supply that space.[57]

As for Africans, industrial education was high on the list of gifts African Americans were supposed to bring for their racial compatriots when they returned to the homeland. Branches of the UNIA established in Africa made the funding of industrial education schools a priority.[58] To supply instructors for those schools, in 1922 Garvey proposed founding a "Booker T. Washington University of the UNIA" in Harlem, its purpose to be the training of "technical missionaries" to send to Africa to spread industrial education.[59] Perhaps it was with Garvey's idea in mind that in 1928 the South African Garveyite leader Wellington Buthelezi sought donations for the establishment of the "Saint Booker

T. Washington Industrial College" for the training of future African leaders.[60] Garveyism, because it was Christian and because it did advocate the spread of industrial education, created an enormous amount of confusion among the ranks of the African Christians who were already promoting industrial education. Garveyism associated the promotion of industrial education with a set of political aspirations many Ethiopianists did not share, and the battle over Garveyism placed advocates of industrial education as cross-purposes.

The misunderstanding that occurred in April 1920 in Sierra Leone, when the local women's branch of the UNIA helped organize an event to raise money for a girl's industrial training school, only later to be snubbed by event organizers fearful about colonial government displeasure, provides an example of the confusion. In that instance, supporters of industrial education took sides against each other. Industrial education had been a tent under which Ethiopianists from different denominations had stood together. Garveyism certainly did not tear down the tent. But advocates of industrial education became much more aware that the person standing next to them under the tent might be pursuing the same educational goal but with a contrary political agenda. In South Africa, the tensions among Ethiopianists became overt. There, Garvey and his message were targeted for disdain and opprobrium by the older generation of Ethiopianists, most significantly Dube, who in *Ilanga* explicitly dissociated himself and his political activities from Garvey's "wild talks."[61]

After Washington's death, the Christian audience in Africa that had listened to Washington began to hear many things to which it as a group could not respond with approbation. Going back to at least the time of Alexander Crummell, African Americans had been taking and sending schemes for Africa's regeneration across the Atlantic to Africa, and some groups of African Christians had welcomed these ideas. As this study has shown, African receptivity to African American ideas reached a high point during the era when Booker T. Washington was most actively promoting Tuskegee as the bridge over which the African race could travel toward regeneration. Garveyism and its idea of pan-Africanism were not the only new African American ideas crossing the Atlantic in the decade after the death of Washington. Du Bois' notions of pan-Africanism also crossed the Atlantic during this time. But the politics and promises of both these men left the people who had been listening to Washington perplexed. They could not see how the ideas of either could lead the

African further toward Christianity. Both Garvey and Du Bois said things that, on the surface, in no way rejected the Ethiopianism upon which reception of Washington's message had been premised. Yet, both men also tried to turn the religious aspirations behind Ethiopianism toward more political goals. In different ways, both sought to secularize Ethiopianism into a political movement. African audiences existed for what Garvey and Du Bois had to say. Some parts of these audiences had previously paid attention to the words of Washington. But a large portion of Washington's audience, the more Christian portion, could not hear or could not understand what Garvey and Du Bois were saying. So this portion stopped listening to either speaker.

Christians who turned away from Garvey and Du Bois thought they heard an echo of Washington in the voice of a former church pastor turned educator, James Emman Kwegyir Aggrey, who returned to Africa after twenty-two years in the United States as part of the first Phelps Stokes Education Commission. Aggrey was born and first educated in the Gold Coast. Much like Faduma, his intellectual ambitions and abilities impelled him toward leaving Africa to study in the United States. He attended Livingstone College in North Carolina, where he studied for the ministry, married, and settled, serving as pastor to two local A.M.E. Zion churches. In the summer of 1904, he met Thomas Jesse Jones, then an assistant chaplain at Hampton Institute. Jones heard Aggrey speak once and was so impressed with Aggrey's conservative political views that Jones recruited him as an associate. Jones moved on from Hampton to work as a statistician for the U.S. Bureau of Education before landing the job of director of education for the Phelps Stokes Fund, an American philanthropy dedicated to African American education. Through all these career developments, Jones maintained his connection with Aggrey, using Phelps Stokes money to help Aggrey complete all of the work but the dissertation for a doctoral degree in sociology from Columbia University under Jones' old mentor, Franklin Giddings. Jones led the two Phelps Stokes Education Commissions that traveled through different parts of Africa in the early years of the 1920s assessing schools, primarily mission schools, from the perspective of the schools' efficiency and effectiveness according to what Jones insisted was the Hampton-Tuskegee model. Aggrey was the only person Jones selected to serve with him on both commissions. Aggrey had instant rapport with African Christians as well as with whites in Africa. He spoke more than one hundred times before audiences on each of the tours, his primary objective being to convince Africans that harmony was possible between the races.[62]

The idea of industrial education that Jones promoted as being taught at Tuskegee was far removed from the idea Washington developed at the school. Washington trained students to avoid openly confronting white political domination but instead to size up and seize economic opportunities. Washington was convinced that the black man with $50,000 to lend would have some political say. According to Jones, Washington taught Tuskegee students to accommodate white domination in the economic as well as the political sphere. Tuskegee taught black people how to adapt to the niches whites designated for them. Jones initially made these claims in his two-volume survey of African American schools, *Negro Education*, published two years after Washington's death.[63]

When Washington was alive, the two men were adversaries. Washington wrote a letter against Jones' appointment as education director of the Phelps Stokes Fund, Washington preferring that his own man, Robert E. Park, get the job.[64] Jones' idea of the Hampton-Tuskegee model actually placed more emphasis on Hampton than Tuskegee because Jones did not believe black people were racially mature enough to run their own schools. In terms of Jones' perspective on African Christians and their role in the civilizing of Africa, the key terms as used in the two Phelps Stokes reports were "Native" and "self-determination." Jones classified all of the Africans discussed in this book as "Natives," meaning people collectively on the anthropological level of primitives. As "educated Natives" these particular men needed also to be classified pejoratively as "denationalized" because of their inclinations to protest against white tutelage. Their protests took the form of movements for "self-determination" in the face of European colonization. Jones made missions culpable for the production of such natives and accepted as valid charges leveled by imperialists that mission Christianity was the true source of rebellion among Africans against colonial rule. Jones was entirely sanguine, however, believing that if missions adopted his approach to industrial education, they could mend their ways and become useful tools of colonial administration.[65]

African Ethiopianists were so ecstatic about having Aggrey, someone whom they literally identified as one of their own,[66] as part of the Phelps Stokes Education Commissions, that they did not pay close attention to what Jones was saying, though in their defense, during the tours, when Jones did speak to African, as distinct from European, audiences, typically it was to introduce Aggrey.[67] In West Africa, especially in the Gold Coast, his birthplace, Aggrey was treated in African newspapers as a world-renowned scholar and dignitary.[68] In South Africa, African newspapers used him more often to reinforce Ethiopianist dismissals of Garvey and Garveyism. Aggrey was quoted to say in *Umteteli wa Bantu* (Voice of the people), the newspaper published in Johannesburg, "If you send money to these fool men, then you are the bigger fools."[69] Ethiopianists saw Aggrey as representing the next generation of African leadership, whose faith would be beyond doubt but who would be also expert in some discipline of European knowledge. An editorial published in *Imvo* in May 1922 speculated that if Aggrey returned to South Africa, to Fort Hare as expected to teach economics and sociology, then the Native College would become the "Mecca or Athens of Native Education in South Africa."[70] Aggrey did not return to South Africa to teach, however. In 1924 he accepted an offer from the British Colonial Office to become vice principal of a new school for the sons of chiefs, Prince of Wales College, to be built in Achimota in the Gold Coast. Aggrey spent some time at Achimota College in 1925–1926 before heading to London to do research on his dissertation and then back to the United States to see his family. In 1927, while attending a function at Columbia University, Aggrey took sick and suddenly died of meningitis. He was fifty-two years old.[71]

Aggrey did not know Booker T. Washington and did not visit Tuskegee's campus until after his return from the first Phelps Stokes Education Commission tour of Africa. And the ideas Aggrey advanced as reflecting Washington's wisdom came from Thomas Jesse Jones, not Washington. Aggrey had no real connection to Washington except in the minds of the many individuals, black as well as white, who, as Lyman Ward preached after Washington death, wanted to affirm that Washington lived on, at least in an approach to racial uplift. That approach was the personification of opportunism. Both Washington and Aggrey believed and taught the need for black people, for black individuals, to seize the day, that is, take whatever opportunities to advance that they saw before themselves. E. Cornelius May thought that Washington's instincts in this regard exalted him above all others save Toussaint Louverture as a race leader.

Many African Ethiopianists wanted to place Aggrey in this company. They had not heard of him before his arrival, and they had only the words of Jones to vouch for his presumed expertise; still, they eagerly read Washington's leadership into his opportunism. Aggrey's early death left them without any validation for their faith, however. From the publication in 1922 of *Education in Africa*, the report Jones wrote about the Phelps Stokes Education Commission first tour, Ethiopianists found themselves defined as the problem mission schools needed to correct. From that time forward, they fought a battle of attrition, not so much against Jones' ideas as against the oversight over all forms of education colonial governments instituted and then justified using Jones' ideas.

The Black Atlantic is one way of conceptualizing the diaspora of African peoples that stretched from Africa to the New World. The concept first emerged as a meaningful construct for Christians and other peoples of African descent. Its embrace by black peoples on either side of the Atlantic provided a passageway for the communication of Christian ideologies of racial regeneration. Colonial governments in Africa achieved some success in shutting down the communication of Christian ideologies from the United States to Africa during the 1920s and 1930s, due in part to cooperation from American and European mission organizations.[72] European efforts at regulating the communication of black Christian thought did not impair the utility of the concept of the Black Atlantic as a bridge, however. The Black Atlantic was reimagined as a secular, racial, and even socioeconomic construct.[73] Black people on both sides of the Atlantic continued to think of themselves as one and to exchange ideas about how to make Africa great. The ideologies being communicated and their points of engagement did change, though. Colonial governments effectively stifled African American Christian missions to Africa but displayed far less control over the movement of West Indian Marxists to and about the continent. Africans looking to the New World for ideas on social development found them emanating from secular ideologies as opposed to Christian ones, from the islands of the Caribbean as opposed to the United States. Industrial education as conceived by people like Thomas Jesse Jones did not disappear, either; it was rethought and incorporated into various notions of community development deemed supportive of colonial regimes and, as such, promoted with government approbation by Western philanthropic agencies.

In retrospect, the one thing that may have been lost in the transition from Christian to secular notions of diaspora was African confidence in the African capacity for technological innovation. During the time when African Christians were listening across the Atlantic to Christian African Americans, the two groups shared a conviction that they could transform African societies so the latter could build their own bridges, construct their own harbors, and light their own cities. Such notions were part of the Protestant ethos of the time. Africans exhibiting the effects of the embrace of this ethos were the ones colonial governments were most inclined to suppress. Schools like Tuskegee were never built in Africa. Africans identified as possessing instincts toward any sort of technological competence were sent to some other continent to train. Most of them never returned. By the mid-twentieth century, world Protestantism had moved away from its celebration of, as Faduma phrased it, "Christ, tools and man." So, when colonialism ended, neither the people nor the ideology behind that conviction remained still to be found.

# Conclusion

Christianity in Africa has been the subject of significant scholarship in numerous research fields. Incongruously, the least-deciphered aspect of the spread of the faith on the continent has been the consciousness of African Christians themselves. The thoughts and motivations of Africans who self-identified as Christians remain dimly understood. The bias and chauvinism transcendent in the Western perspective, which Western scholarship has never outgrown, can be cited as the main obstacle to growth beyond Western assumptions.[1] From the perspective of missionaries writing about the continent through the period under discussion, to the extent to which African expressions of Christian faith were recognized as distinct, African sensibilities and visions for their cultural improvement were stigmatized as deficient. Missionaries condemned most mildly as superstitious, most harshly as primitive, what to their eyes were the imperfect ways Africans essayed to grasp Christian doctrine and practices. European governments and other whites took over the Christian critique and turned it toward their own purposes. To speak only of the permutation pertinent for this discussion, the African appropriations of European culture that missionaries labeled superstitions, white governments castigated as denationalization. Counterintuitively, in using European ideas of political mobilization to organize themselves against European domination, Africans were supposedly guilty of negating their African identity. Western scholarship has continued in this tradition, treating all African appropriations of European culture and values as, to use an expression of the British writer E. D. Morel, "race suicide," that is, things that could only destroy African racial consciousness.[2]

Such assessments have built upon a proprietary notion of European civilization that has taken for granted that only Europeans can experience European culture without psychological trauma. A cultural/chronological index has been imposed on discussions of cultural appropriations, particularly as such discussions pertained to Africans, with European modernity posited as one end and African primitivism as the other. The more primitive, that is, less evolved toward some notion of European modernity an individual was supposed to be, the more psychological damage, it was postulated, the individual could be expected to have experienced attempting to assimilate European culture. Africans who took the initiative and determined themselves the extent of their exposure to the modern culture over which Europeans claimed ownership were scarred psychologically by their inability to cognitively assimilate the culture they had attempted to appropriate. Manifestations of such psychic damage included establishing churches under their own leadership and claiming whites-only privileges, matters that, according to the European sensibilities of the age, Africans had no real capacity or right to do.

One ambition guiding this study has been to reverse the image and show the articulation of African Christian consciousness from the perspective of African Christians themselves. African Christians committed to the African evangelization of Africa, the group discussed in this study as Ethiopianists, strove to introduce what they understood to be modern civilization in Africa as part of their evangelization efforts. To them, modern civilization advanced based upon technological innovation. Thus, they wanted to sponsor the development of technological innovation among Africans. Industrial institutes founded upon the example of Booker T. Washington's Tuskegee Institute appealed to them as the most cost-effective and efficient way to sponsor technological innovation. So they pursued various strategies to build schools like Tuskegee. As the African push for industrial education schools suggests, one of the flaws in the scholarly argument has been the assumption that Europeans provided the only model of modern peoples that Africans sought to copy. Africans themselves saw African Americans as far more viable role models to emulate. Africans were looking for strategies for economic success that worked in the face of European opposition, and the strategies African American had followed appeared tested and proven effective. Shared Protestant Christian values reinforced the attractiveness of the

African American example. African Americans had been challenged by severe hardships as Christian people in ways that signaled God's favor as a factor in their achievements. Shared Ethiopianist objectives cemented African commitment to schools like Tuskegee as the way to build toward the future. Both African American and African Ethiopianists dreamed of the regeneration of Africa. The expression meant different things to members of the two groups, but there was enough common conviction about African agency to facilitate communications between the two.

Another ambition has been to show that the problem confronting Africans who aimed to appropriate and make use of European culture was not psychological scarring but political suppression. No evidence exists in African newspapers to support a view that Ethiopianists experienced any collective psychological stress for attempting to appropriate a type of Western education aimed at producing skills over which European societies at that time sought to assert a monopoly.[3] Rather, the evidence suggests instead that education became an early locus of African mobilization against European overrule. Ethiopianists never found the funding needed to construct technological institutes, but ultimately they did not succeed because white governments did not allow them to succeed. Schools can take decades, and generations of benefactors, to grow self-sustaining roots. Ethiopianists in Africa had at most twenty years, from 1895 to 1915, when Booker T. Washington seemed to turn industrial education into, as the Lagos Standard described it, "something more useful than gold."[4] After that, white governments suppressed Ethiopianist initiatives as sedition. These governments were not concerned with the psychological damage Ethiopianists might inflict upon themselves but with the damage they might do to political regimes structured upon racial domination.

A third goal guiding the study has been to move the discussion of African Christian consciousness away from the notions of alienation and self-negation in which Western scholars have framed it toward some consideration of the self-affirming ways African Christians endeavored to save other African peoples. Christianity could serve as an instrument of European oppression on the African continent. But it also provided African Christians with tools not only to resist racial domination but also to press forward against it. Clearly, Ethiopianists looked upon Christianity from this last vantage. And because they controlled the technology of Western-style mass communication, newspapers, to which all African converts to Christianity became exposed once they learned to read, shaped the discourse between Africans and Europeans about Christianity, as well as other subjects, from the African perspective. This was the cultural process at the heart of what Europeans condemned as denationalization. In response to African newspapers and the Ethiopianist agendas the newspapers advanced, Africans did not accept at face value European self-portrayals of what Europeans were doing in Africa. After reading the newspapers, recently converted Christians could and did become suspicious about the behavioral strictures imposed upon them by missionaries. Africans who learned to read came to reject, primarily by leaving the countryside and heading for the cities, the taxes and labor obligations white governments imposed on them using traditional rulers as proxies. In *Education in Africa*, Thomas Jesse Jones promised his version of industrial education would correct the "impudence" of educated Africans.[5] But that which Jones labeled impudence, Ethiopianists considered the racial sophistication needed to identify and react against the racial domination implicit in European demands. The members of the women's branch of the Sierra Leone UNIA did not see the snub of their efforts to contribute to the start of a girl's industrial school engineered by the British governor as a demonstration of the futility of the African's fight against British colonialism. They saw themselves as a David and the colonial government as a Goliath who had landed a glancing blow. And in reporting their story, the Sierra Leone *Weekly News* was surreptitiously sharing their perspective.[6]

Because Ethiopianists identified missionaries as the originators of the notions of African mental inferiority that Europeans used to justify racial domination, Ethiopianists treated mission education with suspicion and sought to replace mission schools with schools that focused on the communication of technological skills, the skills Europeans insisted only they as a race were intelligent enough to possess. Ethiopianists did not have a clear sense of the features of a school that provided technological skills. They knew that the features were not the same as those of the trade schools run by missionaries, however. Ethiopianists were receptive to what they heard worked in Europe and the United States, an interest that led them first to an investigation of Hampton as an alternative to mission trade schools, second to a grassroots movement in support of Colwyn Bay far away in Wales, and, third, to a determination to construct versions of Tuskegee across Africa. As African newspapers demonstrated, Ethiopianists grew excited about industrial education because it promised to expedite the transformation of

Africans into Western-style entrepreneurs. For all the discussion among scholars about what type of training Tuskegee instituted for its students, of greater importance, Africans understood Tuskegee to provide its students with the equivalent of a modern-day business school education, ideally with an emphasis on commercial agriculture.[7] Assumptions held that students with this sort of education would recognize that the purpose behind their education was the acquisition of skills they could exercise for profit. Further, since Ethiopianists, as other Africans, were very conscious of the huge amounts of money European expatriates were making and taking from the continent, the amassing of wealth by individual Africans could be broadly celebrated as a victory for the African people, if some part of the wealth was channeled back into the social welfare projects late nineteenth-century Protestantism recognized as progress. If Ethiopianists felt any sense of psychological inadequacy, it was for the African failure to live up to Washington's ideal of practical Christianity. The frustrations of Thomas Horatio Jackson and John L. Dube were traceable to their sense that Africans, different from the reported case of African Americans, did not have the commitment to racial advance needed to fund projects like industrial institutes.

Jackson and Dube were being too hard on other Africans. Even in their moments of greatest self-sufficiency, Hampton and Tuskegee were not funded in the ways Armstrong and Washington boasted they were. Revenues from student production did not cover expenditures. The financial success of those two schools always came back to "begging," Armstrong's expression for the relentless pursuit of donations and funding from wealthy philanthropists. Funding schemes such as the one that Jabavu pursued in South Africa or the one that Casely-Hayford promoted in the Gold Coast might have gotten the proposed schools started, but, as Dube learned at Ohlange, ongoing infusions of large amounts of capital were needed to keep industrial schools functioning. Ethiopianists recognized the wealth needed for their various proposals for social and cultural regeneration and were open to contributions to the cause from wealthy European "friends of the African." Alfred L. Jones, the Welsh shipping magnate who helped subsidize Hughes and the African Institute and allowed African students free passage to and from the school, and Andrew Carnegie, the Scottish American who subsidized Washington and Tuskegee and granted Washington his own private expense account, were glorified in African newspapers.[8] The absence of this type of philanthropist at the International Conference on the Negro at Tuskegee in

1912 may be read from a number of different perspectives as a sign of the worsening of the times for dependence on capitalist philanthropy.

Ethiopianists claimed the middle ground in the spectrum of responses by African Christians to what they perceived as mounting racism among missionaries and Europeans in general. They stood between African Christians who acquiesced to missionary oversight and African Christians who invested their faith in African-led churches. Ethiopianists based their occupancy of the middle on promises that the things missionaries were doing wrong could be changed through African Christian initiative. Industrial education schools were supposed to be the most brilliant demonstration of their argument. By 1920, however, it had become clear that the African Christian initiative to build schools like Tuskegee could not compensate for insufficient funding and government and mission opposition. So the Ethiopianist position gradually lost its viability among African Christians who ceased to believe that Ethiopianist objectives could be achieved within an evangelical framework. Political mobilization was required. The pursuit of Ethiopianists by Garvey and Du Bois has already been mentioned. Ethiopianists were more inclined toward indigenous political movements, however. They founded both the National Congress of British West Africa and, in South Africa, the African National Congress. These developments have been well studied by scholars.[9] Less studied but perhaps as important in another direction was the failure of Ethiopianism to keep alive an African idea of European denominational social welfare. To go back to Dwane's message to Turner, for Africans, nothing was more important for the validation of the A.M.E. Church than the establishment in South Africa of an American-style industrial education school.[10] When such a school did not appear, many of the Africans who migrated first from Methodist (Wesleyan) mission churches to the Ethiopianist Church, before accepting membership in the A.M.E. Church, left the A.M.E. Church to establish African independent churches. The social welfare institutions Ethiopianists promised to build functioned to keep many African Christians interested in European notions of church life, which measured church growth by the number of such institutions built and maintained. When Ethiopianists could not keep their promises, the Christians for whom social welfare institutions were important looked back toward European denominations, while the Christians for whom such institutions were not of consequence created and investigated church experiences more in line with their own cultural sensibilities. Beginning in the

1920s, colonial governments asserted their authority to maintain and oversee all social services. In response to Jones and the British Colonial Office follow-up on the recommendations of the reports of the Phelps Stokes Education Commissions, the Ethiopianist agenda essentially was preempted by the state. With state-maintained schools, hospitals, and other social welfare agencies to use when in need of Western-style social welfare, African Christians estranged from European ideas of faith had even less inclination to bother with mission Christianity.

This text has explained what African Christians did with the idea of industrial education. Other groups of people in Africa, European missionaries and colonial governments, pursued objectives with the idea, but their stories should be recognized as separate from, if interrelated with, the story of African Christians. Industrial education was associated in the African Christian mind with more than just Booker T. Washington and Tuskegee. Education had to do with African Americans and the inspirational model they provided, and with other schools, like Hampton Institute and the African Institute at Colwyn Bay. Still, Washington and his school provided African Christians with both a plan and proof that the plan could work. The fervor African Christians came to express for industrial education reflected their admiration for Washington and their conviction that Washington had decoded the program behind European technological supremacy and then recoded it for African utilization. Washington and the school he founded remain subjects of great controversy among scholars of American history. Most of these debates concern his political activities, however.[11] Washington's legacy as an educator should be approached separately from his legacy as a politician. His achievements as an educator occurred first and created the opportunity for his later movement into national and international politics. And while African Christians for the most part feted Washington for his political exploits, what they wanted to introduce in Africa were his educational innovations. Their resolve to do this in turn prompted European colonial governments, led by the British, to commandeer industrial education and put it to work to build up, rather than tear down, colonial rule.[12] Looking forward, it can be argued that colonial school systems, for all the wealth and authority they had at their command, had no more luck than did Ethiopianists in building industrial education schools.[13] Whatever the nature of the magic the wizard of Tuskegee used to create his school, no one else ever figured out how to copy it.

# Notes

CHAPTER I

1 "Africa and Its Future (Mr. R. B. Blaize in Liverpool)," *Lagos Weekly Record*, October 23, 1897, 4.

2 Andrew Porter, "'Commerce and Christianity': The Rise and Fall of a Nineteenth-Century Missionary Slogan," *Historical Journal* 28, no. 3 (1985): 597–621; and Porter, *Religion versus Empire? British Protestant Missionaries and Overseas Expansion, 1700–1914* (Manchester: Manchester University Press, 2004). See also Brian Stanley, *The Bible and the Flag: Protestant Missions and British Imperialism in the Nineteenth and Twentieth Century* (Leicester: Apollos, 1990).

3 See Roland Oliver and G. N. Sanderson, eds., *The Cambridge History of Africa*, vol. 6, *From 1870–1905* (Cambridge: Cambridge University Press, 1985); Thomas Pakenham, *The Scramble for Africa: White Man's Conquest of the Dark Continent* (New York: Avon Books, 1991); A. Adu Boahen, ed. (UNESCO), *General History of Africa*, vol. 7, *Africa under Foreign Domination 1880–1935* (Berkeley: University of California Press, 1999).

4 See the discussion in Karin Barber, *The Anthropology of Texts, Persons and Politics: Oral and Written Culture in Africa and Beyond* (Cambridge: Cambridge University Press), esp. 152–57.

5 See Philip Zachernuk, *Colonial Subjects: An African Intelligentsia and Atlantic Ideas* (Charlottesville: University of Virginia Press), 2003; Vivian Dickford Smith, "The Betrayal of Creole Elites, 1880–1920," in *Black Experience and the Empire*, ed. Philip Morgan and Sean Hawkins (Oxford: Oxford University Press, 2004), 194–227.

6 See, e.g., Alexander M. MacKay, "The Solution to the African Problem," *Weekly News* (Sierra Leone), March 22, 1890, 2–3; see also Editorial, "The Solution to the African Problem," *Weekly News* (Sierra Leone), March 22, 1890, 4.

7 Edward W. Blyden, *Christianity, Islam and the Negro Race* (Edinburgh: Edinburgh University Press, 1967; first published London, 1887). For Blyden on

this point, see Andrew E. Barnes, "*Christianity, Islam and the Negro Race:
E. W.* Blyden, African Diasporas and the Regeneration of Africa," in *Redefining the African Diaspora: Expressive Cultures and Politics from Slavery to
Independence*, ed. Toyin Falola and Danielle Sanchez (Amherst, N.Y.: Cambria,
2016), 125–54.

8  Stephanie Newall, *The Power to Name: A History of Anonymity in Colonial
West Africa* (Athens: Ohio University Press, 2013), 29–61.

9  See, e.g., "American Negro Progress," *Weekly News* (Sierra Leone),
July 6, 1901, 2.

10  John L. Dube, "Fifty Years of Freedom," *Ilanga lase Natal*, November 15, 1912, 4.

11  "Africa and Its Future (Mr. R. B. Blaize in Liverpool)," *Lagos Weekly Record*,
October 23, 1897, 4.

12  John Tengo Jabavu, Editorial, "Native Opinion," *Imvo Zabantsundu*, October 30, 1890, 3.

13  E. Cornelius May, Editorial, "The African in America," *Weekly News* (Sierra
Leone), July 15, 1899, 4.

14  See Edwin S. Redkey, *Black Exodus: Black Nationalist and the Back to Africa
Movement, 1890–1910* (New Haven: Yale University Press, 1971).

15  "Bishop Ingram and African Repatriation," *Lagos Weekly Record*, September 8, 1894.

16  Edward W. Blyden, *The Return of the Exiles and the West African Church: A
Lecture Delivered at the Breadfruit School House, Lagos, West Africa, January 2, 1891* (London: W. B. Whittingham, 1891), 19–20, 23.

17  "Civilized Barbarians," *Weekly News* (Sierra Leone), November 13, 1909, 7.

18  John P. Jackson, Editorial, "The Civilization of Europe," *Lagos Weekly Record*,
May 19, 1906.

19  "American Negro Academy," *Weekly News* (Sierra Leone), April 9, 1898, 6.

20  "The African Poet," *The Gold Coast Leader*, August 6, 1906, 2–3.

21  E. Cornelius May, Editorial, *Weekly News* (Sierra Leone), March 18, 1911, 5.

22  "The Negro Race in the United States," *West African Reporter*, April 23, 1881, 2.

23  John Tengo Jabavu, Editorial, "Notes on Current Events," *Imvo Zabantsundu*,
January 9, 1890.

24  Alexander Crummell, "The Regeneration of Africa," in his *Africa and America:
Addresses and Discourses* (Springfield, Mass.: Willey, 1891), 437.

25  Crummell, "Regeneration of Africa," in *Africa and America*, 432–53, 442.
On Crummell and his ideas on African regeneration, see also Wilson Jeremiah
Moses, *Alexander Crummell: A Study of Civilization and Discontent* (New
York: Oxford University Press, 1989), 52–195; J. R. Oldfield, *Alexander Crummell (1819–1898) and the Creation of an African-American Church in Liberia*
(Lewiston: E. Mellen, 1990), 25–115.

26  Crummell, "Regeneration of Africa," in *Africa and America*, 436–37.

27  Crummell, "Regeneration of Africa," in *Africa and America*, 439.

28  Crummell, "Regeneration of Africa," in *Africa and America*, 440.

29  Crummell, "Regeneration of Africa," in *Africa and America*, 440.

30 Alexander Crummell, "The Relations and Duties of Free Colored Men in America to Africa," in his *The Future of Africa: Being Addresses, Sermons, Etc., Etc., Delivered in the Republic of Liberia* (New York: Scribner's, 1862), 221–22.

31 Crummell, "Relations and Duties of Free Colored Men," in *Future of Africa*, 234–35.

32 See Crummell, "Regeneration of Africa," in *Africa and America*, 441.

33 See Eric Michael Washington, "Heralding South Africa's Redemption: Evangelicalism and Ethiopianism in the Missionary Philosophy of the National Baptist Convention, USA 1880–1930" (Ph.D. diss., 2 vols., Michigan State University, 2010), 255–308.

34 "An Interesting Academy," *Lagos Weekly Record*, July 3, 1897, 3.

35 Edward W. Blyden, "The Religion for the African People," *Weekly News* (Sierra Leone), May 9, 1903, 2. On Agbebi, see Hazel King, "Cooperation in Contextualization: Two Visionaries of the African Church—Mojola Agbebi and William Hughes of the African Institute, Colwyn Bay," *Journal of Religion in Africa* 16, no. 1 (1986): 2–20. See also See David Killingray, "Passing on the Gospel: Indigenous Mission in Africa," *Transformation: An International Journal of Holistic Mission Studies* 28, no. 2 (2011): 96.

36 Taken from the sermon "The Call of Providence to the Sons of Africa in America," in Edward W. Blyden, *Liberia's Offerings: Being Addresses, Sermons* (New York: John Gray, 1862), 70.

37 "Address by Dr. Blyden," *Southern Workman*, January 1883, 9.

38 Reprint taken from Edward Wilmot Blyden, "Keep Out of Politics: That Is What Dr. Edward Wilmot Blyden Advises the Negro to Do," *Weekly News* (Sierra Leone), March 9, 1895, 2.

39 Edward Wilmot Blyden, "Keep Out of Politics: That Is What Dr. Edward Wilmot Blyden Advises the Negro to Do," *Weekly News* (Sierra Leone), March 9, 1895, 2.

40 See Edward W. Blyden, "The Lagos Literary College and Industrial Training Institute," reprinted in Hollis R. Lynch, ed., *Black Spokesman: Selected Published Writings of Edward Wilmot Blyden* (New York: Humanities Press, 1971), 253–64; Thomas Horatio Jackson, "The Problem of Education in Nigeria," *Lagos Weekly Record*, January 15, 1921.

41 The newspapers were the *Weekly News* (Sierra Leone) and the *Lagos Weekly Record*.

42 See chap. 4 below.

43 "Dr. Edward W. Blyden," *Tsala Ea Batho*, April 1, 1911.

44 See obituaries in *Tsala Ea Batho*, March 9, 1912; *Imvo Zabantsundu*, March 12, 1912.

45 See Paul T. Phillips, *A Kingdom on Earth: Anglo American Social Christianity 1880–1940* (University Park: Pennsylvania State Press, 1996), 83–117; Ralph Luker, *The Social Gospel in Black and White: American Racial Reform 1885–1912* (Chapel Hill: University of North Carolina Press, 1991), 9–88; Jeffrey Cox, *The British Missionary Enterprise since 1700* (New York: Routledge, 2010), 171–240; Richard Elphick, *The Equality of Believers: Protestant Missionaries and the Racial Politics of South Africa* (Charlottesville: University of Virginia Press, 2012), 103–78.

46  An interesting discussion of the Christian understanding of industrial education in the second half of the nineteenth century is presented in Brett H. Smith, *Labor's Millennium: Christianity, Industrial Education, and the Founding of the University of Illinois* (Eugene, Ore.: Wipf & Stock, 2010).

47  J. W. E. Bowen, "The Needs and Possibilities of the Student Volunteer Movement for Foreign Missions among the Colored Students of America," in *The Student Missionary Appeal: Addresses at the Third International Convention of the Student Volunteer Movement for Foreign Missions Held at Cleveland, Ohio, February 23–27, 1898* (New York: Student Volunteer Movement for Foreign Missions, 1898), 163.

48  See, e.g., "No Progress," *Ilanga lase Natal*, March 30, 1906, 4; "The Problem of Education in Nigeria," *Lagos Weekly Record*, January 15, 1921.

## CHAPTER 2

1  Samuel Chapman Armstrong, "Hampton Institute," *Lend a Hand* 6 (1891): 32.

2  The following discussion of Armstrong and his work was framed primarily based upon Robert Francis Engs' two works: *Freedom's First Generation: Black Hampton, Virginia, 1861–1890* (New York: Fordham University Press, 2004; first published Philadelphia: University of Pennsylvania, 1979); and *Educating the Disfranchised and Disinherited: Samuel Chapman Armstrong and Hampton Institute, 1839–1893* (Knoxville: University of Tennessee Press, 1999). These have been supplemented by the two older works: Francis Peabody, *Education for Life: The Story of Hampton Institute* (New York: Doubleday, 1918); Lyman Abbott, "General Samuel Armstrong: Educational Pioneer," in *Silhouettes of My Contemporaries* (New York: Doubleday, 1921), 136–54. On industrial education and industriousness, see Engs, *Educating the Disenfranchised*, 80.

3  See C. Kalani Beyer, "The Connection of Samuel Chapman Armstrong as Both Borrower and Architect of Education in Hawai'i," *History of Education Quarterly* 47, no. 1 (2007): 23–47; C. Kalani Beyer, "Setting the Record Straight: Education of the Heart and Mind Existed in the United States before the 1800's," *American Educational History Journal* 37, no. 1 (2010): 149–67.

4  On Hampton Institute and the education of African Americans after the American Civil War, see James D. Anderson, *The Education of Blacks in the South, 1860–1935* (Chapel Hill: University of North Carolina Press, 1988), esp. 33–78; Adam Fairclough, *A Class of Their Own: Black Teachers in the Segregated South* (Cambridge, Mass.: Harvard University Press, 2007), esp. 99–131.

5  For earlier discussions of Armstrong's ideas on the Christian regeneration of African Americans, see Peabody, *Education for Life*, 195–225; Charles Henry Dickinson, "Samuel Armstrong's Contribution to Christian Missions," *International Review of Missions* 10 (1921): 509–24.

6  Samuel Chapman Armstrong, *Ideas on Education as Expressed by Samuel Chapman Armstrong* (Hampton, Va.: Hampton Institute Press), 1908; *Education for Life* (Hampton, Va.: Hampton Institute Press, 1913)

7  Armstrong, *Education for Life*, 37.

8  Armstrong, *Ideas on Education*, 7.

9  Armstrong, *Ideas on Education*, 6.

10  See Max Weber, *The Protestant Ethic and the Spirit of Capitalism* (Florence, Ky.: Routledge, 2001), 53–101.

11  See Engs, *Educating the Disenfranchised*, 103–7; Anderson, *Education of Blacks in the South*, 49–56; Fairclough, *Class of Their Own*, 121–22.

12  Engs, *Educating the Disenfranchised*, 106.

13  Armstrong, "Hampton Institute," 32.

14  See "Hampton Institute," *New York Times*, April 16, 1889.

15  Louis R. Harlan, "*Up from Slavery* as History and Biography," in Brundage, *Booker T. Washington and Black Progress*, 32.

16  Helen W. Ludlow, "The Hampton Normal and Agricultural Institute," *Harper's New Monthly Magazine* 47 (1873): 672–85.

17  Ludlow, "Hampton Normal," 675.

18  Ludlow, "Hampton Normal," 679.

19  Ludlow, "Hampton Normal," 679.

20  "Hampton Institute," *New York Times*, April 16, 1889.

21  "Hampton Institute," *New York Times*, April 16, 1889.

22  "Hampton Institute," *New York Times*, April 16, 1889.

23  "Hampton Institute," *New York Times*, April 16, 1889.

24  Ludlow, "Hampton Normal," 673.

25  H. M. Turner, "Wayside Dots and Jots," *Christian Recorder*, May 2, 1878, 2.

26  Turner, "Wayside Dots and Jots," 2.

27  Turner, "Wayside Dots and Jots," 2.

28  See Anderson, *Education of Blacks in the South*, 63–72.

29  Engs, *Educating the Disenfranchised*, 135.

30  Engs, *Educating the Disenfranchised*, 130–43.

31  For a classic discussion of the adage, see Roland H. Bainton, *Erasmus of Christendom* (New York: Scribner, 1969), 158.

32  The historiography on Washington is simply too large to usefully list in a footnote. For a helpful bibliographic survey of the various biographies of Washington, see Pero Gaglo Dagbovie, " 'Shadow versus Substance': Deconstructing Booker T. Washington," in his *African American History Reconsidered* (Urbana: University of Illinois Press, 2010), 127–57. For a survey of the latest scholarly treatments of Washington and Tuskegee, see W. Fitzhugh Brundage, ed., *Booker T. Washington and Black Progress: "Up from Slavery" One Hundred Years Later* (Gainesville: University of Florida Press, 2003).

33  See the reprinted articles and illustrations in Michael Scott Beize and Marybeth Gasman, eds., *Booker T. Washington Rediscovered* (Baltimore: Johns Hopkins University Press, 2012).

34  Harry Johnston, "The Negro in America I: The Hampton Institute," *Times* (London), January 13, 1909, 8.

35  Harry Johnston, "The Negro in America II: Tuskegee," *Times* (London), January 15, 1909.

36  Anderson, *Education of Blacks in the South*, 34.

37  See the comments and criticisms of Charles W. Eliot, president of Harvard, who believed that the nursing and minister training programs were too rudimentary in their focus, as noted by Louis R. Harlan, *Booker T. Washington: The Wizard of Tuskegee 1901–1915* (New York: Oxford University Press, 1983), 163;

Robert J. Norrell, *Up from History: The Life of Booker T. Washington* (Cambridge, Mass.: Belknap Press of Harvard University Press, 2009), 363.

38  See Andrew Zimmerman, *Alabama in Africa: Booker T. Washington, the German Empire and the Globalization of the New South* (Princeton: Princeton University Press, 2010).

39  Booker T. Washington, "Twenty-Five Years of Tuskegee," in Beize and Gasman, *Booker T. Washington Rediscovered*, 87.

40  Louis R. Harlan, *Booker T. Washington: The Making of a Black Leader 1856–1901* (New York: Oxford University Press, 1972), 235–36; Harlan, *Washington: The Wizard of Tuskegee*, 145.

41  Engs, *Educating the Disenfranchised*, 152.

42  See Harlan, *Washington: The Wizard of Tuskegee*, 135.

43  See Michael B. Boston, *The Business Strategy of Booker T. Washington: Its Development and Implementation* (Gainesville: University of Florida Press, 2010), 114–28.

44  Engs, *Educating the Disenfranchised*, 155–58.

45  See David Sehat, "The Civilizing Mission of Booker T. Washington," *Journal of Southern History* 73, no. 2 (2007): 323–62, 350.

46  Boston, *Business Strategy of Booker T. Washington*, 56–74, 124–28.

47  Engs, *Freedom's First Generation*, 125.

48  Boston, *Business Strategy of Booker T. Washington*, 75–90; Virginia Lantz Denton, *Booker T. Washington and the Adult Education Movement* (Gainesville: University of Florida Press, 1993), 109–14.

49  Louis R. Harlan, "The Secret Life of Washington," *Journal of Southern History* 37, no. 3 (1971): 393–416, 403.

50  Wilson Moses, "More Than an Artichoke: The Pragmatic Religion of Booker T. Washington," in Brundage, *Booker T. Washington and Black Progress*, 107–30, n1.

51  See Booker T. Washington, *Working with the Hands: Being a Sequel to "Up from Slavery," Covering the Author's Experiences in Industrial Training at Tuskegee* (New York: Doubleday, Page, 1904), 192–96.

52  Washington, *Working with the Hands*, 195.

53  Washington, *Working with the Hands*, 195.

54  Washington, *Working with the Hands*, 195–96.

55  See Max Bennett Thrasher, *Tuskegee: Its Story and Its Work* (Boston: Small, Maynard, 1901), 123.

56  Washington, *Working with the Hands*, 196.

57  Norrell, *Up from History*, 109.

58  For discussion of the "Pastor's Class" at Hampton, see "Rev Israel Lafayette Butt," *Christian Recorder*, March 22, 1900; *What Hampton Graduates Are Doing* (Hampton, Va.: Hampton Institute Press, 1904), 84–90; Robert Russa Moton, *Finding a Way Out: An Autobiography* (New York, Doubleday, 1920) 54–55.

59  Engs, *Educating the Disenfranchised*, 165.

60  See Washington's discussion of the training school in his "The Story of Tuskegee," and "Twenty-Five Years of Tuskegee," both reprinted in Beize and

Gasman, *Booker T. Washington Rediscovered*, 8–16 and 74–92. See also Thrasher, *Tuskegee*, 123–28, esp. 127.

61 Washington, *Working with the Hands*, 198.

62 See Anderson, *Education of Blacks in the South*, 53–54; see also Engs, *Educating the Disenfranchised*, 76–77.

63 Anderson, *Education of Blacks in the South*, 53.

64 See Louis R. Harlan, ed., *The Booker T. Washington Papers*, 14 vols. (Urbana: University of Illinois Press, 1972–89), 3:26 (hereafter *BTWP*).

65 See *BTWP*, 4:194.

66 For a good example of Washington using the expression, see Beize and Gasman, *Booker T. Washington Rediscovered*, 174.

67 *BTWP*, 4:195.

68 Norrell, *Up from History*, 108–9; Ralph E. Luker, "Missions, Institutional Churches and Settlement Houses: The Black Experience 1885–1910," *Journal of Negro History* 69, no. 3/4 (1984): 102; and Luker, *Social Gospel in Black and White*, 132–44.

69 *BTWP*, 3:27.

70 Booker T. Washington, "A Remarkable Triple Alliance," *Outlook*, October 28, 1914, in *BTWP*, 13:149–57.

71 Washington, "Remarkable Triple Alliance," *BTWP*, 13:150.

72 Washington, "Remarkable Triple Alliance," *BTWP*, 13:151.

73 Washington, "Remarkable Triple Alliance," *BTWP*, 13:155.

74 Washington, "Twenty-Five Years of Tuskegee."

75 Louis R. Harlan, "Booker T. Washington and the White Man's Burden," *American Historical Review* 71 (1966): 459n73.

76 Washington, "Twenty-Five Years of Tuskegee."

77 Harlan, *Washington: The Wizard of Tuskegee*, 163–65.

78 Bowen, "Needs and Possibilities of the Student Volunteer Movement for Foreign Missions among the Colored Students of America," 163.

79 See W. E. B. Du Bois, "On the Training of Black Men," in *The Oxford W. E. B. Du Bois Reader*, ed. Eric J. Sundquist (New York: Oxford University Press, 1996), 146–55; Du Bois, "The Training of Negroes for Social Power," *Outlook*, October 17, 1903, 409–14.

80 Du Bois, "Training of Negroes for Social Power," 411.

81 Orishetukeh Faduma, "Success and Drawbacks of Missionary Work in Africa by an Eye-Witness," in *Africa and the American Negro*, ed. J. W. E. Bowen (Atlanta: Gammon Theological Seminary, 1896), 125–36, 130 (emphasis in original).

### CHAPTER 3

1 "One Thing and Another," *Sierra Leone Times*, August 27, 1892, 3.

2 E. Cornelius May, Familiar Talks on Familiar Subjects, *Weekly News* (Sierra Leone), November 13, 1915.

3 Bengt Sundkler, *Bantu Prophets of South Africa* (Oxford: Oxford University Press, 1961), esp. chs. 4 and 5.

4 See R. Hunt Davis, "School versus Blanket and Settler: Elijah Makiwane and the Leadership of the Cape School Community," *African Affairs* 78, no. 310 (1979): 12–31, 14.

5 Davis, "School versus Blanket and Settler," 21.

6 For Soga, see Tolly Branford, "World Visions: Native Missionaries, Mission Networks and Critiques of Colonialism in Nineteenth-Century South Africa and Canada," in *Grappling with the Beast: Indigenous Southern African Responses to Colonialism 1840–1930*, ed. Peter Limb, Norman Etherington, and Peter Midgley (Leiden: Brill, 2010), 311–39, esp. 318–25; Andrew F. Walls, "Distinguished Visitors: Tiyo Soga and Behari Lal Singh in Europe and at Home," in Becker and Stanley, *Europe as the Other*, 243–54. On Holy Johnson, see E. A. Ayandele, *Holy Johnson: Pioneer of African Nationalism, 1836–1917* (London: Frank Cass, 1970); Jehu Hanciles, "The Legacy of James Johnson," *International Bulletin of Missionary Research* 21 (1997): 162–67.

7 Hanciles, "Legacy of James Johnson," 167.

8 See James E. Campbell, *Songs of Zion: The African Methodist Episcopal Church in the United States and South Africa* (New York: Oxford University Press, 1995), 233.

9 E. Cornelius May, Familiar Talks on Familiar Subjects, *Weekly News* (Sierra Leone), November 13, 1915.

10 "The Tutelage Nation," *Ilanga lase Natal*, July 24, 1908.

11 "One Thing and Another," 3.

12 See J. Tengo Jabavu, "Native Races of South Africa," in *Papers on Inter-racial Problems Communicated to the First Universal Races Congress Held at University of London, July 26–29, 1911*, ed. G. Spiller (London: P. S. King & Sons, 1911), 336–41, 339.

13 "Dr. Agbebi's Sermon," *Weekly News* (Sierra Leone), March 21, 1903, 4.

14 "One Thing and Another," 3.

15 Edward W. Blyden, "Study and Race," *Weekly News* (Sierra Leone), May 27, 1893, 2–4; Edward W. Blyden, "Study and Race," *Sierra Leone Times*, May 27, 1893, 2; continued June 3, 1893, 1. On the reprint, see *Weekly News* (Sierra Leone), September 30, 1893.

16 Blyden, "Race and Study," 2.

17 "Education of American Indians," *Christian Express*, September 1, 1879, 7.

18 "Hampton Institute. Sixteenth Anniversary for School for Negroes and Indians," *Christian Express*, September 1, 1884, 135.

19 "Native Africans at Hampton," *Observer* (Liberia), April 8, 1880, 2, 2–3.

20 "Industrial Education in Sierra Leone," *Weekly News* (Sierra Leone), January 4, 1890, 3.

21 "Industrial Education in Sierra Leone," *Weekly News* (Sierra Leone), January 4, 1890, 3.

22 "Industrial Education in Sierra Leone," *Weekly News* (Sierra Leone), January 4, 1890, 3.

23 Geo. L. Curtis, "Hampton and Her Daughters," *Weekly News* (Sierra Leone), July 18, 1891, 2–3.

24 Geo. L. Curtis, "Hampton and Her Daughters," *Weekly News* (Sierra Leone), July 18, 1891, 2–3.

25 Geo. L. Curtis, "Hampton and Her Daughters," *Weekly News* (Sierra Leone), July 18, 1891, 2–3.

26 Samuel Chapman Armstrong, "Elevating the Negro," *Imvo Zabantsundu*, August 6, 1891, 3.

27 James Stewart, "'The Educated Kaffir': Industrial Education; A Sequel," *Christian Express*, September 1, 1880, 3–4, 13–14.

28 Samuel Chapman Armstrong, "Elevating the Negro," *Imvo Zabantsundu*, August 6, 1891, 3.

29 John Tengo Jabavu, Editorial, "The Jubilee Singers," *Imvo Zabantsundu*, October 16, 1890, 3.

30 John Tengo Jabavu, Editorial, "Industrial Education," *Imvo Zabantsundu*, April 14, 1892.

31 *Observer*, April 8, 1880, 3.

32 "Address by Dr. Blyden," *Southern Workman*, January 1883, 9.

33 See Gardner W. Allen, *The Trustees of Donations for Education in Liberia: A Story of Philanthropic Endeavor 1850–1923* (Boston: Thomas Todd, 1923), 47–57.

34 On Dube, see Heather Hughes, *The First President: A Life of John L. Dube, Founding President of the ANC* (Johannesburg: Jacana Media, 2011), xx; see also Shula Marks, "The Ambiguities of Dependency: John L. Dube of Natal," *Journal of Southern African Studies* 1, no. 2 (1975): 160–82; Manning Marable, "African Nationalist: The Life of John Langalibalele Dube" (Ph.D. diss., University of Maryland, 1976); R. Hunt Davis, "John L. Dube: A South African Exponent of Booker T. Washington," *Journal of African Studies* 2, no. 4 (1975/1976): 497–528; Heather Hughes, "Doubly Elite: Exploring the Life of John Langalibalele Dube," *Journal of Southern Africa Studies* 27, no. 3 (2001): 445–58.

35 Marable, "African Nationalist," 162–88; Hughes, *First President*, 87–88. See also Manning Marable, "South African Nationalism in Brooklyn: John L. Dube's Activities in New York State, 1887–1899," *Afro-Americans in New York Life and History* 3, no. 1 (1979): 23–34.

36 Mandikane Cele, "Hampton Lessons," *Southern Workman* 45, no. 3 (1916): 186–88.

37 "Native Education. Letter to the Editor," *Imvo Zabantsundu*, October 22, 1891.

38 Akinsola Akiwowo, "The Place of Mojala Agbebi in African Nationalist Movements 1890–1917," *Phylon* 26, no. 2 (1965): 122–39, 123; King, "Cooperation in Contextualization," 1–16.

39 See King, "Cooperation in Contextualization," 3–4; David Killingray, "Godly Examples and Christian Agents: Training African Missionary Workers in British Institutions in the Nineteenth Century," in Becker and Stanley, *Europe as the Other*, 164–95, 192–94. See also Jeffrey Green's helpful website "Colwyn Bay's African Institute: 1889–1912," *Post Card*, http://www.jeffreygreen.co.uk/colwyn-bays-african-institute-1889-1912.

40 For a sense of the excitement that the African Institute created among West African and mobilization that resulted, see "The Civilisation of Africa. An Important Scheme," *Lagos Weekly Record*, February 3, 1894, 2; "The African

Institute," *Weekly News* (Sierra Leone), May 16, 1896, 4–5; "Colwyn Bay Institute for African Students," *Gold Coast Aborigines*, October 29, 1898, 3.

41  "An Appeal from the Rev. W. Hughes, African Institute, Colwyn Bay," *Weekly News* (Sierra Leone), August 13, 1898, 2–3.

42  Notes and Comments, *Gold Coast Aborigines*, April 26, 1902, 2.

43  On the desire of Hughes to build feeder schools in Africa, see Killingray, "Godly Examples and Christian Agents," 193. For an announcement from the time of this intention, see the *Lagos Weekly Record*, December 10, 1892. According to Hazel King, of the eighty-seven Africans who passed through the African Institute, nineteen of them hailed from southern Nigeria, though she does not note how many of them trained first at Agbowa Industrial Mission. Since Agbebi or one of his supporters sponsored most of the Nigerian students, the suspicion has to be most of them probably got their start at Agbowa. See King, "Cooperation in Contextualization," n9.

44  "Death of Rev. J. E. Ricketts," *Lagos Weekly Record*, November 7, 1908, 5; News, Notes and Comments, *Lagos Standard*, November 4, 1908, 6.

45  Killingray, "Godly Examples and Christian Agents," 193.

46  For an African newspaper report of the closing of Colwyn Bay, see "Collapse of the Colwyn Bay African Institute," *Gold Coast Leader*, April 27, 1912, 2; for an account of the libel trial, see "Sequel to Attack on College for Training African Natives," *Gold Coast Leader*, August 10, 1912, 6 (the newspaper page erroneously dates itself July 10).

47  William Hughes, "Extract of Letter Received from Rev. Hughes of the African Training Institute, Colwyn Bay," *Weekly News* (Sierra Leone), July 30, 1910, 5.

48  General Notes, *Imvo Zabantsundu*, July 13, 1915, 5.

49  *Transvaal Advertiser*, February 2, 1891, as noted in Veit Erlmann, " 'A Feeling of Prejudice': Orpheus M. McAdoo and the Virginia Jubilee Singers in South Africa 1890–1898," *Journal of Southern African Studies* 14, no. 3 (1988): 331–50, 335.

50  J. Mutero Chirenje, *Ethiopianism and Afro-Americans in Southern Africa, 1883–1916* (Baton Rouge: Louisiana State Press, 1987), 33–39; Erlmann, "Feeling of Prejudice," 331–32. See also Robert Trent Vinson, *The Americans Are Coming: Dreams of African American Liberation in Segregationist South Africa* (Athens: Ohio University Press, 2012), 13–22.

51  *Leselinyana*, October 1, 1890, as noted in Erlmann, "Feeling of Prejudice," 344.

52  Erlmann, "Feeling of Prejudice," 345.

53  On Ethiopianism in South Africa, see Chirenje, *Ethiopianism and Afro-Americans in Southern Africa*; Les Switzer, *Power and Resistance in an African Society: The Ciskei Xhosa and the Making of South Africa* (Madison: University of Wisconsin Press, 1993); Elphick, *Equality of Believers*.

54  Switzer, *Power and Resistance*, 178–79.

55  Carol A. Page, "Colonial Reaction to AME Missionaries in South Africa," in Jacobs, *Black Americans and the Missionary Movement in Africa*, 177–95, 180.

56  As quoted in Chirenje, *Ethiopianism and Afro-Americans in Southern Africa*, 56.

57  "Goes to Found a Kaffir College," *Christian Recorder*, March 9, 1899.

58  As quoted in Chirenje, *Ethiopianism and Afro-Americans in Southern Africa*, 75.

59  See Campbell, *Songs of Zion*, 246–47.

60  "Bishop Coppin's African Letter," *Christian Recorder*, July 18, 1901.
61  Campbell, *Songs of Zion*, 235–37.
62  Quoted in Campbell, *Songs of Zion*, 240.
63  For Brander, see the entry under his name in the *Dictionary of African Christian Biography*, http://www.dacb.org/stories/southafrica/brander_samuel.html. On Dwane, see Campbell, *Songs of Zion*, 216–22; also Andrew Paterson, "Education and Segregation in a South African Church: James Dwane and the Order of Ethiopia, 1900–1908," *International Journal of African Studies* 36, no. 3 (2003): 585–605.

CHAPTER 4

1  E. Cornelius May, Familiar Talks on Familiar Subjects, *Weekly News* (Sierra Leone), November 13, 1915.
2  See Booker T. Washington, "Professor Booker T. Washington on Education for the Negro," *Lagos Weekly Recorder*, December 18, 1897; "Professor Booker T. Washington on the Negro in the United States," *Lagos Weekly Recorder*, March 11, 1899; Booker T. Washington, "Tuskegee Institute," *Nigerian Chronicle*, September 6 and 13, 1912. The article was reprinted from the *African Times and Orient Review*, August 1912.
3  Samuel Coleridge-Taylor, "In Defense of the Negro: Why He Should Be Treated Reasonably," *Gold Coast Leader*, August 29, 1908, 2–3.
4  Kelly Miller, "A Visit to Tuskegee," *Weekly News* (Sierra Leone), February 6, 1904, 2–3.
5  For the May brothers and their newspaper, see Christopher Fyfe, "The Sierra Leone Press in the Nineteenth Century," *Sierra Leone Studies* 8 (1957): 226–36, 235.
6  On Jackson, see Robert W. July, *The Origins of Modern African Thought* (New York: Praeger, 1967), 345–65; James S. Coleman, *Nigeria: Background to Nationalism* (Berkeley: University of California Press, 1971), 183–86.
7  See J. Ayondele Langley, *Pan Africanism and Nationalism in West Africa* (Oxford: Clarendon, 1973), 153, 188.
8  The article was reprinted from *Pearson's Magazine*. See *Lagos Weekly Record*, February 16, 1901.
9  *Weekly News* (Sierra Leone), November 12, 1910, 4.
10  Robert Payne Jackson, Editorial, *Lagos Weekly Record*, August 15, 1896.
11  *Weekly News* (Sierra Leone), December 4, 1915, 10.
12  "Mfantsipim School," *Gold Coast Leader*, supplement, August 12, 1905, 1.
13  E. Cornelius May, Familiar Talks on Familiar Subjects, *Weekly News* (Sierra Leone), November 20, 1915, 10.
14  E. Cornelius May, Familiar Talks on Familiar Subjects, *Weekly News* (Sierra Leone), November 20, 1915, 10.
15  See Peter A. Coclanis, "What Made Booker Wash(ington)? The Wizard of Tuskegee in Economic Context," in Brundage, *Booker T. Washington and Black Progress*, 81–106; and Michael Rudolph West, *The Education of Booker T. Washington: American Democracy and the Idea of Race Relations* (New York: Columbia University Press, 2006), 125–26.

16 Booker T. Washington, "Professor Booker T. Washington on Education for the Negro," *Lagos Weekly Record*, December 18, 1897, 6.

17 Booker T. Washington, "Professor Booker T. Washington on Education for the Negro," *Lagos Weekly Record*, December 18, 1897, 6.

18 Booker T. Washington, "Professor Booker T. Washington on Education for the Negro," *Lagos Weekly Record*, December 18, 1897, 6.

19 See C. L. Fleischer, "Training for Girls," *Gold Coast Leader*, supplement, May 26, 1906.

20 Professor Council, "The Negro's Future," *Lagos Weekly Record*, September 26, 1896.

21 J. T. E., "The Government's Proposed Establishment of a Secondary School. Is it a Pressing Necessity for the Colony?" *Weekly News* (Sierra Leone), October 26, 1918, 5.

22 "Our London Letter," *Gold Coast Leader*, June 23, 1906, 3 (emphasis in original).

23 "Our London Letter," *Gold Coast Leader*, June 23, 1906, 3.

24 Edward W. Blyden, "The Negro in the United States," *A.M.E. Church Review*, 1900, 308–31, 330.

25 Edward Wilmot Blyden, "Keep Out of Politics: That Is What Dr. Edward Wilmot Blyden Advises the Negro to Do," *Weekly News* (Sierra Leone), March 9, 1895, 2; summarized in the *Lagos Weekly Record*, March 16, 1895; reprinted also in Lynch, *Black Spokesman*, 205–8.

26 See "Appointment of Dr. Blyden as Political Officer in Lagos," *Lagos Weekly Record*, November 11, 1895, 6; "The Education Question," *Weekly News* (Sierra Leone), June 20, 1896.

27 Reprinted in Lynch, *Black Spokesman*, 253–64.

28 Lynch, *Black Spokesman*, 257–58.

29 Lynch, *Black Spokesman*, 258.

30 See entry on J. Claudius May, *Dictionary of African Christian Biography*, http://www.dacb.org/stories/sierraleone/may_joseph.html.

31 E. Cornelius May, Familiar Talks on Familiar Subjects, *Weekly News* (Sierra Leone), November 13, 1915.

32 E. Cornelius May, Familiar Talks on Familiar Subjects, *Weekly News* (Sierra Leone), November 27, 1916.

33 E. Cornelius May, Familiar Talks on Familiar Subjects, *Weekly News* (Sierra Leone), February 26, 1916.

34 E. Cornelius May, Familiar Talks on Familiar Subjects, *Weekly News* (Sierra Leone), December 4, 1915.

35 E. Cornelius May, Familiar Talks on Familiar Subjects, *Weekly News* (Sierra Leone), February 26, 1916.

36 E. Cornelius May, Familiar Talks on Familiar Subjects, *Weekly News* (Sierra Leone), February 26, 1916.

37 E. Cornelius May, Familiar Talks on Familiar Subjects, *Weekly News* (Sierra Leone), January 29, 1916.

38 E. Cornelius May, Familiar Talks on Familiar Subjects, *Weekly News* (Sierra Leone), November 27, 1915.

39 E. Cornelius May, Familiar Talks on Familiar Subjects, *Weekly News* (Sierra Leone), December 4, 1915.
40 E. Cornelius May, Familiar Talks on Familiar Subjects, *Weekly News* (Sierra Leone), November 27, 1915.
41 "Lecture on Industrial Education," *Weekly News* (Sierra Leone), June 27, 1908, 5.
42 *Weekly News* (Sierra Leone), August 1, 1908, 4.
43 See Sven Beckert, "From Tuskegee to Togo: The Problem of Freedom in the Empire of Cotton," *Journal of American History* (September 2005): 498–526; Zimmerman, *Alabama in Africa*.
44 Editorial Notes, *Gold Coast Leader*, October 3, 1908, 2–3.
45 *Weekly News* (Sierra Leone), September 25, 1909, 6–7 (emphasis in original).
46 Orishatukeh Faduma, "What Does the African Movement Stand For?" *Weekly News* (Sierra Leone), October 3, 1914, 6–7; *Gold Coast Leader*, serialized in October 10, October 17, and October 24, 1914, issues.
47 Orishatukeh Faduma, "What Does the African Movement Stand For?" *Weekly News* (Sierra Leone), October 3, 1914, 7; *Gold Coast Leader*, October 24, 1914, 4.
48 Orishetukeh Faduma, "Drawbacks and Successes in African Missionary Work," *Weekly News* (Sierra Leone), July 1, 1916, 8.
49 Orishetukeh Faduma, "Booker T. Washington," *Weekly News* (Sierra Leone), November 20, 19158.
50 Orishetukeh Faduma, "Drawbacks and Successes in African Missionary Work," *Weekly News* (Sierra Leone), July 1, 1916, 8–9.
51 Orishetukeh Faduma, "Drawbacks and Successes in African Missionary Work," *Weekly News* (Sierra Leone), July 1, 1916, 9.
52 See Moses N. Moore, *Orishatukeh Faduma: Liberal Theology and Evangelical Pan-Africanism, 1857–1946* (Lanham, Md.: Scarecrow, 1996); Langley, *Pan Africanism and Nationalism in West Africa*, 41–103.
53 See Richard A. Corby, "The Bo School and Its Graduates in Colonial Sierra Leone," *Canadian Journal of African Studies* 15, no. 2 (1981): 323–33; Corby, "Educating Africans for Inferiority under British Rule: Bo School in Sierra Leone," *Comparative Education Review* 34, no. 3 (1990): 314–49.
54 "An Old Schoolmaster," "Education in Sierra Leone," *Weekly News* (Sierra Leone), October 5, 1907, 2; "Report of Deuptation to the School for Sons of Chiefs and their Nominees—October 1907," *Weekly News* (Sierra Leone), October 26, 1907, 5; "Elementary Education and the Memorial to Lord Elgin," *Weekly News* (Sierra Leone), November 23, 1907, 8.
55 Editorial, "State Aided Education," *Weekly News* (Sierra Leone), October 30, 1909, 6.
56 "Lagos Intelligence," *Weekly News* (Sierra Leone), July 25, 1896, 6.
57 See "Victors—Multum in Parvo," *Weekly News* (Sierra Leone), September 19, 1896, 2.
58 See the articles "Education Scheme," *Lagos Weekly Record*, August 15, 1896; "The Influence of Extraneous Culture by a Young Patriot," *Lagos Weekly Record*, March 13, 1897; C. A. Sarapa Williams, "The Proposed Lagos Government College," *Lagos Weekly Record*, December 8, 1906. See also "Higher

Education," Sierra Leone *Weekly News*, October 7, 1899; "Educational Progress in Lagos," *Lagos Standard*, October 27, 1909.

59 See "A Proposed System of Education for West Africa," *West African Mail*, February 22, 1907, 8–9; Editorial, *West African Mail*, February 22, 1907, 2–3.

60 E. D. Morel, Editorial, *West African Mail*, February 22, 1907, 3.

61 "West African Education," *Weekly News* (Sierra Leone), March 9, 1907, 2; "West African Education," *Lagos Weekly Record*, March 16, 1907, 4–5; "Proposed Scheme for the Education of the Youths of Yorubaland," *Lagos Standard*, March 27, 1907, 4–5.

62 E. Cornelius May, Editorial, *Weekly News* (Sierra Leone), March 9, 1907.

63 "Janus," Lagosian on Dits, *Lagos Standard*, April 29, 1908, 4; "The Education for the Native," May 13, 1908, 5.

64 "A Moribund Scheme," *Lagos Standard*, August 2, 1911, 4–5. See also *Lagos Standard*, April 7, 1915.

65 News Telegram, *Lagos Standard*, January 26, 1910, 6; "Janus," Lagosian on Dits, *Lagos Standard*, February 2, 1910, 4.

66 G. Rome Hall, "Sir Alfred Jones Charity for West Africa," *Lagos Weekly Record*, June 25, 1910, 5; Letter to the Editor, *Lagos Weekly Record*, July 16, 1910, 5.

67 "Janus," Lagosian on Dits, *Lagos Standard*, April 23, 1913.

68 "Conference at Government House, Technical and Industrial Education," *Weekly News* (Sierra Leone), July 7, 1917, 5.

69 "Native Energy," *Lagos Standard*, September 25, 1907, 5.

70 News, Notes and Comments, *Lagos Standard*, October 2, 1907, 3.

71 "The Blyden Memorial, Lagos," *Lagos Standard*, August 28, 1912, 6.

72 The example of the advertisement used here is taken from the *Gold Coast Nation*, March 8, 1919, 4.

73 See "The Girls Industrial and Literary Institute," *Weekly News* (Sierra Leone), November 18, 1922, 5.

74 "Announcement," *Weekly News* (Sierra Leone), April 3, 1920, 10. For a description of the event and a sense of the speeches, see "Vocational Education: A Great Locale Scheme," *Weekly News* (Sierra Leone), April 10, 1920, 8–9.

75 "The Proposed Technical and Industrial School for Girls," *Weekly News* (Sierra Leone), June 12, 1920, 5; Ma Mashado, "The Proposed Technical and Industrial School for Girls," *Weekly News* (Sierra Leone), June 12, 1920, 8.

76 "An Appreciation," *Weekly News* (Sierra Leone), June 19, 1920, 5.

77 "The Industrial School for Girls," *Weekly News* (Sierra Leone), December 11, 1920, 8.

78 *BTWP*, 4:195.

79 Thomas Horatio Jackson, "The Problem of Education in Nigeria," *Lagos Weekly Record*, January 15, 1921, 5.

80 See Thomas Horatio Jackson, "The Problem of Education in Nigeria," *Lagos Weekly Record*, January 15, 1921, 5.

81 Thomas Horatio Jackson, "The Problem of Education in Nigeria," *Lagos Weekly Record*, January 15, 1921, 5.

82 "Mr. Carr's Speech at the Dinner Given by the Reform to the Phelps-Stokes Education Commission," *Nigerian Pioneer*, November 26, 1920, 6.

83  Printed list of Chiefs' requests inserted as pp. 8a and 8b in *Nigerian Pioneer*, March 24, 1922.
84  Langley, *Pan Africanism and Nationalism in West Africa*, 147.

### CHAPTER 5

1  Mahatma Gandhi, *Indian Opinion*, March 17, 1906.
2  On African newspapers in South Africa, see Les Switzer, "The African Christian Community and Its Press in Victorian South Africa," *Cahiers d'Etudes Africaines* 24, no. 96 (1984): 455–76; Switzer, ed., *South Africa's Alternative Press: Voices of Protest and Resistance 1880s–1960s* (Cambridge: Cambridge University Press, 1997).
3  See Chirenje, *Ethiopianism and Afro-Americans in Southern Africa*, 132.
4  See D. D. T. Jabavu, *The Life of John Tengo Jabavu, Editor of Imvo Zabantsundu 1884–1921* (Lovedale, Cape Providence, S. Africa: Lovedale Institute Press, 1922), 110–22.
5  *Ilanga lase Natal*, February, 19, 1909, 4.
6  "Tuskegee," *Ilanga lase Natal*, May 19, 1911.
7  See "The Salvation of the Native," *Ilanga lase Natal*, July 3, 1903, 4.
8  See André Odendaal, *Black Protest Politics in South Africa until 1912* (Totowa, N.J.: Barnes & Noble, 1985), 31–32; Switzer, *Power and Resistance in an African Society*, 156.
9  See Editor's Corner, *Izwi Labantu*, November 5, 1901.
10  "Negro Philistines," *Izwi Labantu*, February 4, 1908, 2.
11  "Negro Leadership at Fault," *Izwi Labantu*, July 28, 1908, 3.
12  "The Same Problem in Two Countries," *Christian Express*, May 1, 1905, 1. For another example of Stewart making the same point, see Campbell, *Songs of Zion*, 215–48, 307. For a rebuttal of the argument by Dube, see "Dr. Washington," *Ilanga lase Natal*, August 21, 1903, 4.
13  "Booker Washington and Tuskegee," *Christian Express*, May 1, 1906, 10 (emphasis in original).
14  See Booker T. Washington, "The Educational and Industrial Emancipation of the Negro I," *Christian Express*, July 1, 1908, 109–10; Booker T. Washington, "The Educational and Industrial Emancipation of the Negro II," *Christian Express*, August 1, 1908, 136–37; Booker T. Washington, "The Educational and Industrial Emancipation of the Negro III," *Christian Express*, September 1, 1908, 150–51.
15  "Booker T. Washington on Country Schools," *Christian Express*, January 1, 1910, 173; "Dr. Booker T. Washington on the Negro Problem," *Christian Express*, January 2, 1911, 8.
16  Editor's Corner, *Izwi Labantu*, November 5, 1901, 3.
17  James Henderson, "Technical Education," *Christian Express*, February 1, 1907, 9.
18  See Sir Harry Johnston, "The Negro in America," *Christian Express*, May 1, 1909, 82.
19  Editorial Notes, *Ilanga lase Natal*, January 8, 1909, 4.
20  Sir Harry Johnston, "The Negro in America," *Christian Express*, March 1, 1909, 82.

21 "Progress and Aims of the Inter-State Native College Scheme," *Christian Express*, March 1, 1907, 47.

22 See "Missionary Raiders," *Christian Express*, April 1, 1898, 45–46; "Missionary Raiders II," *Christian Express*, May 2, 1898, 65–66; "Will a Reformation Be Necessary in Africa?" *Christian Express*, November 1, 1899, 165–66.

23 Chirenje, *Ethiopianism and Afro-Americans in Southern Africa*, 122–26; Elphick, *Equality of Believers*, 87–91.

24 Davis, "John L. Dube," 497–528.

25 See Editorial Notes, *Izwi Labantu*, August 27, 1901, 3; Chirenje, *Ethiopianism and Afro-Americans in Southern Africa*, 136.

26 Quoted from Campbell, *Songs of Zion*, 249.

27 George Shepperson, "Ethiopianism: Past and Present," in Baeta, *Christianity in Tropical Africa*, 250–60, 252.

28 Chirenje, *Ethiopianism and Afro-Americans in Southern Africa*, 126.

29 Chirenje, *Ethiopianism and Afro-Americans in Southern Africa*, 126.

30 Chirenje, *Ethiopianism and Afro-Americans in Southern Africa*, 122.

31 Chirenje, *Ethiopianism and Afro-Americans in Southern Africa*, 101–11.

32 Chirenje, *Ethiopianism and Afro-Americans in Southern Africa*, 122.

33 For the "self defense" comment, see Campbell, *Songs of Zion*, 249.

34 See Chirenje, *Ethiopianism and Afro-Americans in Southern Africa*, 118–43.

35 Chirenje, *Ethiopianism and Afro-Americans in Southern Africa*, 128; but see also Letter to the Editor, *Christian Express*, December 1, 1905, 178.

36 The life of Jabavu has been the focus of surprisingly little historical research. See Switzer, *Power and Resistance in an African Society*, 136–80; Switzer, "African Christian Community," 465–66. See also D. D. T. Jabavu, *Life of John Tengo Jabavu*.

37 See Chirenje, *Ethiopianism and Afro-Americans in Southern Africa*, 132.

38 For an earlier use of Stewart's "apothegm," see "Sir John Rodgers Views," *Imvo Zabantsundu*, February 1, 1910, 1.

39 Jabavu, "Native Races of South Africa," 338.

40 See "Race and Religion," *Imvo Zabantsundu*, May 11, 1898, 5, reprint from *Christian Express*, May 2, 1898.

41 "The Jubilee Singers," *Imvo Zabantsundu*, October 16, 1890, 3.

42 See Chirenje, *Ethiopianism and Afro-Americans in Southern Africa*, esp. 168–72.

43 See "Native Petitions to the High Commissioner and Governors," *Christian Express*, December 1, 1905. See also Odendaal, *Black Protest Politics in South Africa until 1912*, 66–67; Chirenje, *Ethiopianism and Afro-Americans in Southern Africa*, 128–32.

44 Chirenje, *Ethiopianism and Afro-Americans in Southern Africa*, 131; Odendaal, *Black Protest Politics in South Africa until 1912*, 167.

45 According to Chirenje, *Ethiopianism and Afro-Americans in Southern Africa*, by 1907, more than £43,000 had been promised, and by 1914, all £50,000 had been pledged. In the paper he presented at the Universal Congress of Races in 1911, Jabavu noted that, of the £50,000, so far £23,000 had been raised by "European sources," while £17,000 had been raised by "Native sources." See Jabavu, "Native Races of South Africa," 341.

46   Odendaal, *Black Protest Politics in South Africa until 1912*, 66–67; Chirenje, *Ethiopianism and Afro-Americans in Southern Africa*, 128–32.

47   Gandhi, *Indian Opinion*, March 17, 1906.

48   Campbell, *Songs of Zion*, 306–7.

49   Odendaal, *Black Protest Politics in South Africa until 1912*, 67.

50   Odendaal, *Black Protest Politics in South Africa until 1912*, 113.

51   Paul B. Rich, "The Appeal of Tuskegee: James Henderson, Lovedale and the Fortunes of South African Liberalism, 1906–1930," *International Journal of African Historical Studies* 20, no. 2 (1987): 271–92, 276.

52   See, e.g., "The Conference," *Imvo Zabantsundu*, May 5, 1908, 4; "The Conference," *Imvo Zabantsundu*, May 26, 1908, 4; "Basutoland," *Imvo Zabantsundu*, May 26, 1908, 4.

53   "The Native College in the Senate," *Imvo Zabantsundu*, January 3, 1911, 4.

54   "£10,000 for the College," *Imvo Zabantsundu*, February 5, 1907, 6.

55   "Hari-Kari," *Imvo Zabantsundu*, April 8, 1913, 7. The money was later restored. See D. D. T. Jabavu, *Life of John Tengo Jabavu*, 102.

56   See "Lovedale Missionary Institute College Department" advertisement, *Imvo Zabantsundu*, February 7, 1911, 2; Lovedale News, *Christian Express*, August 1, 1910, 130; Lovedale News, *Christian Express*, July 1, 1911, 103.

57   Rich, "Appeal of Tuskegee," 276–78.

58   Rich, "Appeal of Tuskegee," 277.

59   See Catherine Higgs, *The Ghost of Inequality: The Public Lives of D. D. T. Jabavu of South Africa 1885–1959* (Athens: Ohio University Press, 1997), 23–29; D. D. T. Jabavu, *The Black Problem: Papers and Addresses on Various Native Problems* (Lovedale, Cape Providence, S. Africa: Lovedale Institute Press, 1920).

60   "Booker Washington's Methods," *Imvo Zabantsundu*, August 26, 1913, 7. See also "Mr. D. Tengo Jabava," *Imvo Zabantsundu*, July 8, 1913, 9; "A South African Abroad," *Imvo Zabantsundu*, November 18, 1913, 7.

61   David Kerr, *Fort Hare: Evolution of an African College* (London: C. Hurst, 1968), 3–32.

62   Kerr, *Fort Hare*, 92–102.

63   Rich, "Appeal of Tuskegee," 278.

64   "Prof's Kerr's Inaugural," *Imvo Zabantsundu*, March 21, 1916, 5.

65   "Prof's Kerr's Inaugural," *Imvo Zabantsundu*, March 21, 1916, 5.

66   "Another Professor Wanted," *Imvo Zabantsundu*, March 28, 1916, 5.

67   Campbell, *Songs of Zion*, 257.

68   "Land in U.S.A.," *Imvo Zabantsundu*, May 4, 1915.

69   On Dube's life, see Hughes, *First President*, xx. In addition, see Marks, "Ambiguities of Dependency," 160–82; Marable, "African Nationalist"; Hughes, "Doubly Elite," 445–58.

70   D. T. T. Jabavu, *Life of John Tengo Jabavu*, 95.

71   "Teacher of His Tribe: Americanized Zulu Goes to Civilize His People with School and Plowshare," *Washington Post*, April 30, 1899.

72   John L. Dube, "Practical Christianity among the Zulu," *Missionary Review of the World*, May 1907, 370–73, 372.

73   "Teacher of His Tribe"; Dube, "Practical Christianity among the Zulu," 372–73.

74 "Mr. Booker Washington Approached," *Ilanga lase Natal*, June 19, 1903, 3.

75 John L. Dube, "The Salvation of the Native," *Ilanga lase Natal*, July 3, 1903, 3.

76 Dube, "Practical Christianity among the Zulu," 371.

77 W. T. Stead, "Interview on Topics of the Month: 132—An Appeal from the Zulu: Mr. J. L. Dube," *Review of Reviews*, July 1909, 530.

78 See Marable, "South African Nationalism in Brooklyn," 23–34.

79 Marable, "African Nationalist," 162–88; Hughes, *First President*, 87–88.

80 See "A Zulu's Account of a Zulu Enterprise," *Outlook*, 1910, 290–91, 290.

81 Stead, "Interview on Topics of the Month," 530.

82 Dube, "Practical Christianity among the Zulu," 372.

83 "Training of Natives. An Industrial Ideal," *Ilanga lase Natal*, January 8, 1909, 4; Marable, "African Nationalist," 121–61; Hughes, *First President*, 89–104.

84 "Training of Natives. An Industrial Ideal," *Ilanga lase Natal*, January 8, 1909, 4.

85 Marable, "African Nationalist," 122–28.

86 "Education and Training. Evidence before the Commission," *Ilanga lase Natal*, January 10, 1908, 4.

87 "Native Education. An Increasing Demand," *Ilanga lase Natal*, August 18, 1911, 4. See also "Fear Not Improvement," *Ilanga lase Natal* October 12, 1906, 4.

88 "Training of Natives. An Industrial Ideal," *Ilanga lase Natal*, January 8, 1909, 4.

89 "Training of Natives. An Industrial Ideal," *Ilanga lase Natal*, January 8, 1909, 4.

90 Hughes, *First President*, 96.

91 "Training of Natives. An Industrial Ideal," *Ilanga lase Natal*, January 8, 1909, 4.

92 Hughes, *First President*, 97–99.

93 Hughes, *First President*, xx.

94 John L. Dube, "Character Building," *Ilanga lase Natal*, August 2, 1907, 4.

95 John L. Dube, "Fifty Years of Freedom," *Ilanga lase Natal*, November 15, 1912, 4.

96 "Swazi Appreciation of Mr. Dube," *Ilanga lase Natal*, April 30, 1915, 5.

97 *Missionary Review of the World*, August 1914, 628–29.

98 John L. Dube, "The Black Problem in South Africa," *Missionary Review of the World*, March 1916, 205–7. For another example of Dube's absorption with the Native Land Act, see *The Anti-slavery Reporter and Aboriginal's Friend*, vol. 4, 5th ser., 1914–1915, 76–79.

99 Hughes, *First President*, 204.

100 "Ohlange Institute," *Ilanga lase Natal*, January 28, 1921, 4.

101 Hughes, *First President*, 212–13.

102 The title of the treatise in Zulu was *Isita somuntu nguye uqobo Iwakhe*. First published in 1922, the treatise was such a success that Dube published a revised and expanded version in 1928. See Hughes, *First President*, 213–14.

## Chapter 6

1 James Denton, "The Negro Problem in the States. A Solution," *Weekly News* (Sierra Leone), December 28, 1912, 4–5.

2 Booker T. Washington Papers, U.S. Library of Congress (hereafter BTW Papers [LC]).

3 Harlan, "White Man's Burden," 441–67, 465.

4 Booker T. Washington, "Industrial Education in Africa," *Independent*, no. 60, March 15, 1906, 616–19; reprinted in Harlan, *Booker T. Washington Papers*, 8:548–53, 548.
5 Washington, "Industrial Education in Africa," 549.
6 Washington, "Industrial Education in Africa," 548.
7 Washington, "Industrial Education in Africa," 551–52. For Stewart's comparisons between Tuskegee and Lovedale, see "Booker Washington and His Work," *Christian Express*, May 1, 1902, 65–66; "The Same Problem in Two Countries," *Christian Express*, May 1, 1905, 65–66.
8 Washington, "Industrial Education in Africa," 551–52. See also Harlan, "White Man's Burden," 450.
9 "International Conference on Africa," *Tsala Ea Becoana*, February 11, 1911, 1. *Tsala* took the story from the *Washington Bee*.
10 See "A Tuskegee Conference," *Ilanga lase Natal*, February 24, 1911, 4; "International Conference on the Negro," *Imvo Zabansundu*, July 11, 1911, 6; "International Conference on the Negro," *Lagos Weekly Record*, September 16, 1911, 4; "Dr. Booker T. Washington's Invitation," *Gold Coast Leader*, November 18, 1911, 2–3.
11 See Boston, *Business Strategy of Booker T. Washington*, 75–90.
12 Boston, *Business Strategy of Booker T. Washington*, 91–113.
13 "International Conference on the Negro," Tuskegee Records, BTW Papers (LC), reel 716.
14 BTW Papers (LC). See also the articles referenced in n10.
15 Weekly Notes, *Lagos Weekly Record*, September 16, 1911, 3.
16 "Dr. Booker T. Washington's Invitation," *Gold Coast Leader*, November 18, 1911, 3.
17 "A Tuskegee Conference," *Ilanga lase Natal*, February 24, 1911, 4.
18 "International Conference on the Negro," *Imvo Zabantsundu*, July 11, 1911, 6.
19 BTW Papers (LC).
20 A. W. Baker, "The First International Congress of the Negro," *Missionary Review of the World*, June 1912, 440–42.
21 BTW Papers (LC).
22 BTW Papers (LC).
23 BTW Papers (LC).
24 See Robert E. Park, "The International Conference of the Negro," *Southern Workman* 41, no. 6 (1912), 347–52. Park also published a version aimed more at academic audiences. See Robert E. Park, "Tuskegee International Conference of the Negro," *Journal of Race Development* 3 (1912–1913): 117–20. To list only the versions of the article published in journals aimed at African audiences, "The Conference on the Negro in America," *Lagos Weekly Record*, June 1, 1912, 4–7; "The Conference on the Negro in America," *Weekly News* (Sierra Leone), June 29, 1912, 5–6; "International Conference of the Black Man," *Tsala Ea Becoana*, June 1, 1912, 3; "The Negro in Conference at Tuskegee Institute," *African Times and Orient Review*, July 1912, 10–12; "International Conference on the Negro," *Gold Coast Leader*, June 8, 1912, 6; *Ilanga lase Natal*, June 21, 1912; *Lagos Weekly Report*, June 1, 1912.
25 Baker, "First International Congress of the Negro," 440.

26 Baker, "First International Congress of the Negro," 440.

27 BTW Papers (LC).

28 BTW Papers (LC).

29 Baker, "First International Congress of the Negro," 442.

30 F. A. Pinanko, "Report on the International Conference of the Negro Held at Tuskegee April 17, 18, 19, 1912," *Gold Coast Nation*, February 6, 1913.

31 Maurice Evans, "The International Conference of the Negro," *Christian Express*, October 1, 1912.

32 BTW Papers (LC).

33 BTW Papers (LC).

34 The press release did not mention that all power to plan the conference was actually vested in another committee composed of Washington and his two lieutenants, Park and Scott, and Frissell of Hampton. It is not clear that the either committee ever met. See BTW Papers (LC).

35 James Denton, "The Negro Problem in America: A Solution," *Church Missionary Review* 63 (1912): 654–59.

36 See for example, "The Native College," *Imvo Zabantsundu*, September 23, 1913, 7; "College Constitution," *Ilanga lase Natal*, February 5, 1915, 5.

37 E. Cornelius May, "The Acting Principal of Fourah Bay College and Tuskegee in United States of America," *Weekly News* (Sierra Leone), December 28, 1912, 6–7.

38 Ahguyahvee, "Some of Our Present Needs," *Weekly News* (Sierra Leone), March 29, 1913, 8.

39 "A Pronounced View," *Ilanga lase Natal*, November 23, 1915, 5.

40 The Month, *Christian Express*, July 1, 1912, 98–99.

41 Letter to the Editor, *Christian Express*, September 2, 1912, 147–48.

42 "The African Rhetoricals," *Tsala ea Batho*, May 22, 1915, 2.

43 Lagosians On Dits, *Lagos Standard*, November 24, 1915, 4.

44 E. Cornelius May, Familiar Talks on Familiar Subjects, *Weekly News* (Sierra Leone), November 27, 1915.

45 Orishetukeh Faduma, "Booker T. Washington," *Weekly News* (Sierra Leone), November 20, 1915, 9. The piece was reprinted in the *Gold Coast Nation* on December 30, 1915.

46 A. O. Delo-Dosumu, "Booker T. Washington," *Lagos Standard*, December 1, 1915, 5. For Delo-Dosumu's background, see News, Notes, and Comments, *Lagos Standard*, February 17, 1915, 4. Like Faduma's piece, Delo-Domusu's obituary was reprinted in the December 30 issue of the *Gold Coast Nation*.

47 A. O. Delo-Dosumu, "Booker T. Washington," *Lagos Standard*, December 1, 1915, 5.

48 Les Switzer, "*Bantu World* and the Origins of the Captive African Commercial Press in South Africa," *Journal of Southern African Studies* 14, no. 3 (1988): 351–70.

49 "Dr. Booker T. Washington," *Imvo Zabantsundu*, November 23, 1915, 5.

50 "Booker T. Washington. A Character Sketch," *Imvo Zabantsundu*, November 30, 1915, 5.

51 The Month, *Christian Express*, December 1, 1915, 180.

52 "Booker T. Washington, Noted Coloured Educator, Dies," *Ilanga lase Natal*, January 14, 1916, 5.

53 "The Funeral of Booker T. Washington," *Ilanga lase Natal*, February 25, 1916.

54 Langley, *Pan Africanism and Nationalism in West Africa*, 89–103; Vinson, *Americans Are Coming*.

55 "Negro Enterprise," *Lagos Weekly Record*, February 7, 1920, 5.

56 "The Marcus Garvey Movement," *Gold Coast Leader*, December 18, 1920, 4.

57 See Edmund David Cronin, *Black Moses: The Story of Marcus Garvey and Universal Negro Improvement Agency* (Madison: University of Wisconsin Press, 1968); Tony Martin, *Race First: The Ideological and Organizational Struggles of Marcus Garvey and the Universal Negro Improvement Agency* (Norwich, Conn.: Greenwood, 1976); Mary Rolinson, *Grassroots Garveyism: The United Negro Improvement Agency in the Rural South* (Chapel Hill: University of North Carolina Press, 2007). Robert A. Hill, ed., *The Marcus Garvey and Universal Negro Improvement Agency Papers*, 10 vols. (University of California Press, 1983–1995) is the essential source of information on Garvey.

58 See "U.N.I.A. of Lagos," *Lagos Weekly Report*, October 23, 1920, 6.

59 See *Marcus Garvey Papers*, 4:719, 1036; Kevern Verney, *The Art of the Possible: Booker T. Washington and Black Leadership in the United States, 1881–1925* (New York: Routledge, 2001), 113, 124.

60 Vinson, *Americans Are Coming*, 109.

61 "Two Distinguished Visitors," *Ilanga lase Natal*, April 15, 1921, 2.

62 See Sylvia Jacobs, "James Emman Kwegyir Aggrey: An African Intellectual in the United States," *Journal of Negro History* 81, nos. 1–4 (1996): 47–61. In addition, see Kenneth King, *Pan Africanism and Education: A Study of Race Philanthropy and Education in the Southern United States and East Africa* (Oxford: Clarendon, 1971), esp. 95–127; Edward H. Berman, "Education in Africa and America: A History of the Phelps Stokes Fund, 1911–1945" (Ed.D. diss., Columbia University, 1970).

63 See U.S. Department of the Interior, Bureau of Education, *Negro Education: A Study of the Private and Higher Schools for Colored People in the United States*, prepared in cooperation with the Phelps-Stokes Fund under the direction of Thomas Jesse Jones, specialist in the education of racial groups (Washington, D.C.: Government Printing Office, 1917).

64 Berman, "Education in Africa and America," 90; Stephen Taylor Correia, " 'For Their Own Good': An Historical Analysis of the Educational Thought of Thomas Jesse Jones" (Ph.D. diss., Pennsylvania State University 1993), 257.

65 See African Education Committee, *Education in Africa: A Study of West, South, and Equatorial Africa by the African Education Commission, under the Auspices of the Phelps-Stokes Fund and Foreign Mission Societies of North America and Europe*, report prepared by Thomas Jesse Jones, chairman of the commission (New York: Phelps Stokes Fund, 1922), 86; African Education Committee, *Education in East Africa: A Study of East, Central and South Africa by the Second African Education Commission under the Auspices of the Phelps-Stokes Fund, in Cooperation with the International Education Board*, report prepared by Thomas Jesse Jones (New York: Phelps Stokes Fund, 1925), 87–88. See also

Thomas Jesse Jones, "A Good Word for Missionaries," *Current History*, July 1, 1926, 539–44.

66  *Gold Coast Leader*, August 28, 1920, 5.
67  Epitome of the News, *Lagos Weekly Record*, November 13, 1920, 7.
68  See, e.g., "The Education Commission," *Gold Coast Nation*, October 23, 1920, 5.
69  "A Notable Visitor," *Umteteli wa Bantu*, April 9, 1921, 2.
70  "Lovedale and Fort Hare," *Imvo Zabantsundu*, May 12, 1922, 7.
71  Jacobs, "Aggrey," 56.
72  See King, *Pan Africanism and Education*, 87–94.
73  See Paul Gilroy, *The Black Atlantic: Modernity and Double Consciousness* (London: Verso Books, 1993).

## CONCLUSION

1  For extended discussions of this point, with consideration of the relevant bibliography, please see Andrew E. Barnes, "Aryanizing Projects: African Collaborators and Colonial Transcripts," in *Antimonies of Modernity*, ed. Vasant Kaiwar (Durham, N.C.: Duke University Press, 2003), 62–97; Barnes, *Making Headway: The Introduction of Western Civilization in Colonial Northern Nigeria* (Rochester, N.Y.: University of Rochester Press, 2009), chap. 2.
2  E. D. Morel, *Nigeria, Its Peoples, Its Problems* (London: Cass Reprints, 1968), 216.
3  See V. G. Keirnan, *The Lords of Human Kind: Black Man, Yellow Man, and White Man in an Age of Empire* (Boston: Little, Brown, 1969); Douglas Lorimer, *Colour, Class and the Victorians: English Attitudes toward the Negro in the Mid-nineteenth Century* (Leicester: Leicester University Press; New York: Holmes & Meier, 1978); George M. Fredrickson, *White Supremacy: A Comparative Study in American and South African History* (New York: Oxford University Press, 1981); Michael Adas, *Machines as the Measure of Man: Science, Technologies and Ideologies of Western Dominance* (Ithaca, N.Y.: Cornell University Press, 1989).
4  Lagosians on Dits, *Lagos Standard*, November 24, 1915, 4. See chap. 6 above.
5  Thomas Jesse Jones, *Education in Africa*, 39.
6  "The Industrial School for Girls," *Weekly News* (Sierra Leone), December 11, 1920, 8. See chapter 4 above.
7  In addition to Engs, *Educating the Disenfranchised*, 103–7; Anderson, *Education of Blacks in the South*, 49–56; Fairclough, *Class of Their Own*, 121–22; see Donald A. Spivey, "The African Crusade for Black Industrial Schooling," *Journal of Negro History* 63, no. 1 (1978): 1–17; V. P. Franklin, "Pan African Connections, Transnational Connections, Transnational Education, Collective Cultural Capital and Opportunities Industrialization Centers International," *Journal of African American History* 96, no. 1 (2011): 44–61.
8  On Jones, see "Mr. Alfred P. Jones," *Sierra Leone Times*, December 24, 1892, 3; "The New Governor of Lagos," *Lagos Weekly Record*, April 24, 1897, 5. On Carnegie, see "A Millionaire and the Negro Race," *Gold Coast Leader*, June 6, 1903, 4.

9   On West Africa, see Langley, *Pan Africanism and Nationalism in West Africa*. On South Africa, see Chirenje, *Ethiopianism and Afro-Americans in Southern Africa*; Switzer, *Power and Resistance in an African Society*; Hughes, *First President*; Elphick, *Equality of Believers*.

10  See chap. 5 above.

11  For historiography on Washington, chap. 2, n. 32 above.

12  Seppe Sivonen, *White-Collar or Hoe Handle: African Education under British Colonial Policy 1920–1945* (Helsinki: Soumen Historiallinen Seura, 1995); Aaron Windel, "British Colonial Education in Africa: Policy and Practice in the Era of Trusteeship," *History Compass* 7, no. 1 (2009): 9–13.

13  See L. J. Lewis, *Educational Policy and Practice in British Tropical Areas* (London: Thomas Nelson, 1954).

# Works Cited

List of African newspapers accessed online via the World Newspaper Archive (Center for Research Libraries)

*Gold Coast Aborigines*
*Gold Coast Chronicle*
*Gold Coast Independent*
*Gold Coast Leader*
*Gold Coast Nation*
*Gold Coast Times*
*Ilanga Lase Natal*
*Imvo Zabantsundu*
*Izwi Labantu*
*Lagos Observer*
*Lagos Standard*
*Lagos Weekly Record*
*Leselinyana La Lesutho*
*Liberia Recorder*
(Liberia) *Observer*
*Nigerian Chronicle*
*Nigerian Pioneer*
*Sierra Leone Guardian and Foreign Mail*
*Sierra Leone Times*
*Sierra Leone Weekly News*
*Times of Nigeria*

*Tsala Ea Batho*
*Umteteli Wa Bantu*
*West African Mail*
*West African Reporter*

Abbott, Lyman. "General Samuel Armstrong: Educational Pioneer." In *Silhouettes of My Contemporaries*, 136–54. New York: Doubleday, 1921.

Adas, Michael. *Machines as the Measure of Man: Science, Technologies and Ideologies of Western Dominance*. Ithaca, N.Y.: Cornell University Press, 1989.

African Education Committee. *Education in Africa: A Study of West, South, and Equatorial Africa by the African Education Commission, under the Auspices of the Phelps-Stokes Fund and Foreign Mission Societies of North America and Europe*. Report prepared by Thomas Jesse Jones, chairman of the commission. New York: Phelps Stokes Fund, 1922.

———. *Education in East Africa: A Study of East, Central and South Africa by the Second African Education Commission under the Auspices of the Phelps-Stokes Fund, in Cooperation with the International Education Board*. Report prepared by Thomas Jesse Jones. New York: Phelps Stokes Fund, 1925.

Akiwowo, Akinsola. "The Place of Mojala Agbebi in African Nationalist Movements 1890–1917." *Phylon* 26, no. 2 (1965): 122–39.

Anderson, James D. *The Education of Blacks in the South, 1860–1935*. Chapel Hill: University of North Carolina Press, 1988.

Armstrong, Samuel Chapman. *Education for Life*. Hampton, Va.: Hampton Institute Press, 1913.

———. "Hampton Institute." *Lend a Hand* 6 (1891): 32.

———. *Ideas on Education as Expressed by Samuel Chapman Armstrong*. Hampton, Va.: Hampton Institute Press, 1908.

Ayandele, E. A. *Holy Johnson: Pioneer of African Nationalism, 1836–1917*. London: Frank Cass, 1970.

Baeta, C. G., ed. *Christianity in Tropical Africa*. Oxford: Oxford University Press, 1968.

Bainton, Roland H. *Erasmus of Christendom*. New York: Scribner's, 1969.

Baker, A. W. "The First International Congress of the Negro." *Missionary Review of the World*, June 1912 (1935): 440–42.

Barber, Karin. *The Anthropology of Texts, Persons and Politics: Oral and Written Culture in Africa and Beyond.* Cambridge: Cambridge University Press, 2007.

Barnes, Andrew E. "Aryanizing Projects: African Collaborators and Colonial Transcripts." In *Antimonies of Modernity*, edited by Vasant Kaiwar, 62–97. Durham, N.C.: Duke University Press, 2003.

———. "Christianity, Islam and the Negro Race: E. W. Blyden, African Diasporas and the Regeneration of Africa." In *Redefining the African Diaspora: Expressive Cultures and Politics from Slavery to Independence*, edited by Toyin Falola and Danielle Sanchez, 124–50. Amherst, N.Y.: Cambria, 2016.

———. *Making Headway: The Introduction of Western Civilization in Colonial Northern Nigeria.* Rochester, N.Y.: University of Rochester Press, 2009.

Becker, Judith, and Brian Stanley, eds. *Europe as the Other: External Perspectives on European Christianity.* Gottingen: Vanderhoeck & Ruprecht, 2014.

Beckert, Sven. "From Tuskegee to Togo: The Problem of Freedom in the Empire of Cotton." *Journal of American History* (September 2005): 498–526.

Beize, Michael Scott, and Marybeth Gasman, eds. *Booker T. Washington Rediscovered.* Baltimore: Johns Hopkins University Press, 2012.

Berman, Edward H. "Education in Africa and America: A History of the Phelps Stokes Fund, 1911–1945." Ed.D. diss., Columbia University, 1970.

Beyer, C. Kalani. "The Connection of Samuel Chapman Armstrong as Both Borrower and Architect of Education in Hawai'i." *History of Education Quarterly* 47 (2007): 23–47.

———. "Setting the Record Straight: Education of the Heart and Mind Existed in the United States before the 1800's." *American Educational History Journal* 37 (2010): 149–67.

Blyden, Edward W. *Christianity, Islam and the Negro Race.* Edinburgh: Edinburgh University Press, 1967. First published London, 1887.

———. *Liberia's Offerings: Being Addresses, Sermons.* New York: John Gray, 1862.

———. *The Return of the Exiles and the West African Church: A Lecture Delivered at the Breadfruit School House, Lagos, West Africa, January 2, 1891.* London, 1891.

Boahen, A. Adu, ed. (UNESCO). *General History of Africa*. Vol. 7, *Africa under Foreign Domination 1880–1935*. Berkeley: University of California Press, 1999.

Boston, Michael B. *The Business Strategy of Booker T. Washington: Its Development and Implementation*. Gainesville: University of Florida Press, 2010.

Bowen, J. W. E. "The Needs and Possibilities of the Student Volunteer Movement for Foreign Missions among the Colored Students of America." In *The Student Missionary Appeal: Addresses at the Third International Convention of the Student Volunteer Movement for Foreign Missions Held at Cleveland, Ohio, February 23–27, 1898*. New York: Student Volunteer Movement for Foreign Missions, 1898.

Branford, Tolly. "World Visions: Native Missionaries, Mission Networks and Critiques of Colonialism in Nineteenth-Century South Africa and Canada." In *Grappling With the Beast: Indigenous Southern African Responses to Colonialism 1840–1930*, edited by Peter Limb, Norman Etherington and Peter Midgley, 311–39. Leiden: Brill, 2010.

Brundage, W. Fitzhugh, ed. *Booker T. Washington and Black Progress: "Up from Slavery" 100 Years Later*. Gainesville: University of Florida Press, 2003.

Campbell, James E. *Songs of Zion: The African Methodist Episcopal Church in the United States and South Africa*. New York: Oxford University Press, 1995.

Cele, Mandikane. "Hampton Lessons." *Southern Workman* 45, no. 3 (1916): 186–88.

Chirenje, J. Mutero. *Ethiopianism and Afro-Americans in Southern Africa, 1883–1916*. Baton Rouge: Louisiana State University Press, 1987.

Coclanis, Peter A. "What Made Booker Wash(ington)? The Wizard of Tuskegee in Economic Context." In Brundage, *Booker T. Washington and Black Progress*, 81–106.

Coleman, James S. *Nigeria: Background to Nationalism*. Berkeley: University of California Press, 1971.

Corby, Richard A. "The Bo School and Its Graduates in Colonial Sierra Leone." *Canadian Journal of African Studies* 15, no. 2 (1981): 323–33.

———. "Educating Africans for Inferiority under British Rule: Bo School in Sierra Leone." *Comparative Education Review* 34, no. 3 (1990): 314–49.

Correia, Stephen Taylor. " 'For Their Own Good': An Historical Analysis of the Educational Thought of Thomas Jesse Jones." Ph.D. diss., Pennsylvania State University, 1993.

Cox, Jeffrey. *The British Missionary Enterprise since 1700.* New York: Routledge, 2010.

Cronin, Edmund David. *Black Moses: The Story of Marcus Garvey and Universal Negro Improvement Agency.* Madison: University of Wisconsin Press, 1968.

Crummell, Alexander. *Africa and America: Addresses and Discourses.* Springfield, Mass.: Willey, 1891.

———. *The Future of Africa: Being Addresses, Sermons, Etc., Etc., Delivered in the Republic of Liberia.* New York: Scribner's, 1862.

Dagbovie, Pero Gaglo. " 'Shadow versus Substance': Deconstructing Booker T. Washington." In *African American History Reconsidered*, by Pero Gaglo Dagbovie, 127–57. Urbana: University of Illinois Press, 2010.

Davis, R. Hunt. "John L. Dube: A South African Exponent of Booker T. Washington." *Journal of African Studies* 2, no. 4 (1975/1976): 497–528.

———. "School versus Blanket and Settler: Elijah Makiwane and the Leadership of the Cape School Community." *African Affairs* 78, no. 310 (1979): 12–31.

Denton, James. "The Negro Problem in America: A Solution." *Church Missionary Review* 63 (1912): 654–59.

Denton, Virginia Lantz. *Booker T. Washington and the Adult Education Movement.* Gainesville: University of Florida Press, 1993.

Dickinson, Charles Henry. "Samuel Armstrong's Contribution to Christian Missions." *International Review of Missions* 10 (1921): 509–24.

Dube, John L. "The Black Problem in South Africa." *Missionary Review of the World* 1916 (39): 205–7.

———. "Practical Christianity among the Zulu." *Missionary Review of the World*, May 1907, 370–73.

———. "A Zulu's Account of a Zulu Enterprise." *Outlook* 40 (1910): 290–91.

Du Bois, W. E. B. "On the Training of Black Men." In *The Oxford W. E. B. Du Bois Reader*, edited by Eric J. Sundquist, 146–55. New York: Oxford University Press, 1996.

———. "The Training of Negroes for Social Power." *Outlook* 33 (1903): 409–14.

Elphick, Richard. *The Equality of Believers: Protestant Missionaries and the Racial Politics of South Africa*. Charlottesville: University of Virginia Press, 2012.

Engs, Robert Francis. *Educating the Disenfranchised and Disinherited: Samuel Chapman Armstrong and Hampton Institute, 1839–1893*. Knoxville: University of Tennessee Press, 1999.

———. *Freedom's First Generation: Black Hampton, Virginia, 1861–1890*. New York: Fordham University Press, 2004. First published Philadelphia: University of Pennsylvania Press, 1979.

Erlmann, Veit. " 'A Feeling of Prejudice': Orpheus M. McAdoo and the Virginia Jubilee Singers in South Africa 1890–1898." *Journal of Southern African Studies* 14, no. 3 (1988): 331–50.

Evans, Maurice. "The International Conference of the Negro." *Christian Express*, October 1, 1912.

Faduma, Orishetukeh. "Successes and Drawbacks of Missionary Work in Africa by an Eye-Witness." In *Africa and the American Negro*, edited by J. W. E. Bowen, 125–36. Atlanta: Gammon Theological Seminary, 1896.

Fairclough, Adam. *A Class of Their Own: Black Teachers in the Segregated South*. Cambridge, Mass.: Harvard University Press, 2007.

Franklin, V. P. "Pan African Connections, Transnational Connections, Transnational Education, Collective Cultural Capital and Opportunities Industrialization Centers International." *Journal of African American History* 96, no. 1 (2011): 44–61.

Fredrickson, George M. *White Supremacy: A Comparative Study in American and South African History*. New York: Oxford University Press, 1981.

Fyfe, Christopher. "The Sierra Leone Press in the Nineteenth Century." *Sierra Leone Studies* 8 (1957): 226–36.

Gilroy, Paul. *The Black Atlantic: Modernity and Double Consciousness*. London: Verso Books, 1993.

Hanciles, Jehu. "The Legacy of James Johnson." *International Bulletin of Missionary Research* 21 (1997): 162–67.

Harlan, Louis R. *Booker T. Washington: The Making of a Black Leader 1856–1901*. New York: Oxford University Press, 1972.

———. *Booker T. Washington: The Wizard of Tuskegee 1901–1915*. New York: Oxford University Press, 1983.

———. "Booker T. Washington and the White Man's Burden." *American Historical Review* 71 (1966): 441–67.

———, ed. *The Booker T. Washington Papers*. 14 vols. Urbana: University of Illinois Press 1972–89.

———. "The Secret Life of Washington." *Journal of Southern History* 37 (1971): 393–416.

———. "Up from Slavery as History and Biography." In Brundage, *Booker T. Washington and Black Progress*, 37.

Higgs, Catherine. *The Ghost of Inequality: The Public Lives of D. D. T. Jabavu of South Africa 1885–1959*. Athens: Ohio University Press, 1997.

Hill, Robert A., ed. *The Marcus Garvey and Universal Negro Improvement Agency Papers*. 10 vols. Berkeley: University of California Press, 1983–1995.

Hughes, Heather. "Doubly Elite: Exploring the Life of John Langalibalele Dube." *Journal of Southern Africa Studies* 27, no. 3 (2001): 445–58.

———. *The First President: A Life of John L. Dube, Founding President of the ANC*. Johannesburg: Jacana Media, 2011.

"International Conference on the Negro." Tuskegee Records, Booker T. Washington Papers, U.S. Library of Congress, reel 716.

Jabavu, Davidson Don Tengo (D. D. T.). *The Black Problem: Papers and Addresses on Various Native Problems*. Lovedale, Cape Providence, S. Africa: Lovedale Institute Press, 1920.

———. *The Life of John Tengo Jabavu, Editor of Imvo Zabantsundu 1884–1921*. Lovedale, Cape Providence, S. Africa: Lovedale Institute Press, 1922.

Jabavu, John Tengo. "Native Races of South Africa." In *Papers on Interracial Problems Communicated to the First Universal Races Congress Held at University of London, July 26–29, 1911*, edited by G. Spiller, 336–41. London: P. S. King & Son, 1911.

Jacobs, Sylvia. "James Emman Kwegyir Aggrey: An African Intellectual in the United States." *Journal of Negro History* 81, nos. 1–4 (1996): 47–61.

Jones, Thomas Jesse. "A Good Word for Missionaries." *Current History*, July 1, 1926, 539–44.

July, Robert W. *The Origins of Modern African Thought*. New York: Praeger, 1967.

Keirnan, V. G. *The Lords of Human Kind: Black Man, Yellow Man, and White Man in an Age of Empire*. Boston: Little, Brown, 1969.

Kerr, David. *Fort Hare: Evolution of an African College*. London: C. Hurst, 1968.

Killingray, David. "Godly Examples and Christian Agents: Training African Missionary Workers in British Institutions in the Nineteenth Century." In Becker and Stanley, *Europe as the Other*, 164–95.

———. "Passing on the Gospel: Indigenous Mission in Africa." *Transformation: An International Journal of Holistic Mission Studies* 28 (2011): 96.

King, Hazel. "Cooperation in Contextualization: Two Visionaries of the African Church—Mojola Agbebi and William Hughes of the African Institute, Colwyn Bay." *Journal of Religion in Africa* 16, no. 1 (1986): 2–20.

Langley, J. Ayondele. *Pan Africanism and Nationalism in West Africa*. Oxford: Clarendon, 1973.

Lewis, L. J. *Educational Policy and Practice in British Tropical Areas*. London: Thomas Nelson, 1954.

Lorimer, Douglas. *Colour, Class and the Victorians: English Attitudes toward the Negro in the Mid-nineteenth Century*. Leicester: Leicester University Press, 1978.

Ludlow, Helen W. "The Hampton Normal and Agricultural Institute." *Harper's New Monthly Magazine* 47 (1873): 672–85.

Luker, Ralph. "Missions, Institutional Churches, and Settlement Houses: The Black Experience 1885–1910." *Journal of Negro History* 69, no. 3/4 (1984): 101–13.

———. *The Social Gospel in Black and White: American Racial Reform 1885–1912*. Chapel Hill: University of North Carolina Press, 1991.

Lynch, Hollis R., ed. *Black Spokesman: Selected Published Writings of Edward Wilmot Blyden*. New York: Humanities Press, 1971.

Marable, W. Manning. "African Nationalist: The Life of John Langalibalele Dube." Ph.D. diss., University of Maryland, 1976.

———. "South African Nationalism in Brooklyn: John L. Dube's Activities in New York State, 1887–1899." *Afro-Americans in New York Life and History* 3, no. 1 (1979): 23–34.

Marks, Shula. "The Ambiguities of Dependency: John L. Dube of Natal." *Journal of Southern African Studies* 1, no. 2 (1975): 160–82.

Martin, Tony. *Race First: The Ideological and Organizational Struggles of Marcus Garvey and the Universal Negro Improvement Agency*. Norwich, Conn.: Greenwood, 1976.

Moore, Moses N. *Orishatukeh Faduma: Liberal Theology and Evangelical Pan-Africanism, 1857–1946*. Lanham, Md.: Scarecrow, 1996.

Morel, E. D. *Nigeria, Its Peoples, Its Problems.* London: Cass Reprints, 1968.

Moses, Wilson Jeremiah. *Alexander Crummell: A Study of Civilization and Discontent.* New York: Oxford University Press, 1989.

———. "More Than an Artichoke: The Pragmatic Religion of Booker T. Washington." In Brundage, *Booker T. Washington and Black Progress*, 107–30.

Moton, Robert Russa. *Finding a Way Out: An Autobiography.* New York: Doubleday, 1920.

Newall, Stephanie. *The Power to Name: A History of Anonymity in Colonial West Africa.* Athens: Ohio University Press, 2013.

Norrell, Robert J. *Up from History: The Life of Booker T. Washington.* Cambridge, Mass.: Belknap Press of Harvard University Press, 2009.

Odendaal, André. *Black Protest Politics in South Africa until 1912.* Totowa, N.J.: Barnes & Noble, 1985.

Oldfield, J. R. *Alexander Crummell (1819–1898) and the Creation of an African-American Church in Liberia.* Lewiston: E. Mellen, 1990.

Oliver, Roland, and G. N. Sanderson, eds. *The Cambridge History of Africa.* Vol. 6, *From 1870–1905.* Cambridge: Cambridge University Press, 1985.

Page, Carol A. "Colonial Reaction to AME Missionaries in South Africa." In Jacobs, *Black Americans and the Missionary Movement in Africa*, 177–95.

Pakenham, Thomas. *The Scramble for Africa: White Man's Conquest of the Dark Continent.* New York: Avon Books, 1991.

Park, Robert E. "The International Conference on the Negro." *Southern Workman* 41, no. 6 (1912): 347–52.

———. "Tuskegee International Conference of the Negro." *Journal of Race Development* 3 (1912–1913): 117–20.

Paterson, Andrew. "Education and Segregation in a South African Church: James Dwane and the Order of Ethiopia, 1900–1908." *International Journal of African Studies* 36, no. 3 (2003): 585–605.

Peabody, Francis. *Education for Life: The Story of Hampton Institute.* New York: Doubleday, 1918.

Phillips, Paul T. *A Kingdom on Earth: Anglo American Social Christianity 1880–1940.* University Park: Pennsylvania State University Press, 1996.

Porter, Andrew. "'Commerce and Christianity': The Rise and Fall of a Nineteenth-Century Missionary Slogan." *Historical Journal* 28, no. 3 (1985): 597–621.

———. *Religion versus Empire? British Protestant Missionaries and Overseas Expansion, 1700–1914*. Manchester: Manchester University Press, 2004.

Redkey, Edwin S. *Black Exodus: Black Nationalists and the Back to Africa Movement, 1890–1910*. New Haven: Yale University Press, 1971.

Rich, Paul B. "The Appeal of Tuskegee: James Henderson, Lovedale and the Fortunes of South African Liberalism, 1906–1930." *International Journal of African Historical Studies* 20, no. 2 (1987): 271–92.

Rolinson, Mary. *Grassroots Garveyism: The United Negro Improvement Agency in the Rural South*. Chapel Hill: University of North Carolina Press, 2007.

Sehat, David. "The Civilizing Mission of Booker T. Washington." *Journal of Southern History* 73 (2007): 323–62.

Shepperson, George. "Ethiopianism: Past and Present." In Baeta, *Christianity in Tropical Africa*, 250–60.

Sivonen, Seppe. *White-Collar or Hoe Handle: African Education under British Colonial Policy 1920–1945*. Helsinki: Soumen Historiallinen Seura, 1995.

Smith, Brett H. *Labor's Millennium: Christianity, Industrial Education, and the Founding of the University of Illinois*. Eugene, Ore.: Wipf & Stock, 2010.

Smith, Vivian Dickford. "The Betrayal of Creole Elites, 1880–1920." In *Black Experience and the Empire*, edited by Philip Morgan and Sean Hawkins, 194–227. Oxford: Oxford University Press, 2004.

Spivey, Donald A. "The African Crusade for Black Industrial Schooling." *Journal of Negro History* 63, no. 1 (1978): 1–17.

Stanley, Brian. *The Bible and the Flag: Protestant Missions and British Imperialism in the Nineteenth and Twentieth Century*. Leicester: Apollos, 1990.

Sundkler, Bengt. *Bantu Prophets of South Africa*. Oxford: Oxford University Press, 1961.

Sundquist, Eric J., ed. *The Oxford W. E. B. Du Bois Reader*. New York: Oxford University Press, 1996.

Switzer, Les. "The African Christian Community and Its Press in Victorian South Africa." *Cahiers d'Etudes Africaines* 24, no. 96 (1984): 455–76.

———. "*Bantu World* and the Origins of the Captive African Commercial Press in South Africa." *Journal of Southern African Studies* 14, no. 3 (1988): 351–70.

———. *Power and Resistance in an African Society: The Ciskei Xhosa and the Making of South Africa*. Madison: University of Wisconsin Press, 1993.

———, ed. *South Africa's Alternative Press: Voices of Protest and Resistance 1880s–1960s*. Cambridge: Cambridge University Press, 1997.

Thrasher, Max Bennett. *Tuskegee: Its Story and Its Work*. Boston: Small, Maynard, 1901.

Turner, H. M. "Wayside Dots and Jots." *Christian Recorder*, May 2, 1878, 2.

U.S. Department of the Interior, Bureau of Education. *Negro Education: A Study of the Private and Higher Schools for Colored People in the United States*. Prepared in cooperation with the Phelps-Stokes Fund under the direction of Thomas Jesse Jones, specialist in the education of racial groups. Washington, D.C.: Government Printing Office, 1917.

Verney, Kevern. *The Art of the Possible: Booker T. Washington and Black Leadership in the United States, 1881–1925*. New York: Routledge, 2001.

Vinson, Robert Trent. *The Americans Are Coming: Dreams of African American Liberation in Segregationist South Africa*. Athens: Ohio University Press, 2012.

Walls, Andrew F. "Distinguished Visitors: Tiyo Soga and Behari Lal Singh in Europe and at Home." In Becker and Stanley, *Europe as the Other*, 243–54.

Washington, Booker T. "Industrial Education in Africa." *Independent*, no. 60, March 15, 1906, 616–19. Reprinted in Harlan, *Booker T. Washington Papers*, 8:548–53.

———. "The Story of Tuskegee." In Beize and Gasman, *Booker T. Washington Rediscovered*, 8–16.

———. "Twenty-Five Years of Tuskegee." In Beize and Gasman, *Booker T. Washington Rediscovered*, 74–92.

———. *Up from Slavery: An Autobiography* (1903). In Harlan, *Booker T. Washington Papers*, 1:211–389.

———. *Working with the Hands: Being a Sequel to "Up from Slavery," Covering the Author's Experiences in Industrial Training at Tuskegee*. New York: Doubleday, Page, 1904.

Washington, Eric Michael. "Heralding South Africa's Redemption: Evangelicalism and Ethiopianism in the Missionary Philosophy of the National Baptist Convention, USA 1880–1930." Ph.D. diss., 2 vols., Michigan State University, 2010.

Weber, Max. *The Protestant Ethic and the Spirit of Capitalism*. Florence, Ky.: Routledge, 2001.

West, Michael Rudolph. *The Education of Booker T. Washington: American Democracy and the Idea of Race Relations*. New York: Columbia University Press, 2006.

Windel, Aaron. "British Colonial Education in Africa: Policy and Practice in the Era of Trusteeship." *History Compass* 7, no. 1 (2009): 9–13.

Zachernuk, Philip. *Colonial Subjects: An African Intelligentsia and Atlantic Ideas*. Charlottesville: University of Virginia Press, 2003.

Zimmerman, Andrew. *Alabama in Africa: Booker T. Washington, the German Empire and the Globalization of the New South*. Princeton: Princeton University Press, 2010.

# Index